Macroeconomic Accounting and Analysis in Transition Economies

Abdessatar Ouanes and Subhash Thakur

With contributions from
Ian Lienert
Philippe Marciniak
Karen Swiderski

International Monetary Fund
June 1997

Composition: Alicia Etchebarne-Bourdin

Cover and Charts: Sanaa Elaroussi and IMF Graphics Section

Cataloging-in-Publication Data

Ouanes, Abdessatar

Macroeconomic accounting and analysis in transition economies / Abdessatar Ouanes and Subhash Thakur with contributions from Ian Lienert, Philippe Marciniak, Karen Swiderski — [Washington, D.C.] : International Monetary Fund, 1997.

p. cm.

ISBN 1-55775-628-7

1. National income — Poland — Accounting. 2. Poland — Economic policy — 1990- I. Thakur, Subhash Madhav, 1946-

HC340.3.Z9 I516 1997

Price: US$19.00

Please send orders to:

International Monetary Fund, Publication Services
700 19th Street, N.W., Washington, D.C. 20431, U.S.A.
Tel: (202) 623-7430 Telefax: (202) 623-7201
E-mail: publications@imf.org
Internet: http://www.imf.org

recycled paper

Contents

The following symbols have been used throughout this book:

. . . to indicate that data are not available;

— to indicate that the figure is zero or less than half the final digit shown, or that the item does not exist;

– between years or months (e.g., 1994–95 or January–June) to indicate the years or months covered, including the beginning and ending years or months;

/ between years (e.g., 1994/95) to indicate a crop or fiscal (financial) year.

"Billion" means a thousand million.

Minor discrepancies between constituent figures and totals are due to rounding.

The term "country," as used in this book, does not in all cases refer to a territorial entity that is a state as understood by international law and practice; the term also covers some territorial entities that are not states, but for which statistical data are maintained and provided internationally on a separate and independent basis.

Preface

This volume presents the principal elements of macroeconomic accounting and analysis for a transition economy, using a case study of Poland for purposes of illustration. The primary aim of the volume is to provide officials from transition economies participating in the training courses offered by the IMF Institute with a practitioner's guidebook to the core macroeconomic ideas which underlie formulation of economic policies and to provide him or her with directions for a further in-depth exploration of issues. With the latter aim, the volume includes several references for further reading in the core areas covered. Thus, although the primary target audience of the book is that of officials from countries in transition, the bulk of the material can be used by officials and analysts from any country as a guidebook for the main elements of macroeconomic accounting and analysis. The volume covers accounting and analysis for the real, fiscal, monetary, and external sectors as well as the interrelations among these sectors (the flow of funds). The analyses are based on the most up-to-date accounting methodology, primarily the *1993 System of National Accounts* and the Fifth Edition of the *Balance of Payments Manual* (1993), and include a discussion of the differences between the new accounting system and its predecessors. The choice of Poland to illustrate the macroeconomics of a transition economy reflects a number of considerations: Poland's pioneering role among East European economies in instituting comprehensive economic reforms; the widespread attention the Polish economic program invited as a model of the so-called "big bang" approach to reform; the IMF's role in supporting this program with financing and policy advice; the commonality of the issues Poland and other transition economies face; and finally, the availability of data for the Polish economy in recent years.

The design of the volume was motivated by the IMF Institute's efforts to meet the unique needs of officials from IMF member countries in transition for training in policy-oriented macroeconomic analysis. The material also reflects the Institute's recent efforts to integrate its training activities more closely with the work of other departments of the IMF.

Although a knowledge of the specific institutional, historical, and social conditions in the country is obviously a helpful supplement to a purely economic analysis, the principles of macroeconomic analysis presented here are general and have been found to be robust in a variety of country situations. These principles are grounded in macroeconomic accounting as it is applied to market economies, and a clear understanding of the main accounting concepts used in the classification and presentation of economic statistics is an essential prerequisite to applying them.

Chapter 1 presents a brief overview of economic developments and policies in Poland, while Chapter 2, Analysis of the Real Sector, introduces the basic accounting relationships in the real sector and highlights key analytical tools used in the measurement of output, inflation, wages, and unemployment. Chapter 3, Fiscal Accounting and Analysis, covers the framework of fiscal accounts, based on the IMF's Government Finance Statistics (GFS) and includes a discussion of different measures of the fiscal balance; of the macroeconomic effects of alternative methods of financing a fiscal imbalance; and of key concepts in fiscal analysis, such as the inflation tax, debt neutrality, and fiscal sustainability. It also covers the analysis of fiscal revenues and includes guidelines for assessing a tax system and for analyzing public expenditures. Chapter 4, Balance of Payments Accounts and Analysis, introduces the conceptual framework of the balance of payments based on the *Balance of Payments Manual*, Fifth Edition, and presents some analytical tools used in the interpretation of developments in the external position, external debt, and international reserves. Chapter 5, Monetary Accounts and Analysis, begins by presenting the structure of the financial and monetary systems and the main accounting principles that underlie monetary statistics including the monetary survey. The chapter also touches on the role of the central bank and special issues such as capital flows, exchange rate regimes, currency substitution, and financial deregulation. Chapter 6, The Flow of Funds: Macroeconomic Interrelations, presents the framework of the flow of funds accounts and a brief exposition of how these accounts can be useful in macroeconomic analysis.

Each chapter is followed by brief background information on the case study of Poland and a set of exercises and issues for discussion that can be used in a workshop as a review and as a basis for group discussion of the material covered.

All the statistical and background information on Poland used in this volume is based on information published by the IMF, the World Bank, and the Polish Central Statistical Office. These sources include *Poland—Background Paper*, IMF Staff Country Report No. 96/19 (Washington: International Monetary Fund, 1996); *Poland—Statistical Tables*, IMF Country Report No. 96/20 (Washington: International Monetary Fund, 1996); Liam P. Ebrill, *Poland: The Path to a Market Economy*, Occasional Paper No. 113 (Washington: International Monetary Fund, 1994); *Poland: Policies for Growth and Equity*, World Bank Country Study (Washington: World Bank, 1994); and *Quarterly Statistics of the Polish Central Statistical Office* (Warsaw, various issues).

The volume was prepared in the European Division of the IMF Institute, under the leadership and direction of Abdessatar Ouanes, Division Chief, and Subhash Thakur, Deputy Division Chief. Contributions were made by members of the European Division, including Ian Lienert, Philippe Marciniak, and Karen Swiderski. The views expressed are those of the authors and do not necessarily reflect the views of the IMF.

The volume benefited greatly from the guidance and comments of Chorng-Huey Wong, Assistant Director of the IMF Institute, and from the advice of Patrick de Fontenay, former Director of the IMF Institute and Anthony Lanyi, former Deputy Director. The staff of the IMF Institute at headquarters and at the Joint Vienna Institute offered many helpful comments and suggestions. The untiring efforts of Deanna Kaufmann, Maryse Dubé, and Brian Manuel in producing and organizing the documents for publication, and the valuable editorial assistance of Martha Bonilla of the External Relations Department and Emily Chalmers deserve special acknowledgement, as does the assistance of IMF's European I Department, which provided the statistics and other background information on Poland.

CHAPTER

1 Poland's Transition to the Market: An Overview

Poland was one of the first of the former centrally planned economies to launch a comprehensive program of economic transformation in the late 1980s and early 1990s. The Polish experience of liberalization and reform, which is now over five years old, can provide useful lessons for other developing and transition economies that have undertaken, or are just embarking on similar reforms.

First, aside from the fact that it was one of the first efforts at stabilization and reform among the countries of Central and Eastern Europe and the states of the former Soviet Union, the Polish economic program attracted worldwide attention because of its radical and comprehensive approach. Several attempts to reform the centrally planned system in Poland in a gradual and piecemeal fashion undertaken during the 1980s were generally viewed as failures, in part because they were not comprehensive enough, and many believed that these efforts only compounded the imbalances associated with central planning. The Polish authorities therefore explicitly adopted a less gradual, more radical approach—the so-called "shock therapy" or "big bang" approach to economic reform. The success or failure of this approach was to be a decisive factor in the debate on the appropriate scope and speed of economic reform in transition economies.

Second, the Polish economic program was one of the first to be supported with IMF resources. At the request of the Polish authorities, the IMF collaborated closely with the policymakers in the design and monitoring of the program. The IMF also made available a stabilization fund of $1 billion to support Poland's exchange rate policy (see below). The Polish program thus offers valuable insight into the IMF's approach to financial programming in a transition economy.

Third, when the economic program was introduced at the beginning of 1990, many observers regarded it as an instance of the so-called "heterodox" approach to stabilization, which combines fiscal discipline with a (temporary) fixed exchange rate and a tax-based incomes policy that moderates wage behavior. The program's reliance on the exchange rate "anchor" to brake emerging hyperinflationary expectations was a key feature of the approach and attracted much scrutiny and interest. The Polish reform program is a useful case study of the role of exchange rate policy in stabilization programs.

Finally, prior to stabilization, Poland faced macroeconomic and structural imbalances common to many transition economies. These included (i) emerging hyperinflation at the end of 1989; (ii) widespread "dollarization," suggesting a serious loss of confidence in the local currency; (iii) a sharp fall in output in the early phases of the economic reform program; (iv) large fiscal imbalances, the result of declining tax revenues and pressures for higher spending; and (v) structural and institutional rigidities in the fiscal and financial sectors that made adjustment difficult. While the structural weaknesses and the need for fiscal consolidation continue to present challenges for Polish policymakers, the stabilization program succeeded in bringing down the rate of inflation, thereby restoring confidence in the zloty and the deregulation and liberalization measures helped foster a thriving private sector, leading to increased exports and economic growth.[1] This success makes the Polish program particularly instructive.

[1]This chapter draws on a number of published reviews of Poland's experience of transformation, including Jeffrey Sachs, *Poland's Jump to the Market Economy* (Cambridge, Massachusetts: MIT Press, 1993); Olivier Blanchard, Kenneth Froot, and Jeffrey Sachs, eds., "Stabilization and Transition: Poland, 1990–91," *The Transition in Eastern Europe: Country Studies*, Vol. 1 (Chicago: The University of Chicago Press, 1994), and David Lipton and Jeffrey Sachs, "Creating a Market Economy in Eastern Europe: The Case of Poland," *The Brookings Papers on Economic Activity*, Vol. 1 (Washington: Brookings Institution, 1990). For a general review of economic issues in transition economies, see Michael Bruno, "Stabilization and Reform in Eastern Europe," *Staff Papers*, International Monetary Fund, Vol. 39 (December 1992).

The Decades Before 1990

The Decline in Output and the External Debt Buildup

After a period of economic growth in the 1950s and 1960s based on large-scale investment in heavy industry and the absorption of labor from the farm sector, Poland experienced a slump in the 1970s. In response, the authorities launched a massive investment effort financed by imported capital, which led to a surge in industrial output but also created large external current account deficits and heavy accumulation of external debt. The deficit peaked at about 10 percent of GDP in 1975, and external debt rose from practically zero in the early 1970s to 40 percent of GDP at the end of the decade.

The industrial boom collapsed when foreign capital dried up, and import volumes fell by 50 percent during the crisis years of 1979–82. A harsh adjustment was imposed in 1982 under a martial law regime, but growth resumed only at modest rates during 1983–88. On balance, the decade leading up to 1988 was marked by a dismal record of economic performance, with stagnating real output and rising repressed inflation. A notable feature of this period was the state industrial sector's experience. Output and employment fell, but the consumption of energy and raw materials rose sharply, as did the capital stock, suggesting a rapidly rising capital-output ratio and increased energy-intensity in industry. The stagnating of output was vividly reflected in the failure of exports to grow and generate the foreign receipts necessary to service the rising external debt.

The Failure of the Partial Reforms of the 1980s

The Polish authorities, responding to the balance of payments crisis of 1979–81, undertook a series of partial reforms in the 1980s intended to decentralize economic decision making in the areas of production and investment planning, wage setting, enterprise financing, and foreign trade. Attempts were made to give state enterprises progressively greater autonomy over production, investment, and financing decisions. While these decentralization measures probably facilitated the transformation process, they failed to address the issue of economic stagnation, mainly because they failed to create truly free markets where competition could flourish or to bring about the basic change in the structure of relative prices that was needed to reduce shortages.[2] The decentralization of wage setting led to accelerating wage pressures that culminated in wage explosions during the early 1980s and again in 1987–89. Because these large real wage gains were not backed by gains in productivity, they merely created a huge amount of excess demand and intensified existing shortages. Indeed, they may have been accompanied by a fall rather than a rise in living standards.

Decentralization, in practice, only increased problems with the bureaucracy, as direct controls were replaced by a large number of arbitrarily implemented rules under which enterprises bargained for credits, subsidies, tax relief, and access to foreign exchange. These partial reforms proved to be a poor substitute for well-functioning markets. The lack of market discipline, absence of provisions for free entry to and exit from markets, the ongoing protection from foreign competition, and the absence of a capital market to regulate investment and wage decisions meant that efforts to instill discipline in state enterprises failed. Ultimately, the unwillingness of the *nomenklatura* to undertake real reform and the political illegitimacy of the regime led to the failure of this experiment with reform.

The Legacy of Central Planning

The primary legacy of Poland's long period of central planning was the relative impoverishment of the country. By 1989, Poland lagged behind many developing countries in terms of per capita income. Its per capita GNP ($1,850) fell between the averages for low-income developing countries ($1,270) and high-income developing countries ($2,940). The legacy of central planning was also evident in the main structural characteristics of the Polish economy, which explain the reform strategy adopted in the late 1980s and the early results of the reforms. Poland's economy was characterized by the following structural distortions:

- *Overindustrialization.* Poland, like other Eastern European countries, was highly industrialized, too much so for its level of overall economic development. The result was that other sectors, such as the service sector, were deprived of resources in favor of industry.
- *A large, inefficient agriculture sector.* Almost alone in Europe, Poland still had a large agri-

[2]These attempts at partial reform in the 1980s are parallel to the reforms attempted under *perestroika* in the former Soviet Union. Both efforts ended with hyperinflation, intense shortage of goods and services, growing black markets, and falling output.

culture sector with low productivity and a high political profile.

- *State ownership of enterprises and property.* Like most centrally planned economies, Poland's businesses were largely state run, and private ownership was generally forbidden.
- *An absence of small and medium-sized enterprises.* Most business in Poland was conducted by monolithic state-run enterprises. Typically, these firms were monopolies.
- *Barter trade agreements.* Poland traded almost exclusively with other centrally planned economies through the now-defunct Council for Mutual Economic Assistance (CMEA). Much of this trade was conducted in goods and services rather than for currency.
- *Guaranteed incomes and little private wealth.* The majority of workers could not be fired, and salary levels did not diverge widely. While these factors contributed to social stability, they served as disincentives to entrepreneurial activities.

Emerging Hyperinflation in 1989

As the centrally planned economic structures disintegrated along with the communist system, the mechanisms for maintaining financial control over the budget, the banking system, and external finances collapsed in 1988–89. Despite repeated reschedulings of external debt, actual debt service payments remained large, forcing the authorities to restrict imports and squeeze domestic demand. An abortive austerity program in 1988 attempted to cut subsidies and liberalize prices, but in the absence of popular support resulted in a wage-price-exchange rate spiral. This spiral, in turn, pushed Poland into hyperinflation in the second half of 1989, with monthly inflation accelerating from about 9 percent in July to 55 percent in October. The movement toward hyperinflation was reinforced by three events. First, the legalization of the black market in foreign exchange supported the flight from zloty. Second, the adoption of a formal wage-indexing mechanism led to a sharp rise in real wages in the state industrial sector. Third, the sharp cut in food subsidies intensified the wage-price-exchange rate spiral. All in all, in October 1989 the Polish economy stood on the brink of hyperinflation and was further threatened with a collapse of output.

The Reform Strategy

The solidarity-led government that took office in September 1989 had as its principal economic goal a rapid move to a market economy. The authorities' strategy, called a *leap to the market*, involved rapid macroeconomic stabilization, the immediate liberalization of prices and international trade and payments, and a fixing of the exchange rate. Taken together, these steps were intended to reduce decisively inflation expectations and to introduce widespread competition from abroad as quickly as possible.

The new government's stabilization program was based on five mutually reinforcing policies aimed at reducing aggregate demand and anchoring the price level.

- First, the authorities cut subsidies and investment spending sharply to reduce the fiscal deficit.
- Second, they instituted tight controls on net domestic credit of the banking system, partly by raising interest rates.
- Third, they depreciated the exchange rate by 31 percent, pegged it at the new rate, and established current account convertibility.
- Fourth, they put in place a tax-based incomes policy that would limit the rate of growth of nominal wages.
- Finally, they liberalized prices in all but a few regulated sectors (such as public utilities), raising prices in these sectors in a one-time adjustment.

The authorities' economic strategy recognized that macroeconomic stabilization and structural reform are interrelated and complementary processes on the road to a market economy. An effective system of price setting cannot be established until inflation falls and the currency is made convertible. Tighter fiscal policies will not result in real structural adjustment until state assets are sold off, the private sector is freed from regulation, bankruptcy procedures are established, a social safety net is in place, tax reforms are instituted, and the financial sector is overhauled. While recognizing that implementing all the institutional and legislative changes necessary to the structural reform process requires time, the Polish authorities initiated a limited number of structural reform measures.

Some further noteworthy features of the Polish reform program included:

- *The link between price liberalization and trade liberalization.* This link was a key element in the Polish reform strategy. Reformers in Poland and elsewhere had been reluctant to liberalize prices in economies dominated by monopolistic firms, fearing an explosion in monopoly profits. The rapid opening up of foreign trade provided the needed competition in the domestic market, solving the reformers' dilemma.

- *A relatively low initial exchange rate*. The decision to set the exchange rate slightly below the black-market rate raised inflation in the short term. A more appreciated rate would have resulted in less inflation, but the lower exchange rate was easier to defend and provided the needed competitive margin in the early period of reform.
- *Tight monetary policy*. The level of international reserves at the start of the program was very low, making it essential for the authorities to maintain a tight monetary policy. The new policy would force households and enterprises to convert some of their foreign exchange holdings back into zlotys in order to carry out domestic transactions. The return of confidence in the zloty also helped to boost official international reserves, as the central bank sold zlotys for dollars.
- *External financial support*. The reform program attracted strong support from the international financial community. Support for the balance of payments came in the form of an IMF stand-by loan, a Stabilization Fund administered by the IMF, and a bridging loan from the Bank for International Settlements. Moreover, creditor governments provided temporary relief from the burden of external debt servicing by agreeing to reschedule virtually all the principal and interest on Poland's debt through March 1991.

Economic Performance

Viewed in the light of recent history, the Polish big bang approach was basically successful and widely imitated. It succeeded in averting the risk of hyperinflation by bringing inflation down dramatically from over 1,000 percent on an annual basis to about 50 percent. The fiscal balance improved significantly in 1990 and, as a result of a surge in exports, the current account of the balance of payments showed a slight surplus. Nevertheless, the reforms were not fully successful. Inflation remained higher than targeted, and there was a sharp drop in output, reflecting a combination of influences.[3] The impact of the destruction of existing institutions was underestimated and the speed of response of output to the new incentive structures was overestimated. The early phase of transition was marked by slower than expected fiscal adjustment and difficulties in financing the fiscal deficit because of the lack of public trust in the government—reflected in its inability to sell government securities and the phenomenon of dollarization. But by 1994, the government succeeded in significantly restoring public confidence in the currency, and the focus of financial policy shifted from fiscal adjustment to monetary and exchange rate management in order to contain the inflationary impact of external capital inflows. The specific aspects of economic performance are covered in more detail below.

Inflation

The strategy of using an exchange rate anchor supported by a tax-based incomes policy to reduce inflation achieved dramatic success. The inflation rate, measured by the consumer price index (CPI), fell from over 620 percent in 1989 to 250 percent in 1990 and to 60 percent in 1991. Although the rate was reduced slightly in 1992–93, it then remained in the 30 percent range from late 1993 until early 1995 (see Chart 1.1).

The initial upward shock to the price level at the beginning of the reform program was quite large. The exchange rate depreciation, price liberalization, and increases in administered prices produced a corrective burst of price hikes, so that average monthly inflation in January 1990 was more than 78 percent over the previous month. In subsequent months, the inflation rate fell sharply. The government's success in ensuring that the large corrective price increases did not feed into the underlying rate of inflation owed much to the tax-based wage policy, which kept inflation from being incorporated into wages. This heterodox policy, combined with monetary restraint, helped not only to support the nominal exchange rate peg, but, ultimately, to break the momentum of inflation expectations.

The reduction in inflation was achieved despite the fiscal deficits, which needed considerable monetary financing. Key to this success was a sharp rise in the demand for broad money that reflected growing confidence in the zloty. As the zloty gained favor, the share of private savings in domestic currency held in the form of bank deposits increased. With private savings rechanneled into the banking system, the authorities had some room to maneuver in their efforts to reduce monetary financing of the deficit. Chart 1.2 illustrates the sharp fall in the ve-

[3]See E. Borensztein and J. Ostry, "Structural and Macroeconomic Determinants of the Output Decline in Czechoslovakia and Poland," IMF Working Paper 92/86 (Washington: International Monetary Fund, 1992). See also Guillermo A. Calvo, "Money, Exchange Rates and Output" (Cambridge, Massachusetts: MIT Press, 1996).

locity of zloty money during the period of disinflation in 1990–91.

Consumption, Output, and Unemployment

Real Incomes and Consumption

The official statistics suggesting that the cost of the stabilization effort in Poland has been high—a fall in real incomes of one-third—should be interpreted with caution. The fall in real wages—the index of real wages fell by over 30 percent during 1990—in part simply offset the large increases in real wages of 1987–89. More importantly, real wages do not correspond to living standards in an economy in which shortages are pervasive, because the official price index does not reflect the shortages, queues, or high black-market prices caused by excess demand. Thus, the real wage increases of 1987–89 did not make workers better off, and the fall in real wages in 1990 did not reflect a comparable fall in real consumption, since more and better consumer goods became available after 1990, reducing both queues and the importance of black markets. Data on household consumption expenditures in Poland strongly suggest that there was no sharp fall in living standards as a result of the 1990 price liberalization. Public opinion surveys also refute the notion that living standards declined in the early phases of reform.

Industrial Output

All the previously centrally planned economies of Central and Eastern Europe and the states of the former Soviet Union have experienced a fall in industrial output, irrespective of the pace of individual countries' reform efforts. Poland's fall in industrial output was among the smallest but was nevertheless substantial.

The fall in output of over 11 percent in 1990 reflected the impact of the fiscal balance's sharp swing into surplus and the resultant squeeze on domestic demand; the dislocation brought on by the hyperinflationary period of 1989; the collapse of the central planning structure; and cutbacks in production by large "heavy" industries, which lacked customers. A further fall of 8 percent in 1991 was caused largely by the external shock of the collapse of the CMEA and the accompanying worsening of the terms of trade. Growth resumed in 1992 and accelerated to 4 percent in 1993, supported by a buoyant private sector and expansion of exports.

Other factors influenced the fall in industrial output. In all the transition economies, resources—in-

Chart 1.1. Poland: Inflation and Real GDP
(In percent)

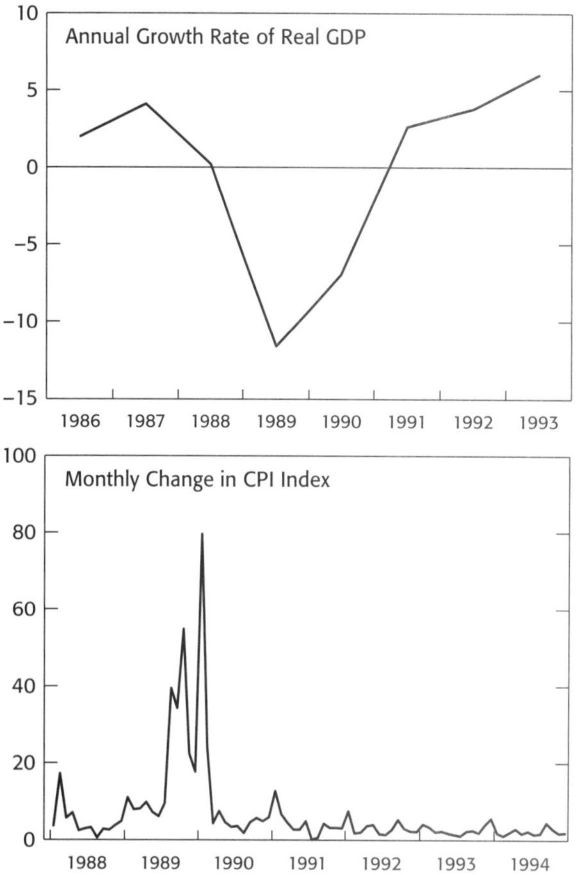

Sources: IMF Institute database and Tables 2.2 and 2.5.

Chart 1.2. Poland: Velocity of Money[1]

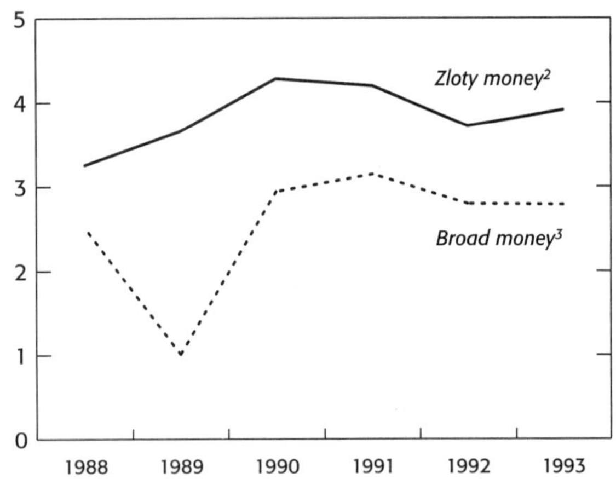

Source: IMF Institute database.

[1]Velocity is measured as nominal GDP divided by average of broad money or zloty money.

[2]Zloty money comprises of currency and all zloty deposits.

[3]Broad money comprises of currency, zloty deposits (demand, savings, and time), and foreign currency deposits.

cluding workers—from the overdeveloped industrial sector were shifted to the service sectors, including wholesale and retail trade and finance. The resulting gains in the service sector's output, which in many transition economies were not reflected in official statistics, helped to offset the fall in industrial output.[4] In fact, the decline was concentrated in the military-industrial complex, and the engineering and transport equipment sectors, while industries such as building materials and food processing registered healthy increases in output. There was also an explosion of new small, private businesses in the trade, services, and small-scale manufacturing sectors—activity the official statistics did not adequately reflect.

All in all, the economic statistics, properly interpreted and supplemented with other relevant information, suggest that a fundamental economic transformation has been occurring in Poland since 1991. While it is undeniable that there have been "losers" as well as "winners" in this process, the basic direction of change has been toward an economy able to provide far higher standards of living for everyone, on the basis of real productivity gains rather than the artificial stimulation of demand by the government. The hallmarks of this transformation have been the creation of large-scale private ownership of productive resources; a market system; a thriving export sector; an end to shortages; a decisive shift from heavy industry to consumer goods and services; and prospects for closer integration with the world economy.

Unemployment

One consequence of the reforms was an initial rise in unemployment. The unemployment rate rose from very low levels in 1990 to 13 percent at the end of 1991. Again, however, the data are suspect: a significant number of those counted as unemployed were working in the "second" economy or on farms while collecting unemployment compensation. For this reason, the pessimistic forecasts of a "catastrophic rise" in unemployment turned out to be wrong. The lesson of the Polish experience is that if firm wage restraint is maintained to prevent wage gains from exceeding productivity gains, and if the private sector is allowed to grow without restraints, then stabilization and restructuring are compatible with unchanged or even declining unemployment.

[4]Indeed, the national accounts of these countries were still being compiled primarily on the basis of the central planning methodology (the Material Product System, or MPS), which did not count services but focused on the net material product.

Financial Policies

Strong fiscal adjustment efforts supported by a tight monetary policy was the key feature of the Polish authorities' stabilization program. The strength of the fiscal adjustment soon became evident in the turnaround in the government's fiscal position. The deficit disappeared, falling from 7.4 percent of GDP in 1989 to zero, and a surplus of 3.1 percent emerged in 1990. Most of this massive adjustment came from the large cuts in expenditures—over 7 percentage points of GDP—achieved through sharp cutbacks in subsidies on food and energy and restraint in raising government wages. Although this fiscal adjustment was reversed in 1991, in part because of the contraction in output attendant on the collapse of CMEA trade and in part because of large wage increases, the authorities managed to regain the momentum of the fiscal adjustment in 1992–93, stabilizing the general government deficit at about 3 percent of GDP.

Monetary policy, especially the peg to the U.S. dollar, supported fiscal restraint, especially in the early phases of the reforms. Despite heavy borrowing from the banking sector to finance the deficit, the authorities succeeded in reducing inflation. One factor in this decline was the rising demand for money as private savings moved into the banking system, attracted by positive real rates of interest on bank deposits. The loosening of interest rate regulation and the success in reducing inflation helped to keep interest rates on deposits broadly positive and to reduce dollarization in the initial stages of the stabilization program (Charts 1.3, 1.4, and 1.5).

Exchange Rate Policy

The Polish experience of exchange rate management offers a number of lessons for policymakers in liberalizing economies.

First, if it is supported by appropriate monetary and wage restraint, an exchange rate peg can provide a valuable instrument of disinflation.

Second, the level at which the rate is pegged is the major determinant of the peg's success in reconciling the objectives of lowering inflation and maintaining competitiveness and of its durability.

Third, the timing of the so-called "exit" from a peg to a more flexible exchange rate is important in preventing the crisis of confidence that can be brought about by speculative attacks on the pegged exchange rate.

Fourth, under a crawling exchange rate regime, a rate of crawl lower than the inflation differential can help reduce inflation without sacrificing competitiveness.

Chart 1.3. Poland: Money and Inflation[1]

(Year-on-year percent change)

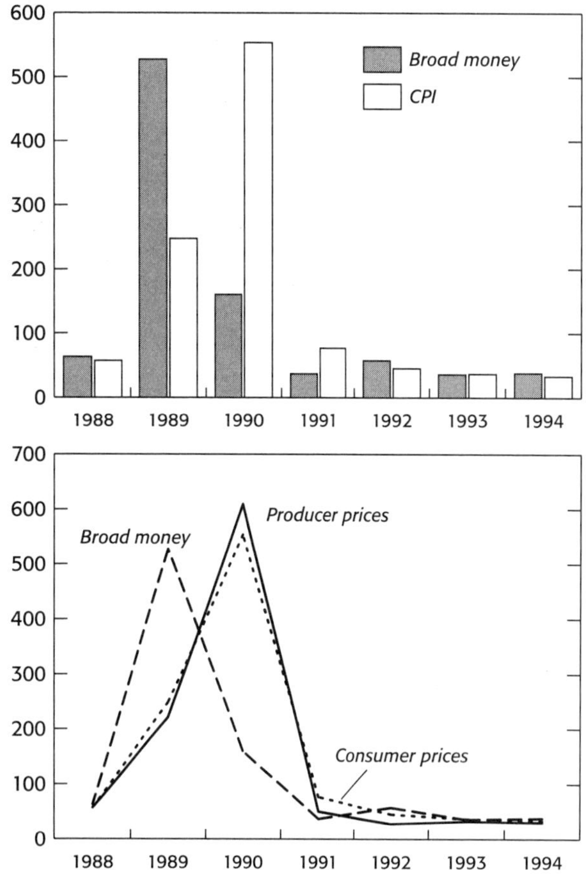

Sources: IMF Institute database and Tables 2.5 and 5.1.

[1]Broad money is defined as zloty broad money plus foreign currency deposits. Inflation is measured by the CPI.

Fifth, a partial solution to the problem of monetary expansion fueled by capital inflows is a move to greater flexibility in the exchange rate (see below).

Trade Liberalization

In the prereform period, Poland traded almost exclusively with other CMEA countries. Trade was governed by bilateral barter and based on prices fixed by governments. The trading environment at the onset of reforms was burdened by administrative impediments, limited freedom of entry, high tariffs, numerous nontariff barriers, and a currency that was not convertible. The radical reforms announced in January 1990 involved sharply reducing or eliminating most tariffs and nontariff barriers, lifting import and export licensing requirements and making the zloty convertible for current account transactions at the new devalued exchange rate. At the beginning of 1990, the General Agreement on Tariffs and Trade (GATT; now the World Trade Organization, or WTO) declared the Polish trade regime to be one of the most liberal in Europe.

This trade liberalization was partially reversed in early 1991 in the face of a worsening current account deficit, and several tariffs were raised and some nontariff barriers reimposed. During 1992–93, Poland returned to the path of liberalization; however, in contrast to the unilateral decisions of 1990 that reduced both tariffs and nontariff barriers, the liberalization took place in the context of negotiations with Poland's trading partners. The consultations culminated in free trade agreements with the countries of the European Union, the European Free Trade Area (EFTA), and the Central European Free Trade Area (CEFTA) covering industrial goods and raw materials. As the deep-seated anti-export bias of the old regime—reflected in an overvalued exchange rate, chronic excess domestic demand, and explicit trade barriers that included quantitative restrictions on exports—was removed, exports (especially to Western markets) boomed.

Chart 1.4. Poland: Nominal Interest Rates
(In percent)

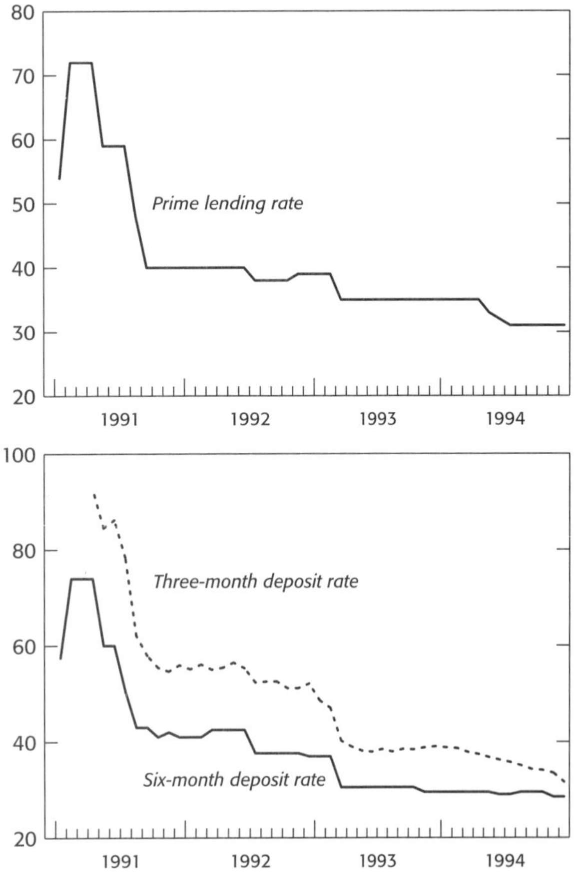

Sources: IMF Institute database and Table 5.3.

Recent Challenges to Macroeconomic Policy

Since 1993, Poland has experienced strong economic growth, sustained by gains in productivity and a positive export performance. In 1994, Poland's economy expanded at an annual rate of 6 percent. Growth has not been hindered, as it often was in the past, by a balance of payments constraint. Indeed, taking into account estimated unrecorded trade, the current account recorded a surplus of over 2 percent of GDP in 1994, and official reserves have continued to rise.

The buildup of international reserves, which reflected the sizable capital inflows of early 1995, caused the money supply to expand faster than planned. The monetary authorities' efforts to sterilize the inflows met with only partial success, and the rapid monetary expansion contributed to the persistent inflation that hovered at about 30 percent a year. The authorities, concerned about the inflationary impact of the capital inflows, first reacted by reducing the rate of the exchange rate crawl from 1.4 percent to 1.2 percent a month in February 1995. When this step did not ease the pressure on monetary expansion, in May 1995, the authorities announced the move to a managed float, which allowed the exchange rate to fluctuate within a band of ± 7 percent on either side of the official rate. The zloty has been allowed to appreciate by 5 percent within the band, helping to put downward pressure on inflation. Despite these policy adaptations, the goal of reducing inflation to less than 20 percent a year has proved difficult to achieve.

The fiscal policy stance has been broadly supportive of the macroeconomic adjustment, although here, too, the pace of adjustment has slowed in recent years. The general government deficit, which stood at about 6.5 percent of GDP in 1991–92, was reduced to under 3 percent of GDP by 1993–94, but further reductions have proved harder to achieve. The downward trend in national saving, which have declined as a proportion of GDP from 20 percent in 1991 to about 15 percent in 1993 (in current prices), highlights the need to increase private saving. The fall in saving may in part reflect a sharp rise in consumption after several years of repressed demand for consumer goods. Should the downward trend continue, however, it could pose a challenge to macroeconomic policy in Poland, as there is a continuing need for noninflationary financing of the fiscal deficits and access to foreign saving may be limited.

The persistence of inflation in Poland reflects a challenge to economic policy confronting a number of countries in transition. The challenge is how to move from moderate to low inflation at an acceptable cost in lost output.[5] It is now well understood that besides the monetary causes of inflation dis-

Chart 1.5. Poland: Foreign Currency Deposits
(In billions of U.S. dollars)

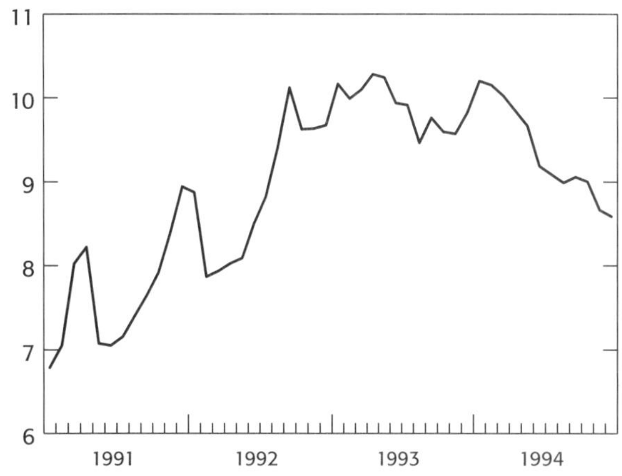

Sources: IMF Institute database and Tables 5.1 and 5.2.

[5]See "Moving from Moderate to Low Inflation in Poland," *IMF Survey*, February 5, 1996. For a broader coverage of this issue, see Sharmini Coorey, M. Mecagni, and Erik Offerdal, "Disinflation in Transition Economies: The Role of Relative Price Adjustments," IMF Working Paper 96/138 (Washington: International Monetary Fund, December 1996).

cussed above, some "real" factors such as relative price adjustment, indexation mechanisms, and enterprise restructuring also play a key role in the inflation process in the transition economies.

The necessity of large relative price adjustments creates an inflationary bias in these economies, because while firms and sectors facing large shocks raise their prices, there are no offsetting decreases in prices elsewhere in the economy. The impact on inflation is also exacerbated by the existence of wage and price indexation. The resulting inflexibility in prices forces the monetary authorities to accommodate inflation to a greater extent than they would otherwise prefer to do, because of the high output costs of nonaccommodation. The authorities are also concerned that the burden of a tight monetary policy should not be borne disproportionately by the emerging private sector. To avoid this risk, a faster restructuring of traditionally dominant industries and the imposition of a hard budget constraint on state enterprises are essential. Thus, the ideal anti-inflationary strategy would combine a tight monetary policy with faster restructuring and gradual elimination of indexation, in order to make the needed relative price adjustment compatible with progress from moderate to low inflation.

Goals and Strategies of Transition[6]

With the collapse of central planning throughout Central and Eastern Europe and the states of the former Soviet Union, a number of countries besides Poland embarked on programs of economic reform that would lead to market-based regimes. The economic strategies these countries employed had several interrelated objectives that would support the overall goal of making a successful *transition* from central planning to a market economy, including *macroeconomic stabilization*, *structural reform*, and the *liberalization of prices and the trade regime*. Each country's strategy was influenced by the degree of emphasis the government placed on the individual objectives, which in turn was dictated by initial conditions, existing economic structures, the severity of the macroeconomic imbalances confronting the authorities, and any broad social and political objectives. The case of Poland illustrates how an individual country's transition strategies are shaped by its own history, institutions, and wider sociopolitical conditions and objectives.

The desire to make the *transition* to a mode of economic organization based on market signals rather than on central directives reflects the recent worldwide consensus that a market-based economy is the more efficient and dynamic way of generating and allocating resources. Centrally planned economies are handicapped by perverse incentives, a lack of information, bureaucratization, and the associated risks of corruption and the abuse of power. While it is widely recognized that markets can fail and that there are circumstances in which government intervention is justified, on balance the market allocates an economy's resources to alternative activities far more efficiently than the government. Moreover, a market economy provides individuals with certain rights—to choose an occupation, consume the goods and services one prefers, and take risks—which are widely seen as fundamental not only to a desirable standard of living, but, also, to individual liberty.

Macroeconomic *stabilization* is concerned with macroeconomic variables such as output, employment, inflation, the balance of payments, and public debt. Since many transition economies have suffered from severe macroeconomic imbalances that have manifested themselves in high inflation and falling output, stabilization has been a high priority among economic policymakers. Progress in macroeconomic stabilization—particularly in bringing down the rate of inflation—is often a precondition for the structural reforms that will support the successful transition to a market economy.

The process of transition to the market encompasses three sets of reforms:

- Stabilization needs to be accompanied by freeing of prices, trade, and entry to markets. Liberalization is a precondition for realizing the other benefits of structural and institutional reforms.
- Clarification of property rights and privatization are essential if individuals and businesses are to respond efficiently to market forces.
- Reshaping of social services and the social safety net with a view to ease the pain of transition is the third critical aspect of the reform process. It is the key to sustaining popular support for the reform process over the long run.

Economic Agents and the Transition to a Market Economy

The transition to an open market-based economy entails changes in virtually all areas of the economy

[6]For a comprehensive review of the experience of transition and the preliminary lessons of this experience, see "From Plan to Market," *World Development Report 1996* (Washington: World Bank, 1996); and the Annual Reports of the European Bank for Reconstruction and Development.

and significantly alters the activities of the key economic players. The new roles are outlined briefly below.

- In a market economy, the *government's role* is not eliminated, but it is drastically transformed from what it was under central planning. Rather than allocating resources and setting quotas for output, the state provides certain "public" goods and services, such as a national defense, law enforcement, environmental protection, and social safety nets for vulnerable sections of the population. It ensures that markets function properly and enforces the rules governing economic operations. Enforcing the rules involves supervising the behavior of enterprises and financial institutions and maintaining legal structures that ensure property rights, regulate private contracts, and promote the smooth functioning of markets.
- The principal productive activities in any free market economy are carried out by *privately owned enterprises* whose owners seek to maximize their profits. Because the search for profits constitutes the main driving force in the economy, the share of total output the private sector generates is often regarded as the key indicator of progress in the transition to a free market. Similarly, privatizing the previously state-owned enterprises is a major element in policies aimed at making a successful transition.
- For an economy to operate efficiently, markets must perform their role in a transparent and legitimate fashion. *Well-functioning markets* are characterized by free trade in a range of goods and services; clear information about prices and quality; flexible prices; and, most importantly, competition, which is ensured if new firms can easily gain entry. Many of the benefits a market economy offers in terms of efficiency and innovation hinge on the existence of competitive markets. Opening the economy to international trade is often the surest means of ensuring competition in domestic markets.
- *Financial institutions* play a pivotal role in a market economy by channeling saving and investment. Financial markets allocate and assess risks, provide a payments mechanism, and ensure that enterprises maintain financial discipline. Fostering a private financial sector that can offer intermediation services in the saving-investment process is therefore a key part of making the transition to the market. But profit-oriented financial institutions are central to a transition economy for another reason. Under central planning, banks were required to provide credit to public enterprises operating under a "soft" budget constraint. The result was an increasing number of "bad" bank loans. Financial institutions must be able to act autonomously and to enforce a "hard" budget constraint on enterprises (with the ultimate sanction of bankruptcy).

Economic Strategies for Transition Economies

The experiences of countries in different parts of the world suggest that there is no one "right" path for making a successful market economy. The sequencing of reforms and the speed with which they are implemented depend largely on country-specific factors such as initial conditions, political constraints, and institutional history. Nevertheless, there is growing consensus on the main points. It is clear from the available evidence on transition economies in Central and Eastern Europe and the states of the former Soviet Union that those countries which have enjoyed the most success have pressed ahead on several fronts, including stabilization, liberalization, privatization, and restructuring. Not only have they made relatively rapid gains in their move to a market-based economy, but they have also seen a rapid reduction in inflation and a more moderate decline in output. In some sectors, however, the pace of change is necessarily slower and requires a gradual approach. Overhauling legislation, legal and judicial structures, and related institutions, for instance, takes time. Gradualism in such areas is effective if the country's overall transition strategy succeeds in gaining (and maintaining) credibility among domestic and international investors. Thus, the authorities must be committed not just to the reform process; they must also be willing to build popular coalitions in support of a consensus on economic reforms.

CHAPTER

2 Analysis of the Real Sector

Macroeconomics focuses on the analysis of macroeconomic variables such as the economy's total output, the rates of inflation and unemployment, the balance of payments, and the exchange rate. It attempts to explain developments in these aggregates and to guide policymakers in their pursuit of economic objectives and efforts to respond to changes in the economic environment. An accurate analysis of events, and consequently the design of appropriate policies, requires accurate economic information and statistics that are made available in a systematic and timely fashion.

The System of National Accounts (SNA)

The System of National Accounts (SNA) was developed as an accounting framework within which macroeconomic data can be compiled and presented for economic analysis. It provides an internationally recognized system for organizing a continuous flow of information that is indispensable to the analysis, evaluation, and monitoring of a country's economic performance.[1] Other important uses of the SNA include:

- *Macroeconomic analysis.* Flexible enough to accommodate different economic theories and models and to meet the needs of countries at various stages of development, the SNA is a suitable statistical framework for such analysis.
- *Intertemporal comparisons.* The SNA is a coherent system for tracking the performance of key macroeconomic aggregates such as output and employment over time.
- *International comparisons.* The SNA is used for reporting to international organizations national accounts data that conform to internationally accepted definitions and classifications. These data allow for comparisons of national accounts that are useful in many areas—for example, in determining eligibility for concessional assistance, in calculating quotas for IMF member countries, and, more generally, in measuring the relative economic power of countries. Such comparisons require that measures of output be converted into a common currency.[2]

The SNA accounting framework, the principles underlying it, and its application to the Polish national accounts data are set out briefly in the appendix to this chapter. The reader needs to become familiar with this accounting framework to understand the macroeconomic accounting and analysis presented in this chapter.

The sections that follow discuss the main macroeconomic aggregates and the basic macroeconomic relationships. Also covered are the issues related to the measurement and analysis of inflation; a discussion of the concepts of employment, unemployment, real wages, and pricing and incomes policies, with special emphasis on the transition economies; an overview of the developments in output, employment, prices, and wages in Poland in recent years; and exercises and issues for discussion.

The Key Macroeconomic Aggregates

This section discusses the main macroeconomic sectors and aggregates, the alternative approaches to gross domestic product (GDP), and the basic national

[1]This section is based on the revised SNA as described in the *System of National Accounts*, Commission of European Communities, International Monetary Fund, Organization for Economic Cooperation and Development, United Nations, and The World Bank, 1993. The previous version of SNA was published in 1968, United Nations, Statistical Office, *A System of National Accounts*, Studies in Methods, Series F, Number 2, Revision 3 (New York: United Nations, 1968). A summary of the main differences between the two versions of the SNA is shown in Appendix Table 2.10.

[2]See Anne-Marie Gulde and Marianne Schulze-Ghattas, "Purchasing Power Parity Based Weights for the World Economic Outlook," *Staff Studies for the World Economic Outlook* (Washington: International Monetary Fund, December 1993).

accounting relationships such as the one between the aggregate income and absorption and the external current account balance.

The Main Economic Sectors

There are five key economic sectors: households, enterprises, the financial sector, the government, and the rest of the world.

Households supply land, labor, and capital to various *factor markets* and demand goods and services in the *market for products*, but they may also work as producers by forming unincorporated enterprises. They make decisions about how much to spend on consumption and how much to save, and how much to invest in the *financial markets* based on their perception of the prevailing economic environment and their expectations about future developments.

Enterprises employ factors of production such as land, labor, and capital to produce goods and services for the market. They make production and investment decisions with a view to maximizing their profits.

The *financial sector* provides financial intermediation services for the economy. It includes all entities whose main activity is financial intermediation, including the banking system and other financial institutions such as mutual funds, credit unions, pension funds, and insurance companies.

The *government's* economic role involves creating an effective regulatory and legal framework; providing certain public goods, such as education, infrastructure, and a social safety net; overseeing the tax system; and managing government expenditures.

The rest of the world sector groups together all of an economy's transactions with nonresidents.

The Main Aggregates

The macroeconomic concepts that follow, which play a central role in macroeconomic analysis, are defined in the framework of the SNA.

Gross output (Q) is the value of all goods and services produced in the economy. This concept is a problematic one because of what is called double-counting. For example, the value of wheat may be counted twice: first, when it is used in the production of bread, and again as the value of bread output.

Value added (VA) is the value of gross output less the value of intermediate consumption. Economists use the concept of value added to measure a country's output. Nonmarket output is distinguished from market output; nonmarket output includes mostly own-account production, such as subsistence farming and owner-occupied housing.

Consumption is divided into two distinct kinds: intermediate and final consumption. Intermediate consumption refers to inputs into production, while final consumption refers to goods and services—both imported and domestically produced—used by households and the government sector.

Gross domestic product (GDP) is defined as the sum of value added across all sectors in the economy. GDP measures the value of *final* goods and services in an economy.

Investment (gross capital formation), in macroeconomic terms, refers to additions to the physical stock of capital in an economy. It is also sometimes defined as output produced during the current year but not used for present consumption. Investment in the macroeconomic sense includes the building of machinery, factories, and houses and changes in inventories.[3] Thus, purchase of a bond or buying a stock that is called investment from an individual's standpoint in everyday language is not investment in the macroeconomic sense, because these transactions reflect only the transfer of financial assets among economic agents.[4]

Depreciation is used to differentiate *net* from *gross* investment and is sometimes called the *consumption of fixed capital*. Since capital stock wears out over time, depreciation, or the cost of replacing the capital used up during a period, is subtracted from gross investment to derive net investment. This relation can be written as:

$$\textit{Net investment} = \textit{Gross investment} - \textit{Depreciation}.$$

Net investment is a more accurate measure of the addition to productive capacity than gross investment.

Net exports, which are equal to the value of exports of goods and services less the value of imports of goods and services, are used to measure the impact of foreign trade on aggregate demand.[5] Net exports are a component of the total demand for domestic goods and services and can play an important role in determining GDP.

[3]Includes inventories of *finished goods* and *work in progress* only. Inventories of intermediate inputs are *not* included.

[4]In a broader sense, any current activity that increases the economy's ability to produce output in the future can be called investment. In this sense, education can be regarded as investment in human capital, since it enhances the ability of the labor force to produce goods and services.

[5]There are different concepts of net exports, depending on what is included in services. A distinction is often made between factor and nonfactor services. Factor services in this context refer to income received from or paid to nonresidents for services provided by a factor of production, such as labor (wages) or capital (interest).

Absorption (*A*), also called aggregate domestic demand, is defined as the sum of total final consumption (C) and gross investment (*I*): $A = C + I$.

The Circular Flow of Income and Spending

The circular flow shown in Chart 2.1 captures important relationships among the key economic sectors and markets. Income flows are shown in the bottom half of the diagram and spending flows in the top half. The main monetary flow is between enterprises and households; money flows from enterprises to households as income and from households to enterprises as spending. At various points in the circular flow, money can be diverted from this stream in what are called *leakages*. Private sector tax payments and spending on imports are leakages from the domestic spending stream. They are offset by *injections* of income and spending into the mainstream—for example, spending by entities other than domestic households; government transfers and purchases; investment; and exports. The sum of all leakages *equals* the sum of all injections.

Alternative Approaches to Determining GDP

The most basic macroeconomic aggregate, the GDP, can be determined using three basic approaches: the production approach, the income approach, and the expenditure approach. These alternative approaches yield equivalent results.

The Production Approach[6]

According to the production approach, GDP equals the sum of gross value added for the economy, or the difference between the value of production (output) and the value of all goods and services used up in the production process (i.e., intermediate consumption). Thus,

$$GDP = \Sigma VA \quad (2.1)$$

where

ΣVA = *sum of value added across all sectors in the economy*.

It should be noted that GDP is based on the notion of residency, so that only production by residents is captured. It should also be noted that it is a *gross concept*, in that it includes depreciation (consumption of fixed capital). The corresponding concept of net production is the *net domestic product* (*NDP*), which can be defined as

$$NDP = GDP - D \quad (2.2)$$

where

D = *depreciation or consumption of fixed capital*.

Depreciation at the level of the whole economy, however, is difficult to measure precisely and is available only with some lag. For this reason, GDP has been the preferred aggregate for measuring total output, even though it may overestimate production.

The Income Approach

GDP can also be considered as equal to the sum of incomes generated by resident producers. Thus,

$$GDP = W + OS + TSP \quad (2.3)$$

where

W = compensation of employees, including wages, salaries, and other labor costs (employers' social security contributions plus employees' social security contributions)

OS = gross operating surplus of enterprises (including profits, rents, interest, and depreciation)[7]

TSP = taxes less subsidies on products.[8]

The Expenditure Approach

Using this approach, GDP is equal to the sum of its final uses. Thus,

$$GDP = C + I + (X - M) \quad (2.4)$$

where

C = final consumption of the government and nongovernment sectors

I = gross investment (fixed capital formation and changes in inventories)

X = exports of goods and nonfactor services

M = imports of goods and nonfactor services.

Box 2.1 summarizes the three approaches and highlights the relationships among the key macroeconomic aggregates.

[6]The identities used here hold only if the components are valued according to the SNA. For a summary of the issues involved in valuation, see the appendix to this chapter.

[7]The operating surplus also includes any statistical discrepancies.

[8]Called "indirect taxes less subsidies" under the previous version of the SNA. The term *indirect taxes* is no longer used to refer to taxes on production and consumption, because it is difficult to determine the real incidence of different kinds of taxes, making the distinction between direct and indirect taxes arbitrary (see Chapter 7, Section C, of the 1993 *System of National Accounts*).

Chart 2.1. The Circular Flow of Income, Expenditure, and Financing[1]

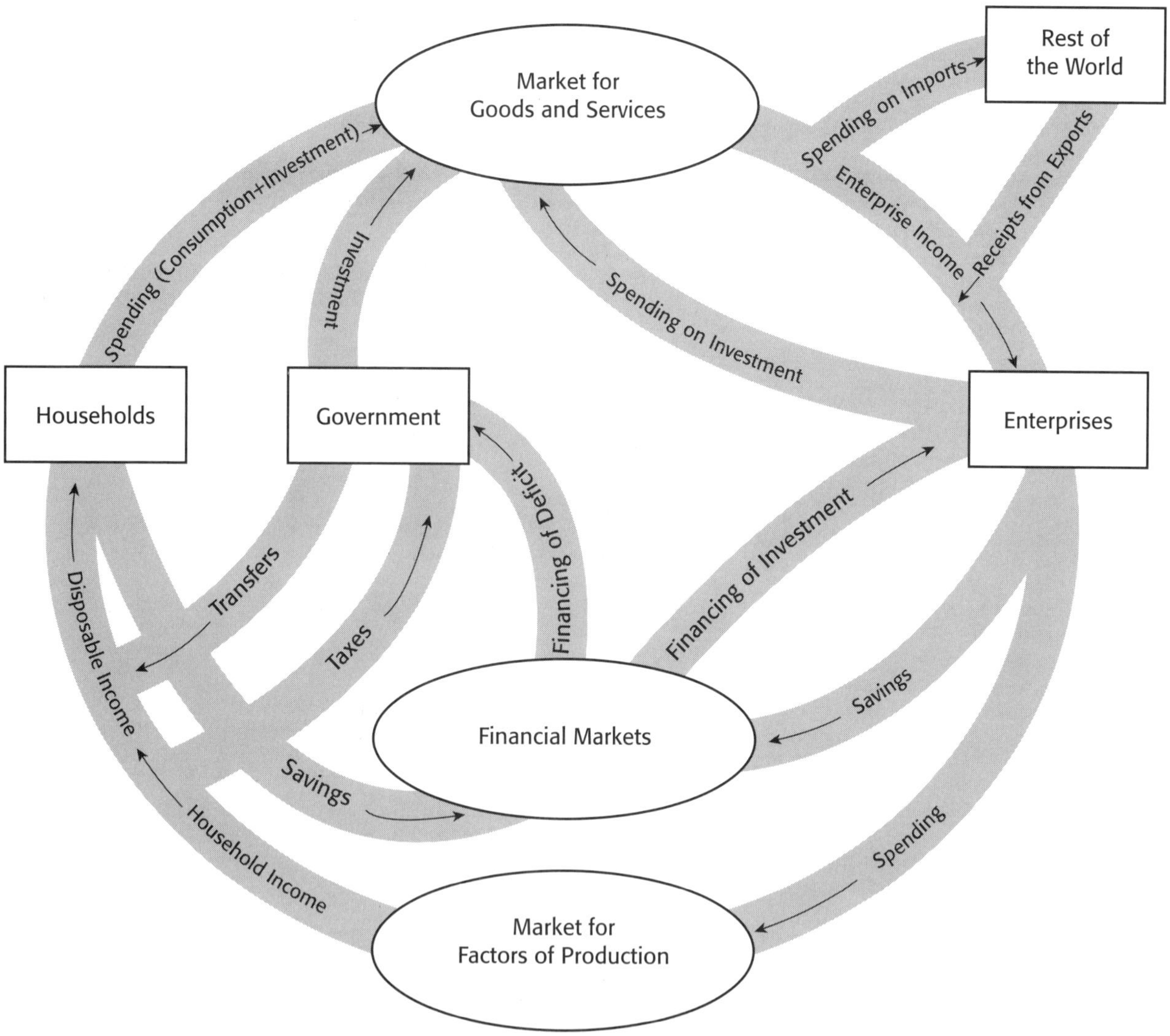

[1]The chart, in the interest of simplicity, shows only financing from domestic financial markets. In reality, households, enterprises, and government have access to external financing as well.

Other Standard Aggregates

Because GDP measures only the income derived from *domestic production*, it does not fully cover the economy's overall income from all sources, which has a key influence on aggregate demand. Accordingly, the SNA defines two additional income aggregates: *gross national income* (GNI), and *gross national disposable income* (GNDI). These aggregates are established on a *national* rather than *domestic* basis because they exclude income generated locally but paid to nonresidents and include incomes generated abroad but paid to residents.

Gross National Income

Because GDP measures final output produced by residents, it ignores income received from or paid to nonresidents. In contrast, gross national income (GNI) also captures *net factor income from abroad* (Y_f). Thus, GNI is equal to GDP *less* factor incomes payable to nonresidents *plus* factor incomes receiv-

Box 2.1.
SNA: Key Aggregates

Production	Income	Expenditure[1]
Value added by: Agriculture Industry Services Government Services = *GDP* (at basic prices) + Taxes less subsidies on products (*TSP*)	Compensation of employees (W) + Operating surplus of enterprises (OS) (including depreciation) = GDP (at basic prices) + Taxes less subsidies on products (*TSP*)	Private consumption (CP) + General government consumption (CG) + Gross investment (*I*) + Exports of goods and nonfactor services (*X*) – Imports of goods and nonfactor services (M)[2]
Gross domestic product = *GDP* (at market prices)	= *GDP* (at market prices)	= *GDP* (at market prices)
	+ Net factor income from abroad (Y_f)	+ Net factor income from abroad (Y_f)
	= Gross national income (*GNI*) (at market prices)	= *GNI* (at market prices)
	+ Net current transfers (TR_f)	+ Net current transfers (TR_f)
	= Gross national disposable income *GNDI* (at market prices)	= *GNDI* (at market prices)
	– Depreciation (*D*)	– Depreciation (*D*)
	= Net national disposable income (*NNDI*) (at market prices)	= *NNDI* (at market prices)

[1]Valued at purchaser's prices.
[2]Unlike other components of expenditure that are valued at purchaser's prices, imports are valued f.o.b., but not at purchaser's prices; in particular, they do not include taxes plus subsidies on imports (see appendix to this chapter).

able from nonresidents. Such factor incomes are primarily (i) capital income, which includes investment income in the form of dividends on direct investment and interest on external borrowing or lending; (ii) labor income of migrant and seasonal workers; and (iii) service income on land, building rentals, and royalties. Thus,

$$GNI = GDP + Y_f. \tag{2.5}$$

Note that unlike GDP, which is a concept of both production and income, GNI is a concept only of income (primary income). In previous versions of the SNA, the GNI at market prices was called the *gross national product* (*GNP*).

Gross National Disposable Income

The total income available to residents for either final consumption or saving is the *gross national disposable income* (*GNDI*). It is obtained by adding *net current transfers* received from abroad (TR_f) to *gross national income* (*GNI*).

$$GNDI = GNI + TR_f. \tag{2.6}$$

Net current transfers from abroad are equal to current transfers received from nonresidents, which are unrelated to income earned with factors of production, *minus* such transfers remitted abroad. These transfers may be either private or public. Private transfers include mostly workers' remittances, public transfers, mostly government grants. The distinction between current and capital transfers is often blurred, potentially affecting the calculation of aggregate saving.

Gross National Saving

Gross national saving (*S*) is defined as the difference between gross national disposable income (*GNDI*) and final consumption (*C*).[9] Thus,

[9]Although net national disposable income (NNDI) is the aggregate that should be used for analysis of the generation of income and wealth, for practical reasons gross national disposable

$$S = GNDI - C. \quad (2.7)$$

Basic Accounting Relationships

The national income accounting framework yields two important relations that lie at the heart of macroeconomic analysis and therefore deserve special emphasis. These key relations are derived from the identity linking GDP with its expenditure counterparts. The first highlights the links between *aggregate income and demand* and the *external current account balance*.[10] The second focuses on the linkages between *aggregate saving and investment* and *the external current account balance*.

Aggregate Income and Absorption and the External Current Account Balance

A first set of interrelations between the national accounts and balance of payments aggregates can be derived from the basic identities defining GDP, GNI, and GNDI. As detailed in Box 2.2, the current account balance (*CAB*) is, ex post, identical to the gap between GNDI and absorption (*A*), or:

$$GNDI - A = CAB. \quad (2.8)$$

This identity forms the basis for the so-called *absorption approach* to the balance of payments. The intuitive interpretation of this relation is that a current account deficit occurs whenever a country spends beyond its means or absorbs more than it produces. In other words, current account deficits mirror an excess of absorption over income. Accordingly, to reduce a current account deficit, the country's income must be increased and/or absorption must be reduced. Increasing output (and therefore income) in the short term requires unused production capacity, and in the medium term, adequate structural policies. Domestic absorption can be reduced by contracting final consumption (*C*) and/or gross investment (*I*). Although the income-absorption identity has important implications for the design of adjustment programs, it remains only an accounting relationship and does not provide a theory of current account behavior. Other factors (such as exchange rates, interest rates, and exogenous shocks) must be introduced to explain current account developments.

A second way to develop a relationship between the national account aggregates and the current account balance is through the saving-investment balance of the economy. As detailed in Box 2.2, the current account of the balance of payments (*CAB*) is, ex post, equivalent to the gap between the saving (*S*) and investment (*I*) of the economy.

Thus,

$$S - I = CAB \quad (2.9)$$

or

$$\begin{matrix} \textit{Economywide} & & \textit{Current} & & \textit{Use of} \\ \textit{saving} - \textit{Investment} & = & \textit{account} & = & \textit{foreign} \\ \textit{gap} & & \textit{balance} & & \textit{saving}. \end{matrix} \quad (2.10)$$

In other words, the economy's saving-investment balance and the external current account balance, which can be viewed as the country's use of foreign saving, are equivalent.

In a closed economy, ex-post aggregate saving is necessarily equal to aggregate investment. In an open economy, however, the difference between aggregate saving and investment is the current account balance. Put differently, any economywide excess of investment over saving must be covered, ex post, by foreign saving. In principle, then, a current account deficit can be reduced by increasing saving and/or reducing investment. When investment exceeds saving, the country must borrow the difference from abroad—that is, it must use foreign saving. As seen in Box 2.2, the identity between the saving-investment balance and the current account balance is a corollary to the income-absorption identity. These relationships are ex post identities that always hold, but they do not provide an explanation of any imbalances in the economy, the underlying behavior of economic agents, or the desirability (or otherwise) of a particular imbalance.

The Resource Gap of the Nongovernment Sector and Its Financing

In the sectoral framework of the national income accounts, the real sector is identified as the sum of the household and enterprise sectors—that is, the nongovernment, nonbank sector, or simply the private sector. As it does for other sectors, the budget constraint links this sector's income-expenditure gap and its financing. This can be seen as follows. Private sector saving (*Sp*) is the difference between the sector's disposable income (*GNDIp*) and its consumption (*Cp*). This relation can be written as:

income (GNDI) is more widely used and is more appropriate for flow-of-funds analysis because receipts and expenditures in the macroeconomic accounts are expressed on a gross basis. Another aggregate sometimes used is *gross domestic saving*, defined as *S* *minus* net current transfers from abroad (TR_f) and net factor income from abroad (Y_f).

[10]The external current account balance is analyzed in more detail in Chapter 4. It is defined as exports of goods and services *minus* imports of goods and services *plus* net factor income from abroad *plus* net current transfers from abroad.

Box 2.2.
Relations Between Aggregate Income and Demand and the External Current Account Balance

Basic Income and Expenditure Aggregates[1]

Gross domestic product (GDP)	=	$C + I + (X - M) = A + (X - M)$	(1)
Gross national income (GNI)	=	$GDP + Y_f = C + I + (X - M + Y_f)$	(2)
	=	$A + (X - M + Y_f)$	(3)
Gross national disposable income (GNDI)	=	$GNI + TR_f$	(4)
	=	$C + I + (X - M + Y_f + TR_f)$	(5)
	=	$A + (X - M + Y_f + TR_f)$	(6)
or $GNDI - A$	=	$X - M + Y_f + TR_f$	(7)
$GNDI - A$	=	current account balance (CAB).	
Since $GNDI - C$	=	S by definition, it follows	
that $GNDI - C$	=	$I + X - M + Y_f + TR_f = S.$	(8)

Therefore

$$S - I = X - M + Y_f + TR_f = CAB \quad (9)$$

where

A = Domestic absorption ($A = C + I$) or domestic demand
X = Exports of goods and nonfactor services
M = Imports of goods and nonfactor services
Y_f = Net factor income from abroad
TR_f = Net transfers from abroad
C = Final consumption
I = Gross investment (including changes in inventories)
S = Gross national saving.

[1]In interpreting these identities, it is important to keep in mind the valuation issues discussed in the appendix.

$$S_p = GNDI_p - C_p \quad (2.11)$$

and the sector's absorption as

$$A_p = C_p + I_p$$

where I_p is private sector gross investment. It follows that

$$GNDI_p - A_p = (S_p - I_p), \text{ or} \quad (2.12)$$

$$F_p = -(S_p - I_p), \quad (2.13)$$

where F_p = *financing gap*.

Put differently, the private sector's resource gap reflects an excess of absorption over income. This gap must then be financed by the rest of the economy, including the rest of the world sector; the analyst's task is to identify the ways in which this resource gap is financed or, alternatively, the ways in which savings are utilized. A financing gap can be covered by foreign direct investment from abroad (FDI_p), net borrowing by this sector from abroad (NFB_p) and private sector borrowing from the banking system, which is identical to the net credit from the banking system to the private sector (ΔNDC_p). These financial inflows are offset by financial outflows from the private sector—that is, its lending to the banking system in the form of increased currency holdings and deposits ($\Delta M2$); and its lending to the government, or the nonbank borrowing of the government from the private sector (NB). Therefore,

$$F_p = FDI_p + NFB_p + \Delta NDC_p - \Delta M2 - NB. \quad (2.14)$$

From equation 2.13, it follows that

$$S_p - I_p + FDI_p + NFB_p + \Delta NDC_p - \Delta M2 - NB = 0. \quad (2.15)$$

Analysts wanting to see how the private sector affects and is affected by the rest of the economy need to understand these accounting relationships. This understanding also paves the way for the fuller exposition of the flow of funds among economic sectors that is discussed in Chapter 6.

Nominal and Real GDP

As noted earlier, nominal GDP measures the value of output for a given year in the prices of that year. Changes over time in nominal GDP will therefore reflect changes both in prices and in physical output. To capture only the changes in physical output, economists deflate the nominal GDP by an overall price index (the implicit GDP deflator). Thus:

- *Nominal GDP* measures the value of the output of the economy at *current prices*.
- *Real GDP*, referred to as "GDP at constant prices" in the *SNA*, measures the value of an economy's output using the prices of a fixed base year. Real GDP is useful in capturing real output growth, and, while it is not an ideal measure of real income or living standards, real GDP is by and large the most widely used measure of real income.
- The *implicit GDP deflator* is an index that measures the average price level of an economy's output relative to the base year. The index has a value of 100 in the base year. Thus, the percentage change in the GDP deflator measures the rate of price increases for all goods and services in the economy.

Nominal and real GDP and the implicit price deflator are linked by the following relationships:[11]

$$\text{Nominal GDP} = \text{Real GDP} \times \text{GDP Deflator}/100 \quad (2.16)$$

or

$$\text{Real GDP} = \frac{\text{Nominal GDP}}{\text{GDP Deflator}} \times 100 \quad (2.17)$$

or

$$\text{GDP Deflator} = \frac{\text{Nominal GDP}}{\text{Real GDP}} \times 100. \quad (2.18)$$

In terms of rates of growth:

$$(1 + v) \approx (1 + g) \times (1 + p) \quad (2.19)$$

where

v = rate of growth of nominal GDP in percent

g = rate of real GDP growth in percent

p = rate of inflation as measured by the GDP deflator in percent.

Problems of GDP Measurement[12]

Although GDP data are widely used to measure production and even the economic welfare of residents, the outcomes are imperfect, for four reasons:

- First, *some types of output are inaccurately measured because they are not traded in the market.* Examples of such output are government services; nonmarket activities such as volunteer work; subsistence farming; and the value of owner-occupied housing.
- Second, *the improvements in the quality of goods are not adequately reflected in the national accounts.* For example, the prices of computers may fall in spite of dramatic improvements in quality.
- Third, *some economic activities, although regarded as adding to real GDP, actually represent the use of resources to offset the impact of undesirable activities ("bads") such as crime, pollution, or threats to national security.* The GDP concept does not net out these "bads."
- Finally, the national accounts do not take into account environmental pollution or the degradation of natural resources, issues that are particularly important in developing and transition economies.

There is another major reason why economic output is often mismeasured: the *black market*, with its underground or concealed transactions. Economic agents attempt to conceal transactions for a variety of reasons: to avoid taxes, to evade laws or government regulations, or to hide illegal activities such as drug trafficking and smuggling. In many countries, the size of the underground economy is perceived as quite large, and there has been an explosion of research into this unofficial sector. Because black-market transactions are conducted mostly in cash, holdings of currency are often used to estimate the market's size. Alternative estimates are based on inconsistencies in the national account measures of GDP—that is, the difference between total income and total expenditures. If the underground economy grows relative to official measures of the economy,

[11]In transition economies, because of rapid changes in production and consumption patterns and the lack of reliable price indicators, it is often preferable to derive real GDP data using volume or quantity indicators rather than using a GDP deflator to deflate GDP at current prices.

[12]Based on Rudiger Dornbusch and Stanley Fischer, *Macroeconomies* (New York, NY: McGraw-Hill, 6th ed., 1994).

the measured growth rate of output is below the true growth rate. As the next section explains, many observers believe that transition economies harbor large black markets because of persistent controls and regulations in the official economy.

Special Measurement Problems in Transition Economies[13]

Underreporting of Output

The economies in transition have undergone dramatic changes in recent years. The limitations of available economic statistics, however, have led to considerable uncertainty about the actual effects of the adjustment process in these economies. Many observers believe that the size of the decline in output in the early stages of the reform programs may have been overstated by official statistics, and, conversely, that the strength of the subsequent recoveries is likely to be understated, for several reasons.

- *The underreporting of private output.* The key problem with measuring real output during the transition process is that the economies are changing rapidly in ways that the traditional statistics were not designed to capture. Relative declines in traditionally favored activities, such as state-owned industry, are accompanied by growth in areas the traditional statistical systems have neglected, such as private services. The result is that private sector growth is often underreported, while any weakness in overall economic activity or decline in living standards is exaggerated. An indication of how important the underreporting of private sector activity can be is provided by a close examination of employment figures in transition economies.
- *The inadequacy of existing statistical systems.* Traditional statistical systems, which were designed to monitor the activities of a small number of state trading organizations, have been overwhelmed by the explosion of small-scale private trading activity. For example, in 1995 foreigners made an estimated 100 million visits to Poland. Many of these visitors were involved in cross-border transactions in the formal and informal markets in commodities such as textiles, food, gasoline, and other consumer goods. These transactions were generally not recorded in official statistics, and similar reporting problems remain for some of the other transition countries.
- *Index number biases.* In addition to the direct underreporting of activity, an intractable index number problem arises during a transition. An index of total real output requires comparisons of the values of different physical outputs. In a market economy, the prices of goods provide the measure of their relative values and are used to construct output indexes. In a transition economy, however, prereform prices did not reflect the relative values of different goods. Although prices tended to reflect production costs, costs themselves did not reflect relative scarcities. Moreover, prior to reform, there were no mechanisms to bring relative costs into line with the value of output to consumers.[14]
- *Changes in the type and quality of output.* It is not clear how the large number of new goods and services should be valued or how dramatic changes in quality should be assessed. Although such problems exist in all countries, they are particularly severe in the countries in transition, where new, high-quality goods and the end of shortages imply higher standards of living and, in the case of capital goods, more efficient investment that go unrecorded. Further, before liberalization, some production could not be sold because of lack of demand but was nevertheless counted as output. After liberalization, production of this sort stopped, and measured production fell. But because these goods had no true economic value before liberalization, their disappearance from the market should not have been counted as a reduction in output.

There is very little direct evidence on the magnitude of these measurement problems, but it is clear that the errors are potentially huge. Attempts have been made to use indicators that are less biased against new activities than traditional statistics, such as data from household consumption surveys, which cover sales from private sector retailers. One study has suggested that Polish real GDP fell 5–8

[13]This section is adapted from the IMF's *World Economic Outlook* (Washington: International Monetary Fund, 1994). For a more technical discussion of national accounts measurement issues, see Adriaan M. Bloem, Paul Cotterell, and Terry Gigantes, "National Accounts in Transition Economies: Distortions and Biases," IMF Working Paper 96/130 (Washington: International Monetary Fund, 1996).

[14]See Kent Osband, "Index Number Biases During Price Liberalization," *Staff Papers*, International Monetary Fund, Vol. 39 (June 1992), pp. 287–309; and Vincent Koen, "Measuring the Transition: A User's View on National Accounts in Russia," IMF Working Paper 94/6 (Washington: International Monetary Fund, 1994).

percent from 1989 to 1990, with consumption falling substantially less than GDP; yet official estimates recorded a substantially higher decline (12 percent) in GDP.[15] Another study examined a variety of problems with the Polish statistics and concluded that the cumulative fall in real output from 1989 to 1992 was about 5–10 percent, in contrast to the "official" 18 percent decline.[16]

At a minimum, it is clear that any user of official statistics must be extremely cautious, keeping in mind the sources and coverage of the data. More generally, broad conclusions about the impact of economic reform programs in the countries in transition, and especially conclusions about the effects of reforms on standards of living, need to take account of the potentially large measurement problems.

The Transition from the MPS to the SNA

The centrally planned economies developed their own method of calculating national accounts, and several economies in transition still use the Material Product System (MPS) as the main economic accounting framework. Although in recent years international organizations have tried to improve the links between the SNA and the MPS, it will take some time for all countries to move to the SNA. In many cases, the GDP of transition economies is still scaled up from basic estimates derived from MPS concepts. The main issues that arise in comparing SNA and MPS estimates are summarized in Box 2.3.

Inflation

Measuring Inflation

A sustained and persistent increase in an economy's overall price level is generally called *inflation*. The increase in the average prices of all goods and services in the economy has to be distinguished from a change in the *relative prices* of individual goods and services. Generally, an overall increase in the price level is accompanied by a change in the structure of relative prices, but it is only the overall increase, not the relative price change, that constitutes inflation. A change in the relative price of a key good (such as oil) can often initiate a process that leads to generalized inflation, although appropriate policy actions can keep inflation from worsening. The GDP deflator (the ratio of nominal to real GDP) measures the prices of all goods and services produced.

Another important distinction must be made between a one-time increase in the price level and underlying inflation. For example, a rise in administered prices will raise the overall level of prices in the first instance. However, this increase will in turn bring about the needed relative price changes without necessarily adding to *underlying*, or *core inflation*, which reflects the basic changes in the overall price level, abstracting from unusual, one-time increases caused by events such as increases in administered prices and excise taxes or discrete devaluations of the exchange rate. While the underlying rate of inflation is not always easy to measure precisely, it can be estimated and may provide a better guide to policy than the measured rate of price inflation. Especially in the transition economies, analysts should focus on the underlying rate of inflation rather than on the measured rate of inflation because of the structural changes and reforms taking place, which inevitably result in a number of discrete adjustments in the prices of many goods and services.

It is, of course, possible for a one-time increase in the prices of certain goods, especially of key products such as energy, to trigger a chain of price (and wage) increases throughout the economy. If monetary policy is not sufficiently firm, a one-time increase in the price level can become a sustained increase in inflation (the cost-push phenomenon described in the following section). There are several examples of this type of initial cost-push phenomenon transforming into persistent inflation. A case in point was the worldwide increase in oil prices that triggered bouts of inflation in a number of oil-importing countries in the mid-1970s and the early 1980s. However, Japan which was a large importer of energy and therefore experienced a huge price shock, managed to keep inflation under control because the authorities followed nonaccommodating financial policies and the population accepted a temporary reduction in real incomes.

A commonly used measure of inflation, the *consumer price index* (*CPI*) measures the prices of a representative basket of goods and services purchased by the average consumer. The CPI is generally calculated on the basis of periodic surveys of consumer prices. There are three main differences between the GDP deflator and the CPI. The first lies in the types of the goods and services each index covers. The CPI takes into account only a subset of all goods and services in the economy

[15]Andrew Berg and Jeffrey Sachs, "Structural Adjustment and International Trade in Eastern Europe: The Case of Poland," *Economic Policy*, Vol. 14 (April 1992), pp. 117–73.

[16]Zenon Raweski, "National Income," *Results of the Polish Economic Transformation*, edited by L. Zienkowski (Warsaw: Glowny Urzad Statystyczny/Polish Academy of Sciences, 1993).

Box 2.3.
The Material Product System (MPS)

Gross domestic product (GDP) vs. gross material product (GMP)

Unlike the SNA, the MPS excludes "nonmaterial services" from the measure of aggregate output and income. Accordingly, under the MPS, only the activities of the "material sphere" contribute to the creation of national income.

- *Nonmaterial services*. These include government services, education, health care, personal services, and transportation not related to production of material goods.
- *Material product*. This measure includes production of both material goods and services. Material services comprise mostly the transport of goods, trade, and maintenance and repair.

Gross domestic product (GDP) and net material product (NMP)

- *Measure of capital depreciation*. The SNA and MPS also differ in their treatment of the depreciation of fixed assets. The SNA recommends estimating the depreciation of fixed assets on the basis of replacement values; the MPS relies on historical costs, which are generally much lower than replacement values. The basic output aggregate in the MPS is the *net material product (NMP)*, which is expressed net of the depreciation of all fixed assets. The NMP generally overstates the value of output because it relies on acquisition prices (*historical costs*) rather than on replacement values to measure the depreciation of fixed assets.
- *Other differences*. The MPS tends to overstate changes in inventories that it values at acquisition prices. The high inflation prevailing in many transition economies results in holding gains and losses on inventories that distort investment estimates. Other items that are treated differently include personal transportation, military expenditures, housing services, capital repairs, and scrapped fixed assets.

Deriving GDP "estimates" from NMP

Deriving GDP from NMP estimates requires that the following types of adjustment be made:

(1)	Net material product (NMP)
+ (2)	Depreciation and losses on fixed assets
(3) = (1) + (2)	Gross material product (GMP)
+ (4)	Value added in nonmaterial sphere
– (5)	Nonmaterial inputs used for material production
+ (6)	Adjustments for differences in classification
= (7) = (3) + (4) – (5) + (6)	Gross domestic product (GDP).

(those bought by consumers). Thus, an increase in the price of goods and services bought by firms or the government, such as machinery, will show up in the GDP deflator but not in the CPI.

Second, the GDP deflator includes only domestically produced goods. *Imported final goods* are not covered, and therefore a change in the prices of imported goods does not have a direct impact on the GDP deflator in the short run. The CPI, however, is affected by changes in the prices of imported goods to the extent that the goods are a part of the CPI "basket."

The third difference concerns the way the prices of different goods are aggregated in the two price indexes. The CPI is based on a set basket of goods and services that are assigned fixed weights (*Laspeyres price index*). The goods in the GDP deflator "basket" are allowed to change over time as the composition of GDP changes (*Paasche price index*). In other words, the CPI uses base year quantities as weights, while the GDP deflator uses current-year quantities. For example, if a drought destroys the corn crop, the output of corn falls to zero, and the price of corn rises sharply. In this case, corn (which is not produced) drops out of the GDP deflator but continues to be included in the CPI, contributing to a substantial rise in the latter index.

The difference between the two indexes is not large if inflation is low and stable but can be substantial in the presence of large relative price changes and movements in import prices that differ from those of domestically produced goods and services. The fixed weight index (Laspeyres index) ignores the so-called substitution effects among products, which are important if consumers can substitute products with lower price increases for those with higher price increases. It therefore tends to overstate inflation. Other fixed weight price indexes (the *wholesale price index (WPI)* and the *producer price index (PPI)*, which measure the prices of goods at the wholesale and producer levels, respectively) also tend to overstate inflation. The flexible weight index (Paasche index), on the other hand, tends to understate the extent of inflation (see Box 2.4).

Box 2.4.
Price Index Formulas[1]

The consumer price index (CPI) and the wholesale price index (WPI) compare the current and base year costs of a basket of goods of *fixed* composition. Denoting the base year quantities of the various goods by q_o^i and their base year prices by p_o^i results in a cost for the basket in the base year of $\Sigma p_o^i q_o^i$, where the summation (Σ) is over all the goods in the basket. The cost of a basket of the *same* quantities but at today's prices is $\Sigma p_t^i q_o^i$, where p_t^i is today's price. The CPI or WPI is the ratio of today's cost to the base year cost, or

$$\text{Consumer or wholesale price index} = \frac{\Sigma p_t^i q_o^i}{\Sigma p_o^i q_o^i} \times 100.$$

This price index is a *Laspeyres* or *base-weighted* index.

The GDP deflator, by contrast, may use the weights of the current period to calculate the price index. Let q_t^i be the quantities of the different goods produced in the current year. Then

$$\textit{GDP deflator} = \frac{\textit{GDP measured in current prices}}{\textit{GDP measured in base year prices}} = \frac{\Sigma p_t^i q_t^i}{\Sigma p_o^i q_t^i} \times 100.$$

This is known as a *Paasche*, or *current-weighted*, price index.

The two formulas differ only in that q_o^i (or the base year quantities) appears in both the numerator and denominator of the CPI and WPI formula, whereas q_t^i appears in the formula for the deflator. In practice, the CPI, WPI, and GDP deflator indexes also differ because they involve different collections of goods.[2]

[1]For details, see Chapter XVI of the 1993 *SNA*.

[2]In transition economies experiencing high inflation, a third index (the Sauerbeck index) is sometimes used. Although it uses base-period weights like the Laspeyres index, this index compares current prices with those in the previous month. See V. Koen, "Measuring the Transition: A User's View on National Accounts in Russia," IMF Working Paper 94/6 (Washington: International Monetary Fund, 1994).

Analyzing Inflation

There are many types of inflation. The broadest categories are discussed below.

- *Policy-induced inflation*, which is often caused by expansionary monetary measures that reflect excessive fiscal deficits and their monetary financing, is often at the root of high inflations. The classic hyperinflations, such as those in Austria and Germany in the 1920s, reflected excessive monetary expansion. *Non-policy induced inflation* is caused by exogenous factors and may reflect, for instance, a drought.
- *Cost-push inflation* is caused by rising costs and may develop even when unemployment is high and resource utilization low. Because wages are frequently the most important cost of production, a rise in wages that is out of line with growth in productivity can initiate the inflation process. But cost-push inflation cannot persist if monetary policy refuses to accommodate it, in which case the wage increases lead to higher unemployment rather than higher inflation.
- *Demand-pull inflation* is caused by excess aggregate demand pushing up the overall price level. The boost to demand can come from internal or external shocks but frequently results from overly expansionary monetary and fiscal policies.
- *Inertial inflation* tends to persist at the same rate until economic events cause it to change. If inflation is steady, the prevailing rate is anticipated and is therefore embedded in wage and financial contracts, which further perpetuate it. Most modern inflation is classified as inertial. The inertial inflation rate is sometimes referred to as the *core* or *underlying* inflation rate (described in the previous section).

Frequently, shocks to the economy from either the supply or demand side cause the actual inflation rate to move above or below the underlying inflation rate. Major supply-side shocks include oil price changes and poor harvests; major demand-side shocks include rapid increases in aggregate demand due to expectations that incomes will rise.

Policy-induced, demand-pull inflation is found in many transition economies, as a result of insufficiently restrictive fiscal policies and monetary financing of the resulting fiscal deficits. Often, external shocks such as those stemming from a rise in energy prices or a contraction of trade with traditional partners have tended to add to the inflation pressures.

Incomes and Employment

Real Wages

Real wages are obtained by deflating nominal wages by an appropriate price index. A distinction should be made between *real wages* and *real incomes.* Real wages reflect the actual purchasing power of nominal money incomes received as direct remuneration by the wage earner. Real incomes include, in addition, in-kind transfers and a variety of fringe benefits. This distinction is especially important in transition economies, where non-wage transfers such as subsidized food and housing are a significant source of income. As a result, movements in real wages in these countries may not be a good indicator of the changes in living standards. In the long run, the growth of real wages depends heavily on the rate of growth of the economy's productivity (see Box 2.5).

Employment and Unemployment

Some of the key concepts and definitions widely used in the analysis of unemployment are described below.

- The *labor force* is defined to include all individuals of working age (usually 16 or older) who are either working or looking for work. Those persons in the labor force who are without regular employment and are looking for work are considered *unemployed.*
- The *unemployment rate* measures the percentage of those in the labor force who do not have regular employment and are seeking work. Thus,

$$\textit{Unemployment rate} = \frac{\textit{Number of unemployed}}{\textit{Labor force}}.$$

- *Discouraged workers* are important to employment analysis. People who are unemployed for long periods of time and cannot find work often stop looking and drop out of the labor force, therefore, they are not counted as unemployed. An unemployment rate that does not include discouraged workers understates the true magnitude of joblessness in the economy.
- The *labor force participation rate* is defined as:

$$\textit{Participation rate} = \frac{\textit{Labor force}}{\textit{Working age population}}.$$

Changes in the participation rate, such as those caused by women's entry into the labor market, can significantly influence the rate of unemployment.

- *Full employment* denotes the optimum employment level of an economy. It does not refer to zero unemployment. In a market economy, where shifts in demand, technology, and products are constantly occurring, there will always be some unemployment. Many observers believe that shifts in the composition of the labor force and institutional changes in the labor market have caused the full employment rate to rise in many countries in recent years, resulting in relatively high and persistent unemployment.
- The Non-Accelerating Inflation Rate of Unemployment, or NAIRU, is an equilibrium rate of unemployment. The NAIRU is defined as the rate of joblessness that is compatible with a stable rate of inflation.

Analytically, it is helpful to classify unemployment according to its causes. Five categories are usually distinguished:

- *Seasonal unemployment,* which is caused by shifts in the supply and demand for labor (typically in agriculture, construction, or tourism) during the calendar year.
- *Frictional unemployment,* which emerges when job vacancies remain unfilled for significant periods of time because both employers and workers need time to explore the market. This type of unemployment generally does not last long and can contribute to a better match between job and worker.
- *Cyclical unemployment,* which is caused by falling output during recessions. Recessions are part of the business cycle in a market economy. Government policies to stimulate demand during a recession can have a more positive impact on this type of unemployment than on other kinds.

Box 2.5.
Wages, Prices, and Productivity

In any economy, the rates of price and wage inflation and the rate of productivity growth are closely related. This relationship, which is crucial to macroeconomic analysis, can be formalized as follows. If P is the general price level, W the average wage rate, L the total labor input measured in man-hours, and Y the level of real output, then Y/L = labor productivity, WL is the total wage bill, and WL/Y is the unit labor cost (ULC). The following relationship can be shown to hold:[1]

$$\frac{\dot{P}}{P} = \frac{\dot{W}}{W} + \left(\frac{\dot{L}}{L} - \frac{\dot{Y}}{Y}\right) \quad (1)$$

or

$$\frac{\dot{P}}{P} = \frac{\dot{W}}{W} - \left(\frac{\dot{(Y/L)}}{Y/L}\right), \text{ or} \quad (2)$$

rate of inflation = rate of wage growth – rate of productivity growth.[2]

Or

$$\frac{\dot{W}}{W} - \frac{\dot{P}}{P} = \left(\frac{\dot{Y}}{Y} - \frac{\dot{L}}{L}\right) \quad (3)$$

In other words

$$\frac{\dot{(W/P)}}{(W/P)} = \frac{\dot{(Y/L)}}{(Y/L)} \quad (4)$$

rate of growth of real wages = rate of growth of productivity.[2]

In the above illustration, if labor productivity is growing at 2 percent a year, then wage growth of 6 percent a year will be consistent with an inflation rate of 4 percent a year. Thus, the rate of productivity growth fixes the upper boundary of the rate of wage growth that is compatible with stable prices.

[1]As we have seen, nominal income (PY) is equal to wage income (WL) plus nonwage income. If β is the ratio of nonwage to wage income, then

$$PY = WL + \beta WL \text{ or } PY = WL(1 + \beta).$$

Assuming β to be constant, it follows that

$$\frac{\dot{P}}{P} + \frac{\dot{Y}}{Y} = \frac{\dot{W}}{W} + \frac{\dot{L}}{L}, \text{ which can be rewritten as equation 1.}$$

[2]All rates of growth are expressed in percent.

- *Structural unemployment* is caused by a mismatch of skills or geographic locations. Changing patterns of demand and technology, for example, reduce the demand for certain types of skills. Structural unemployment can also occur when an industry in a region shuts down and is not replaced. This type of unemployment is harder to eliminate than other kinds because it requires retraining unemployed workers or improving their mobility.
- *Disguised unemployment* develops when a worker's marginal contribution to output is zero or negative, so that the economy is better off by explicitly recognizing this and moving him to more productive employment.

Pricing Policies

An important aspect of reform in most transition economies has been the effort to move to a market-based system of determining prices, generally by liberalizing previously controlled prices. Price liberalization offers several important economic benefits. First, it increases the availability of goods and services. Second, it is necessary to the credible long-term hardening of the budget constraint. In other words, ensuring that the budget constraints facing enterprises are *binding* and cannot be circumvented or made "soft" by a recourse to government or bank financing. Third, it gives investors proper signals. In the absence of an early price liberalization that corrects relative prices to reflect relative scarcities, relative prices may mislead investors, who may then invest in inappropriate sectors. Finally, it helps to develop competitive markets. However, in order to be effective, price liberalization needs to be accompanied by domestic deregulation and demonopolization of the production, transport, distribution, and trade systems.

One important aspect of pricing policies—eliminating distortions in the pricing of foreign exchange and credit—depends on reforms aimed at correcting overvalued exchange rates and reducing hidden credit subsidies. A rational price system reflects world prices. Therefore, an open trading system and a convertible currency (on the current account) are the fastest means of establishing a rational relative price structure. However, the sudden price hikes that may result from price liberalization underline the importance of establishing a social safety net to protect the vulnerable sections of the population, such as the disabled and the elderly.

The liberalization of the price system and the move away from a highly distorted price structure are key steps in moving to a market economy. Virtually all the transition countries have made considerable progress toward formal price liberalization. But it is important to take several considerations into account, as follows:

- For an overall domestic price measure such as the CPI, convergence toward market economy price levels will be a prolonged process in most countries.
- An important policy implication is that the gradual process of price convergence will continue to exert pressure on inflation and, in the absence of adequate exchange rate flexibility, will contribute to real exchange appreciation.
- For nontradables and particularly for services, price convergence can take more time. Increases in the prices of services typically lag behind adjustments in the prices of goods before broad-based liberalization occurs, not only because of deliberate pricing policies but also because price controls are easier to enforce on services than on goods. In many cases, the initial jump in prices associated with large-scale price decontrol entails a further, sharp drop in the relative price of services, as many of them remain administered and are only partially adjusted. There is a subsequent catch-up period as some subsidies are reduced and as structural reforms reduce the role of the public sector in areas such as health care and housing.

In many transition economies, the initial depreciation of the real exchange rate in the wake of price and exchange rate liberalization went far beyond what might have been considered appropriate in light of the prevailing productivity differentials. This initial depreciation, however, was typically followed by a rapid real appreciation, often reflecting high inflation relative to trading partners and occasionally a nominal appreciation. In the process, the wide initial gap between domestic and international price levels narrowed significantly, although in many countries it has remained large three or four years into the transition. As a result, and even in the presence of appropriately tight financial policies, substantial inflationary pressures persist. The implied real appreciation is sustainable only if it is supported by corresponding productivity gains in the tradables sector.

Incomes Policy

Alternative Approaches

Incomes policies are an important component of stabilization programs and are motivated by both macroeconomic and microeconomic concerns. The justification for using incomes policies in transition economies seems stronger than in market economies. Incomes policies are used for several reasons:

- To break inflationary inertia and prevent the emergence of cost-push inflation;[17]
- To prevent the decapitalization of firms by reducing uncertainty regarding ownership and governance of firms; and
- To strengthen the credibility of governments and guarantee the sustainability of the exchange rate anchor.

[17]Inertial inflation is inherited, very often as a result of past excess demand inflation or exogenous price shocks that have been perpetuated through contracts and wage commitments (including indexation).

- Transition economies have experimented with various approaches to incomes policies. The three major approaches to incomes policies involve guidelines, social contracts, and tax-incentive policies.
- Under the *guideline approach*, the government sets norms for the growth of nominal wages and prices, with the aim of reducing inflation through symmetrical reductions such as wage and price freezes. If the objective is to stabilize the price level, money wages must grow at the same rate as average labor productivity.[18]
- *The social contract approach* requires that the government, employers, and labor agree collectively to restrain wage growth.
- *Tax-based incomes policies (TIPs)* penalize deviations from and reward compliance with wage and price norms by levying taxes on employers who do not conform to government standards.

Designing and Enforcing Wage Controls in Transition Economies

Designing wage controls in transition economies is a four-step process that includes (i) selecting the wage norm; (ii) determining how the norm is to be adjusted in response to inflation (the indexation issue); (iii) establishing coverage; and (iv) enforcing controls.

- *The wage norm.* The key element in selecting a wage norm is the need to achieve set macroeconomic objectives with a minimum of microeconomic distortions. There are several possible wage norms and several variations on them.[19] However, two norms have been tested more often than others: the *wage bill norm* and the *average wage norm*. The wage bill norm has three main advantages: it leaves enterprises more flexibility in determining relative wages, it can be administered through the tax system, and it creates an incentive for shedding labor. Average wage norms remove the incentive to lay off workers but encourage firms to hire less-skilled, low-wage workers.
- *Indexation mechanisms.* If wage norms are fully indexed to past inflation, they cannot act as a nominal anchor. But if they are not indexed, the result may be an unacceptably large cut in real wages. Therefore, many transition economies opted for wage controls based on a partial, forward-looking indexation scheme that relies on projected rather than past inflation.
- *Coverage.* The issue here is whether wage controls should apply to both public and private enterprises. Many have argued that in the context of anti-inflationary policies, it is desirable to apply a uniform policy across all sectors of the economy, private and public. However, in transition economies, the need for wage controls is related to the problem of weak governance in state-owned firms. In particular, uncertainties about ownership, soft budget constraints, and a lack of financial discipline have provided strong incentives for these firms to decapitalize, indulge in excessive borrowing, and pay high wages—even if the enterprises in question are insolvent.
- *Enforcement.* In many transition economies, the main instrument for enforcing wage controls has been a tax on excess wages—that is, a tax levied on enterprises paying wages above the norm. Another approach is to seek a "social pact" or a consensus between the government and the labor unions regarding the appropriate wage norm.

It should be noted, however, that while wage controls can help secure macroeconomic objectives, they also carry economic costs—for example, they distort the structure of wages and are responsible for wage indexation.[20] Further, support for wage controls in IMF-supported adjustment programs has been limited. In general, such controls are approved as temporary measures in heterodox stabilization programs and in transition economies when a compelling argument can be made that their benefits outweigh the costs. Experience with wage controls shows that they can play an important temporary role in a strong disinflation program but tend to lose their effectiveness rapidly. The challenge to policymakers is therefore to ensure that wage controls are temporary and to minimize the distortions that inevitably result.

[18]This conventional wage guideline is derived using the assumption that the relative shares of wage and nonwage income in GDP remain unchanged.

[19]See Fabrizio Coricelli and Ana Revenga, eds., "Wage Policy During the Transition to a Market Economy: Poland, 1990–91," World Bank Discussion Paper 158 (Washington: World Bank, 1992).

[20]For a more detailed discussion of wage controls in transition economies, see Susan Schadler, ed., and others, *IMF Conditionality: Experience Under Stand-By and Extended Arrangements*, IMF Occasional Paper No. 129 (Washington: International Monetary Fund, 1995), pp. 107–24. See also Simon Commander and Fabrizio Corricelli, eds., *Unemployment, Restructuring, and Labor Markets in Eastern Europe and Russia* (Washington: World Bank, 1995).

Real Sector Developments

Output and Demand

Poland's economic performance weakened considerably in the 1980s with the failure of several attempts to reform the economic system by addressing the inadequacies of the centrally planned regime. By 1989, Poland was on the brink of hyperinflation; the monthly inflation rate reached 55 percent in October, with virtually no real growth. In response, the government embarked on an ambitious program of reform aimed at stabilizing the economy and launching it decisively on a path to a market economy.[21] This program, which has been characterized as a "somewhat heterodox" approach to stabilization, included tightened financial policies; a temporary fixed exchange rate that would act as a nominal anchor and therefore prevent the emergence of hyperinflation; and a tax-based incomes policy to restrain wage increases.

Real GDP fell sharply in 1990–91 as the economy underwent a deep recession. The recession caught analysts off guard and generated a large body of research into its root causes.[22] It has been generally agreed that the causes of the output collapse can be grouped into three broad categories: (i) macroeconomic factors; (ii) institutional factors; and (iii) measurement factors.

- *Macroeconomic factors.* These include the disintegration of the Council for Mutual Economic Assistance (CMEA) trading system in 1991 and the concomitant terms-of-trade deterioration; a sharp contraction in demand for output from state-owned industries; declines in inventories as liberalization and hard budget constraints eliminated incentives to hoard; fiscal restructuring; and a policy-induced "credit crunch."

  The fiscal restructuring was particularly destabilizing. The traditional mainstay of Poland's revenue base—receipts from state enterprises—disappeared as the enterprises' financial situation deteriorated. On the expenditure side, subsidies were rapidly reduced, but transfer payments increased rapidly as a social safety net was put in place.

- *Institutional factors.* Replacing the previous systems of control with market-based institutions has not only taken longer than expected but also affected the speed with which the ownership laws are reformed. Combined with the absence of incentives, these developments have prevented a normal supply response.

- *Measurement factors.* Problems in accurately measuring Poland's output may have led to an overstatement of the actual decline. Conversely, the recovery may well have been understated because of inadequate private sector data and unreliable price indicators.

The output collapse bottomed out in 1991 and the economy began an impressive recovery with real GDP growing by 2.6 percent in 1992, by about 4 percent in 1993, and by some 6 percent in 1994. Industrial production, which accounts for about 40 percent of Poland's GDP, provided the main basis for the recovery in GDP growth.

The growth in output since 1992 represents an impressive supply-side response and is associated with significant gains in productivity primarily driven by increased domestic demand, particularly consumption. Consumption rose strongly throughout the 1992–93 period before slowing in 1994. However, rapid export growth also made an important contribution to growth, especially in 1993–94. Exports, including unrecorded cross-border trade, increased in real terms at annual rates of over 30 percent through 1994. Growth in fixed investment has also been positive, driven largely by private sector activity.

The increase in real consumption has been mirrored in a marked decline in national saving, from the very high levels of the pretransition era. National saving as a proportion of GDP is estimated to have declined by about 10 percentage points of GDP at the onset of the transition (from 40 percent of GDP to about 30 percent during 1990) and by a further 15 percentage points in 1991. This decline can be explained, in part, by the fall in output and income and the deterioration in public finances. National saving began to improve in 1992, increasing to 16.5 percent of GDP in 1994—a reflection of subdued consumption during the period.

[21]Details on the nature of earlier reform efforts and the events leading to the economic crisis of the late 1980s can be found in T.D. Lane, "Inflation, Stabilization and Economic Transformation in Poland: The First Year," IMF Working Paper 91/70 (Washington: International Monetary Fund, 1991); and T.A. Wolf, "The Lessons of Limited Market-Oriented Reform," *Journal of Economic Perspectives* Vol. 5 (Fall 1991), pp. 45–58.

[22]See, for example, D. Rodrik, "Making Sense of the Soviet Trade Shock in Eastern Europe: A Framework and Some Estimates," *Eastern Europe in Transition: From Recession to Growth?* Discussion Paper No. 196 (Washington: World Bank, 1993); and E. Borenzstein and J. Ostry, "Structural and Macroeconomic Determinants of the Output Decline in Czechoslovakia and Poland" (mimeograph; Washington: International Monetary Fund, 1992). See also G. Calvo and F. Coricelli, "Output Collapse in Eastern Europe: The Role of Credit," and A. Berg, "Measurement and Mismeasurement of Economic Activity During Transition to the Market," *Eastern Europe in Transition: From Recession to Growth?* Discussion Paper No. 196 (Washington: World Bank, 1993).

Prices and Wages

Prices

The movement to a new system of price controls began as early as 1982, when a three-tier price system (administered, regulated, and contract) was introduced. Administered prices were set directly by the authorities, regulated prices were closely monitored, and contract prices were, in principle, free to fluctuate. It was not until the reform program of 1989–90, however, that prices were decisively liberalized. A major reduction in subsidies accompanied price liberalization.

With the wholesale liberalization at the beginning of 1990, recorded inflation (as measured by the CPI), jumped to a monthly rate of close to 80 percent in January 1990—the highest recorded in Poland in recent years. Overall, average annual inflation in 1990 reached over 550 percent. During 1991–93, price liberalization continued, but the adjustment was less dramatic than it had been initially. By 1992, a new system of prices emerged that allowed the market to determine the costs of all but a few "socially sensitive" consumer items.[23] The authorities' policy of adjusting administered prices, together with the ongoing adjustments in relative prices, continued to influence (although less intensely) the overall inflation rate.[24] Starting in 1991, inflation measured by the CPI fell sharply to 70 percent a year in 1991, and further to 43 percent in 1992, and to 38 percent in 1993. Since then, it has proven increasingly difficult to bring it down further and has remained at 30–35 percent annually. Thus while the risk for hyperinflation was eliminated, inflation remained high.

Incomes Policy and Wages

Like many other transition economies, Poland has instituted wage controls. Initially, the rationale for these wage controls was that they would help the authorities meet macroeconomic objectives, most notably aid in the task of containing inflation by restraining wage growth, especially in state enterprises which were no longer under the direct control of the authorities. Poland's wage controls, the so-called *popiwek* system, took the form of the Excess Wage Tax (EWT), which was imposed on enterprises that exceeded the wage norms. Initially, the wage norm was the wage bill, but in 1991, the average wage was adopted as the norm, with some adjustments to reflect productivity growth, with the inflation indexation coefficient on the norm being 60 percent. The EWT was progressive, with rates ranging between 100 percent (for amounts exceeding the norm by up to 3 percent) and 500 percent (for amounts exceeding the norm by more than 5 percent). This maximum rate was reduced to 300 percent in 1993. The norm was adjusted using an ex post partial indexation. Firms with more than 50 percent private ownership were exempt. While it is difficult to demonstrate that the EWT played a key role in reducing real wages, it is clear that the wage controls, high unemployment, low profits, and a hardening of financial constraints have reinforced one another in determining wage developments in Poland.

It has been widely recognized that the microeconomic costs of wage controls—that is, the distortions they create in the labor market—begin to rise sharply after a short period. Over time, problems with enforcement (particularly increasing exemptions) tend to undermine their effectiveness. Whether or not this situation developed in Poland, the excess wage tax was discontinued at the end of 1994 and replaced by a new incomes policy based on the idea of "social partnership." This new system of collective bargaining is guided by indicative norms, set by a commission made up of representatives of government, industry, and labor, that are based on macroeconomic indicators such as growth and inflation. State-owned enterprises that allow wage increases to exceed the norms are subject to sanctions.[25]

Real wages, after declining in the early phases of the stabilization effort, stabilized and in 1994 registered some gains. As discussed earlier, official statistics may have overstated the extent of the fall in real income in 1990 for several reasons, including the unsustainable level real wages reached in 1989 (after two years of very rapid gains) and the importance of in-kind benefits in workers' total incomes. Despite these gains, real wages have lagged behind

[23]The government continued to administer prices for electricity, gas, central heating, basic medicines, and rent in locally administered housing units, as well as television fees. The prices of some other goods, such as engine fuel, beer, wine, and cigarettes, were directly influenced by excises.

[24]For a detailed discussion of the sectoral aspects of inflation in Poland, see *Poland—Background Paper*, IMF Staff Country Report No. 96/19 (Washington: International Monetary Fund, 1996). See also Liam P. Ebrill and others, *Poland: The Path to a Market Economy*, Occasional Paper No. 113 (Washington: International Monetary Fund, 1994).

[25]In setting up institutions for determining wages, it is important to consider the impact of the collective bargaining structure on both macroeconomic performance and microeconomic efficiency in the labor market and the role of minimum wage laws and employment regulations. For a discussion of these issues, see Robert J. Flanagan, "Institutional Structure and Labor Market Outcomes: Western Lessons for European Countries," IMF Working Paper 95/63 (Washington: International Monetary Fund, 1995).

gains in productivity, especially in the industrial sector, where anecdotal evidence suggests that the adoption of new technology associated with foreign investment and the shedding of labor in some sectors have contributed to significant improvements in productivity.

Unemployment

Because of the pervasiveness of "labor hoarding" by Polish firms prior to 1990 (disguised unemployment was estimated at 20 percent of the labor force), the economic reforms resulted in massive layoffs and a subsequent sharp rise in official unemployment. Employment dropped significantly in the public sector in 1990, but by substantially less than production. The figures show that joblessness climbed from practically zero at the beginning of 1989 to over 6 percent of the labor force by the end of 1990, and over 11 percent by end-1991. This doubling in the unemployment rate during 1991 marked the low point of the transition in Poland and caused serious social concerns. As output stabilized in 1992, firms continued to shed labor, a trend that continued into 1993 when output growth accelerated. The rate of increase in unemployment tapered off in 1993–94, and the unemployment rate stabilized at about 15–16 percent of the labor force.

Chart 2.2. Poland: Inflation and Real GDP
(In percent)

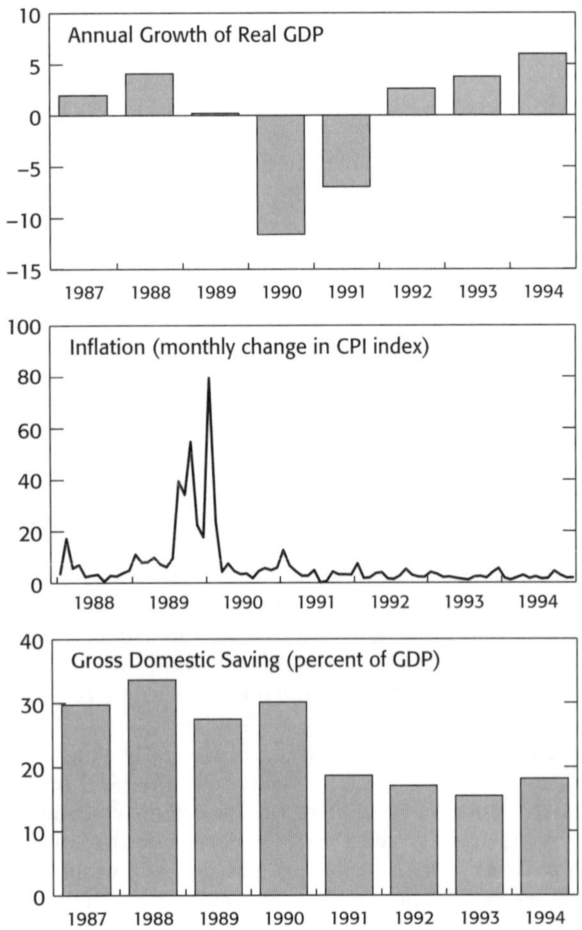

Sources: IMF Institute database and Tables 2.2 and 2.5.

Exercises and Issues for Discussion

Exercises

1. On the basis of the Polish national accounts data for 1993 as shown below, derive the sequence of SNA accounts using the format of Table 2.8.
   Using the national accounts data, verify that the main macroeconomic aggregates derived from 1993, e.g., GDP, GNI, GNDI, and gross saving are consistent with those provided in Table 2.3. Also, verify that equations 1 through 9 of Box 2.2 hold for the above data.

2. Using the format of Table 2.8, construct the sequence of accounts for the government sector for 1992 on the basis of the data found in Tables 2.9–2.14. Interpret the balancing item for this sector and comment on its overall position.

3. Show how Table 2.15 highlights the three approaches to GDP by tracing in the table the production approach, income approach, and expenditure approach.

Polish National Account Data (1993)
(In trillions of zlotys)

Final consumption	1,300.3
Gross capital formation	242.3
Taxes on income	248.1
Taxes on production	128.5
Customs and taxes linked to imports	121.6
Intermediate consumption	1,833.6
Other current transfers, payable	171.6
Interest income, payable	295.2
Property income received	294.1
Subsidies	32.1
Gross output	3,269.8
Capital transfers	9.8
Dividend, payable	62.3
Social security and other social transfers	324.8
Transfers, received	223.1
Compensation of employees	688.1
Imports of goods and services	342.1
Exports of goods and services	357.3
Net income from abroad	−63.4
Current transfers from abroad, net	51.5

4. Tables 2.1 and 2.3 show Poland's main macroeconomic aggregates at current prices while Tables 2.2 and 2.4 show the same aggregate GDP at constant prices.

   (a) Using Table 2.2, comment on the overall and sectoral developments of GDP at constant prices during 1990–94. In your opinion, what accounted for Poland's output collapse in 1990–91 and for the subsequent recovery in 1992–94? To what extent might the output collapse have been overstated and the recovery understated by official statistics?

   (b) Comment on the developments in domestic absorption during 1990–94.

   (c) On the basis of Tables 2.1 and 2.2, derive the implicit GDP deflator for 1990–94. Compare your results with those reported in the bottom of Table 2.2.

   (d) Assuming a real growth rate of 6 percent in 1995 and a level for the GDP deflator (1990=100) of 468.3, derive the nominal GDP for 1995 and show that equation 2.19 holds.

5. Verify that the economywide saving-investment gap is identical to the current account balance for the period 1990–94. Interpret the meaning of this identity for Poland and comment on the evolution of the saving-investment gap over the period.

6. On the basis of Chart 2.2 and Table 2.3, analyze the trend in saving in Poland during the 1992–94 recovery. Should policymakers in Poland have been concerned about the observed trend? Why?

7. On the basis of the illustrative data described below, derive the CPI index (base 1990) according to Laspeyres and Paasche formulas. Compute the inflation rate in both cases and comment on the results.

	1990	1991	1992
Good 1			
Price ($)	1	2	3
Quantity (kg)	5	10	12
Good 2			
Price ($)	3	4	5
Quantity (kg)	8	5	4

8. Table 2.5 contains data on consumer prices, producer prices, and average wages in Poland. Compare annual average and end-of-period measures of inflation during 1990–94. Comment on the differences. What are the main problems affecting the reliability of price index numbers in transition economies?

9. Compare price changes in Poland as measured by the following indicators: the CPI, the PPI, and the GDP deflator. What accounts for the differences between these measures? Explain how they might be used to measure different aspects of inflation in Poland.

10. Comment on the changes in nominal and real wages in Poland during 1990–94. Do you believe that wage increases were responsible for higher inflation during this period? Are real wage indicators adequate to monitor income developments? What additional information is required?

11. On the basis of Tables 2.4 and 2.6, calculate the productivity per unit of labor in Poland (real output/employment), assuming that the number of hours worked per person is unchanged from year to year. Comment on the changes in productivity during 1990–94. Compare the percentage changes in productivity to percentage changes in nominal wages. What implications does this comparison have for the inflation rate in Poland, in

the light of the discussion in Box 2.5? Assuming that the relationship given in the box holds, what should the objective for nominal wage growth be in 1993 and 1994 in order to remain compatible with inflation rates of 30 percent and 25 percent, respectively?

Issues for Discussion

1. Discuss the extent of the GDP measurement problem the underground economy creates in your own country. How should economic policy be formulated to take account of this sector? In particular, how can economic activities in this sector be shifted into official channels?
2. Discuss the factors behind the collapse of output in the early stages of the transition, with special reference to your economy. To what extent was the collapse inevitable? Was it entirely undesirable? If yes, why? If not, why not?
3. Discuss the importance of *underlying* or *core inflation* in a transition economy undergoing rapid price liberalization. In Poland, a number of factors (such as financial policies, price liberalization, changes in taxation, and the exchange rate) influenced the recorded rate of inflation. What, in your view, was the underlying rate of inflation in Poland in 1990? What was it in 1994? Please explain.
4. Discuss the difficulties for analysis and policy that arise when a transition economy's relative price structure moves toward convergence with world prices. Is the process of price convergence likely to be different in the tradable and nontradable services sectors? What are the implications of this phenomenon for exchange rate policy? Discuss with reference to Poland.
5. Discuss the difference between the concepts of real wages and real income, drawing on the experience of your economy. How does this difference affect the analysis of stabilization policies and their consequences?
6. Discuss the pros and cons of the Excess Wage Tax (EWT) in Poland. In particular, did the EWT play an important role in restraining real wage growth during 1990–94? What is the rationale for excluding the private sector from wage controls in transition economies? What alternative policies to restrain wage growth are available in the transition economies?
7. Discuss the concepts of open and disguised unemployment and their relevance to analysis and policy formulation in a transition economy.

Table 2.1.
Poland: Sectoral Distribution of Gross Domestic Product (at Current Market Prices)[1]

	1989	1990	1991	1992	1993	1994
	(In trillions of zlotys; at current prices)					
Agriculture and forestry	15.3	47.6	55.8	79.3	104.4	130.9
Industry	52.2	251.6	325.1	395.4	509.4	677.1
Construction	9.6	51.5	82.5	82.7	91.9	120.1
Services	41.3	209.6	345.4	592.0	852.1	1,176.0
Transport and communications	5.5	26.9	45.3	60.9	82.6	. . .
Trade	19.3	71.2	106.0	143.7	219.6	. . .
Other services	16.5	111.5	194.1	387.4	549.9	. . .
GDP at market prices	**118.4**	**560.3**	**808.8**	**1,149.4**	**1,557.8**	**2,104.1**
	(Annual growth rates in percent)					
Agriculture and forestry	292.1	211.1	17.2	42.1	31.7	25.4
Industry	321.9	382.0	29.2	21.6	28.8	32.9
Construction	206.8	436.5	60.2	0.2	11.1	30.7
Services	303.4	407.5	64.8	71.4	43.9	38.0
Transport and communications	222.3	389.1	68.4	34.4	35.6	. . .
Trade	375.2	268.9	48.9	35.6	52.8	. . .
Other services	268.4	575.8	74.1	99.6	41.9	. . .
GDP at market prices	**299.3**	**373.2**	**44.4**	**42.1**	**35.5**	**35.1**
	(In percent of total GDP)					
Agriculture and forestry	12.9	8.5	6.9	6.9	6.7	6.2
Industry	44.1	44.9	40.2	34.4	32.7	32.2
Construction	8.1	9.2	10.2	7.2	5.9	5.7
Services	34.9	37.4	42.7	51.5	54.7	55.9
Transport and communications	4.6	4.8	5.6	5.3	5.3	. . .
Trade	16.3	12.7	13.1	12.5	14.1	. . .
Other services	13.9	19.9	24.0	33.7	35.3	. . .
GDP at market prices	**100.0**	**100.0**	**100.0**	**100.0**	**100.0**	**100.0**

Sources: IMF Institute database, based on published data by the Polish Central Statistical Office (GUS); *Poland–Statistical Tables*, IMF Staff Country Report No. 96/20 (Washington: International Monetary Fund, 1996); Liam P. Ebrill, *Poland: The Path to a Market Economy*, Occasional Paper No. 113 (Washington: International Monetary Fund, 1994); and IMF Institute staff estimates.

[1]Starting in 1990, GDP follows the 1993 SNA methodology; 1994 GDP figures are preliminary estimates.

Table 2.2.
Poland: Sectoral Distribution of Gross Domestic Product (at Constant 1990 Prices), and Implicit Deflators

	1989	1990	1991	1992	1993	1994
		(In trillions of zlotys; at constant 1990 prices)				
Agriculture and forestry	48.6	47.6	48.2	43.7	44.8	40.6
Industry	322.7	251.7	208.5	214.1	227.1	254.1
Construction	60.2	51.5	55.0	57.1	58.2	58.3
Services	202.2	209.5	209.4	220.0	225.1	230.0
Transport and communications	30.8	26.9	21.5	22.2	21.8	. . .
Trade	70.7	71.2	76.8	76.7	85.9	. . .
Other services[1]	100.8	111.5	111.2	121.2	117.4	. . .
GDP at market prices	**633.7**	**560.3**	**521.1**	**534.9**	**555.2**	**582.9**
		(Annual growth rates in percent)				
Agriculture and forestry	1.0	–2.1	1.3	–9.3	2.5	-9.3
Industry	–2.1	–22.0	–17.2	2.7	6.1	11.9
Construction	–0.3	–14.5	6.8	3.8	1.9	0.2
Services	4.1	3.6	–0.0	5.1	2.3	2.2
Transport and communications	1.1	–12.7	–20.1	3.3	–1.8	. . .
Trade	4.7	0.7	7.9	–0.1	12.0	. . .
Other services[1]	4.5	10.6	–0.3	9.0	–3.1	. . .
GDP at market prices	**0.2**	**–11.6**	**–7.0**	**2.6**	**3.8**	**5.0**
		(Implicit deflators 1990 =100)				
Agriculture and forestry	31.5	100.0	115.8	181.5	233.0	322.1
Industry	16.2	100.0	155.9	184.7	224.3	266.4
Construction	15.9	100.0	150.0	144.8	157.9	205.9
Services	20.4	100.0	164.9	269.1	378.5	511.3
Transport and communications	17.2	100.0	210.7	274.3	378.9	. . .
Trade	27.3	100.0	138.0	187.4	255.6	. . .
Other services[1]	16.5	100.0	174.6	319.6	468.4	. . .
GDP at market prices	**18.7**	**100.0**	**155.2**	**214.9**	**280.6**	**361.0**

Sources: IMF Institute database, based on published data by the Polish Central Statistical Office (GUS); *Poland–Statistical Tables*, IMF Staff Country Report No. 96/20 (Washington: International Monetary Fund, 1996); Liam P. Ebrill, *Poland: The Path to a Market Economy*, Occasional Paper No. 113 (Washington: International Monetary Fund, 1994); and IMF Institute staff estimates.

[1]Starting in 1990, GDP follows the 1993 SNA methodology; 1994 data are preliminary estimates.

Table 2.3.
Poland: Components of Aggregate Demand (at Current Market Prices)

	1989	1990	1991	1992	1993	1994
	(In trillions of zlotys; at current market prices)					
Gross domestic product (GDP)[1]	**118.4**	**560.3**	**808.8**	**1,149.4**	**1,557.8**	**2,104.1**
Absorption (A)	113.4	520.3	824.3	1,131.8	1,542.6	2,086.8
Consumption (C)	67.8	376.8	663.3	957.4	1,300.3	1,751.0
Public	7.1	108.1	195.2	289.6	318.3	386.9
Private	60.7	268.7	468.1	667.8	982.0	1,364.1
Gross investment (I)	45.6	143.5	161.0	174.4	242.3	335.8
Fixed investment	19.4	117.6	157.7	193.0	239.8	341.1
Public	4.1	21.6	26.1	39.3	51.0	67.9
Private	15.3	96.0	131.6	153.7	188.8	273.2
Changes in inventories	26.2	25.9	3.3	−18.6	2.5	−5.3
Foreign balance[2] (X−M)	5.0	40.0	−15.5	17.6	15.2	17.3
Exports of goods and services (X)	22.6	160.5	190.3	272.4	357.3	515.0
Imports of goods and services (M)	−17.6	−120.5	−205.8	−254.8	−342.1	−497.7
Income from abroad (net)(Y_f)	−4.6	−31.9	−30.1	−54.4	−63.4	−33.8
Gross national income (GNI)	113.8	528.4	778.7	1,095.0	1,494.4	2,070.3
Current transfers (net)(TR_f)	1.8	18.4	12.8	39.9	51.5	26.9
Gross national disposable income (GNDI)	**115.6**	**546.8**	**791.5**	**1,134.9**	**1,545.9**	**2,097.2**
Memorandum items:						
Gross domestic saving (S_d)[3]	50.6	183.5	145.5	192.0	257.5	353.1
Gross national saving (S)[4]	47.8	170.0	128.2	177.5	245.6	346.2
	(In percent of GDP)					
Consumption	57.3	67.2	82.0	83.3	83.5	83.2
Gross investment	38.5	25.6	19.9	15.2	15.6	16.0
Foreign balance	4.2	7.1	−1.9	1.5	1.0	0.8
Gross national saving	40.4	30.3	15.9	15.4	15.8	16.5

Sources: IMF Institute database, based on published data by the Polish Central Statistical Office (GUS); *Poland–Statistical Tables*, IMF Staff Country Report No. 96/20 (Washington: International Monetary Fund, 1996); Liam P. Ebrill, *Poland: The Path to a Market Economy*, Occasional Paper No. 113 (Washington: International Monetary Fund, 1994); and IMF Institute staff estimates.

[1]Data for 1994 are preliminary estimates.

[2]On an accrual basis, including adjustments for unrecorded trade.

[3]Defined as GDP net of final consumption.

[4]Defined as GNDI net of final consumption.

Table 2.4.
Poland: Components of Aggregate Demand (in Constant 1990 Prices)

	1989	1990	1991	1992	1993	1994
	(In trillions of zlotys; at constant 1990 prices)					
Gross domestic product (GDP)	**633.8**	**560.3**	**521.2**	**534.9**	**555.2**	**582.9**
Domestic demand	628.5	520.3	519.5	518.8	555.0	579.7
Consumption (C)	437.6	376.7	404.9	419.1	440.4	454.3
Public	107.2	108.1	119.1	126.8	131.9	133.1
Private	330.4	268.7	285.7	292.3	308.6	321.3
Gross investment (I)	190.9	143.5	114.7	99.7	114.6	125.4
Fixed investment	130.4	117.6	112.4	115.0	118.4	129.1
Public	27.4	21.6	18.6	23.4	24.4	25.0
Private	102.9	96.0	93.8	91.6	94.0	104.1
Changes in inventories	60.6	25.9	2.2	−15.3	−3.8	−3.7
Foreign balance[1]	5.2	40.0	1.7	16.1	0.1	3.2
Exports of goods and services	139.0	160.5	157.9	174.9	180.3	210.3
Imports of goods and services	−133.8	−120.5	−156.2	−158.8	−180.2	−207.1
Gross domestic saving	196.2	183.5	116.3	115.8	114.7	128.6
Income from abroad (net)	−26.0	−31.9	−9.9	−14.8	−11.8	−28.5
Gross national income	607.8	528.4	511.3	520.1	543.4	554.4
Current transfers (net)	12.4	18.4	3.3	4.7	8.5	17.0
Gross national disposable income	**620.2**	**546.7**	**514.6**	**524.8**	**551.8**	**571.4**
Gross national saving	182.6	170.0	109.7	105.8	111.4	117.1

Sources: IMF Institute database, based on published data by the Polish Central Statistical Office (GUS); *Poland–Statistical Tables,* IMF Staff Country Report No. 96/20 (Washington: International Monetary Fund, 1996); Liam P. Ebrill, *Poland: The Path to a Market Economy,* Occasional Paper No. 113 (Washington: International Monetary Fund, 1994); and IMF Institute staff estimates.

[1]On an accrual basis, including adjustments for unrecorded trade.

Table 2.5.
Poland: Price and Wage Indicators
(1990 = 100)

	Consumer Price Index				Producer Prices: Industry				Real Wages[1] (deflated by CPI)			
	End period	Percent changes	Period average	Percent changes	End period	Percent changes	Period average	Percent changes	Period average	Percent changes	Period average	Percent changes
1988	**5.3**		**4.4**		**5.3**		**4.1**		**5.6**		**125.0**	
Q1	3.9		3.6		4.0		3.8		4.4		122.4	
Q2	4.4	12.8	4.3	19.6	4.2	5.2	4.0	6.2	4.6	4.3	106.7	−12.8
Q3	4.8	7.0	4.7	7.7	4.6	8.9	4.1	3.7	5.2	12.3	111.3	4.3
Q4	5.3	11.9	5.1	9.2	5.3	15.6	4.4	6.7	8.1	56.7	159.8	43.6
1989	**39.4**	**643.4**	**15.3**	**244.6**	**39.8**	**652.6**	**8.9**	**117.8**	**21.5**	**284.3**	**143.0**	**14.3**
Q1	6.9	29.0	6.4	24.8	6.5	22.4	6.4	44.0	8.6	6.1	136.9	−14.3
Q2	8.5	23.8	8.0	26.0	8.0	23.2	7.0	9.3	10.9	26.5	137.4	0.4
Q3	17.6	106.6	13.4	66.7	14.6	83.1	8.4	20.7	21.4	95.8	161.4	17.5
Q4	39.4	124.2	33.3	149.4	39.8	172.7	13.8	64.6	45.1	110.5	136.3	−15.6
1990	**128.4**	**225.9**	**100.0**	**555.4**	**116.0**	**191.5**	**100.0**	**1,023.5**	**100.0**	**364.9**	**100.0**	**−30.1**
Q1	84.6	114.6	78.5	135.6	89.6	125.2	96.0	593.5	76.9	70.6	98.7	−27.6
Q2	98.0	15.8	94.2	20.0	93.3	4.2	97.4	1.5	87.7	14.1	93.8	−5.0
Q3	109.4	11.7	105.6	12.1	101.4	8.6	100.5	3.2	100.6	14.7	96.0	2.3
Q4	128.4	17.4	121.8	15.4	116.0	14.4	105.9	5.4	134.8	34.1	111.5	16.2
1991	**205.9**	**60.4**	**176.7**	**76.7**	**161.6**	**39.3**	**141.9**	**42.0**	**167.1**	**67.1**	**95.3**	**−4.7**
Q1	161.5	25.8	153.6	26.2	139.6	20.3	135.9	28.3	152.9	13.4	100.2	−10.1
Q2	178.5	10.5	171.5	11.6	147.7	5.8	139.7	2.8	155.8	1.9	91.5	−8.8
Q3	187.5	5.0	181.9	6.1	155.6	5.3	143.9	3.0	164.6	5.7	91.1	−0.4
Q4	205.9	9.8	199.7	9.8	161.6	3.9	148.1	2.9	195.2	18.6	98.4	8.1
1992	**297.3**	**44.4**	**256.8**	**45.3**	**211.8**	**31.1**	**189.6**	**33.6**	**228.5**	**36.7**	**89.3**	**−6.3**
Q1	230.0	11.7	225.6	12.9	175.0	8.3	170.3	15.0	198.5	1.7	88.6	−10.0
Q2	251.9	9.5	246.1	9.1	188.7	7.8	184.4	8.3	209.2	5.4	85.6	−3.4
Q3	276.2	9.6	264.6	7.5	199.2	5.6	195.4	5.9	229.4	9.6	87.3	2.0
Q4	297.3	7.7	290.9	9.9	211.8	6.3	208.4	6.7	276.8	20.7	95.8	9.8
1993	**409.4**	**37.7**	**351.5**	**36.9**	**287.8**	**35.9**	**250.7**	**32.2**	**320.0**	**40.1**	**91.5**	**2.4**
Q1	326.7	9.9	319.0	9.6	227.3	7.3	224.2	7.6	284.1	2.6	89.7	−6.4
Q2	345.0	5.6	339.8	6.5	240.9	6.0	236.7	5.6	302.3	6.4	89.6	−0.1
Q3	365.8	6.0	357.2	5.1	268.0	11.2	262.0	10.7	314.8	4.1	88.8	−0.9
Q4	409.4	11.9	390.0	9.2	287.8	7.4	280.1	6.9	378.8	20.3	97.8	10.2
1994	**530.0**	**29.5**	**468.4**	**33.3**	**366.0**	**27.9**	**292.0**	**16.5**	**421.4**	**31.7**	**90.8**	**−0.7**
Q1	429.9	5.0	422.7	8.4	304.7	5.9	273.9	−2.2	395.6	4.4	94.2	−3.7
Q2	460.3	7.1	450.8	6.7	317.1	4.1	280.3	2.3	411.7	4.1	92.0	−2.4
Q3	496.5	7.9	479.6	6.4	342.4	8.0	298.4	6.5	424.8	3.2	89.2	−3.0
Q4	530.0	6.7	520.3	8.5	368.0	7.5	315.5	5.7	453.5	6.8	87.8	−1.6

Source: IMF, *International Financial Statistics.*
[1]Social sector, excludes outworkers.

Table 2.6.
Poland: Employment by Sector

	1989	1990	1991	1992	1993	1994
			(In thousands of persons)			
Total employment	**17,129.8**	**16,511.4**	**15,601.4**	**14,974.2**	**14,584.1**	**14,922.5**
(of which: private sector)	7,511.4	7,441.7	7,830.3	8,036.6	8,291.1	. . .
Agriculture and forestry	4,671.4	4,558.9	4,382.8	4,136.0	3,762.8	4,016.8
Industry	4,894.3	4,619.9	4,249.9	3,882.1	3,696.9	3,634.0
Construction	1,318.3	1,242.7	1,116.3	1,066.2	897.9	833.8
Services	6,245.8	6,089.9	5,852.4	5,889.9	6,226.5	6,437.9
Transport and communications	978.6	932.1	842.9	773.1	730.3	838.0
Trade	1,458.7	1,388.5	1,560.8	1,605.3	2,028.4	2,407.3
Other	3,808.5	3,769.3	3,448.7	3,511.5	3,467.8	3,192.6
			(Percent change)			
Total employment	**0.6**	**–3.6**	**–5.5**	**–4.0**	**–2.6**	**2.3**
(of which: private sector)	(. . .)	–0.9	5.2	2.6	3.2	. . .
Agriculture and forestry	1.2	–2.4	–3.9	–5.6	–9.0	6.8
Industry	—	–5.6	–8.0	–8.7	–4.8	–1.7
Construction	–2.3	–5.7	–10.2	–4.5	–15.8	–7.1
Services	1.4	–2.5	–3.9	0.6	5.7	3.4
Transport and communications	–5.3	–4.8	–9.6	–8.3	–5.5	14.7
Trade	–1.3	–4.8	12.4	2.9	26.4	18.7
Other	4.3	–1.0	–8.5	1.8	–1.2	–7.9
Registered unemployment (end of period)						
In thousands of persons	10.0	1,126.1	2,155.6	2,509.3	2,889.6	. . .
In percent of total labor force	0.1	6.3	11.8	13.6	16.4	16.0

Sources: IMF Institute database, based on published data by the Polish Central Statistical Office (GUS); *Poland–Statistical Tables*, IMF Staff Country Report No. 96/20 (Washington: International Monetary Fund, 1996); Liam P. Ebrill, *Poland: The Path to a Market Economy*, Occasional Paper No. 113 (Washington: International Monetary Fund, 1994); and IMF Institute staff estimates.

Appendix

The 1993 SNA Accounting Framework

The 1993 System of National Accounts

As noted earlier, the System of National Accounts (SNA) is a group of integrated accounts that provide an overview of a country's economic performance. This appendix attempts to present, in a summary fashion, the 1993 SNA accounting framework as it applies to Poland. The accounts are a convenient way to present a large volume of detailed information, which is organized according to internationally accepted economic principles and conventions about the working of an economy. The accounts are interconnected and linked to different types of economic activity over a period of time—that is, they are *flow accounts*. Each account is related to a particular kind of activity, such as production, distribution, or use of income, and is balanced by introducing an item defined residually as the difference between total resources and their uses (the *balancing item*). The balancing item from one account is carried forward as the first item in the succeeding account, making the accounts sequential.[1]

In the 1993 SNA, the flow accounts have been structured in two groups: *current accounts* and *accumulation accounts*. In addition to the flow accounts, the 1993 SNA structure includes a number of *balance sheets*.

- *Current account* comprises *production accounts* and *income accounts*. The former record the production of goods and services, the latter record the generation of distribution of the income generated during the production process as well as the use of income for consumption and saving purposes. The income accounts include the Generation of Income Account, the Allocation of Income Account, and Redistribution of Income Account. Table 2.7 summarizes the purpose of each of these accounts and identifies the balancing item. The section below interprets the accounts in the case of Poland and sheds light on their linkages.
- The *accumulation accounts* detail the acquisition and disposal of financial and nonfinancial assets and liabilities. These accounts are linked to the current account through saving, which is used to acquire financial and nonfinancial assets. The accumulation accounts include the main accounts, namely the *capital account*, the *financial accounts*, and *other changes in assets accounts*.
- The *balance sheet* records the values of the stocks of assets and liabilities sectors held at the beginning and end of the period.

All the above accounts are prepared for the main institutional sectors in the economy. For the purposes of the SNA, there are five of these mutually exclusive sectors: (i) nonfinancial corporations; (ii) financial corporations; (iii) governmental units; (iv) nonprofit institutions serving households; and (v) households.

These five sectors make up the total economy. However, while the SNA does not require that accounts be compiled for economic activity taking place in the rest of the world, all transactions between resident and nonresident units must be recorded in order to obtain a complete accounting of the economic behavior of resident units.[2] Transactions between residents and nonresidents are grouped together in a single account, *the rest of the world*. Specifically, in order for the system to be closed, this sector must be included to capture those flows that are not reflected as "uses" or "resources" for two resident units but rather only for one. The accounts in the rest of the world sector capture the full range of transactions, including the external account of goods and services, the external account of primary incomes and current transfers, the external accumulation accounts, and the external assets and liabilities accounts.

Basic Accounting Principles

The basic accounting principles and conventions that underlie the SNA system of recording flows and stocks are discussed below. An understanding of

[1]See *SNA*, Section I, 1993.

[2]See *SNA*, Chapter XIV, External Transactions Account, 1993.

these principles is essential to the interpretation and use of macroeconomic statistics.

Types of Transactions

The basic purpose of a system of national accounts is to record economic flows (transactions) and stocks (of assets or liabilities). Transactions are grouped into three categories: (1) transactions in *goods and services*, originating from either domestic production or external trade; (2) *distributive* transactions related either to production (primary income) or to income redistribution (secondary income); and (3) *financial* transactions reflecting changes in financial assets and liabilities.

Assets and liabilities are stocks held by economic operators at one point in time. These stocks represent the accumulation of prior transactions and are affected by changes in both the volume of transactions and their prices (valuation changes).

Main Accounting Conventions

Double-entry recording. All macroeconomic accounts use this form of bookkeeping. For every transaction, there are two accounting entries, a credit and a debit. For unrequited transactions (such as transfers or grants) that flow one way only, a corresponding entry is made on the opposite side of the "ledger."

Timing. Transactions are recorded when claims and obligations arise, are transformed, or are canceled (not at the time of their settlement) on what is called an *accrual basis.*

Types of Transactors

There are two types of transactors: residents and nonresidents. Resident transactors must have been in a country for more than a year and regard it as the *main center of their interest.*[3] Exceptions apply mostly to economic "enclaves," such as embassies and military bases. Resident transactors are included under institutional sectors, while nonresident transactors are grouped under the rest of the world.

[3]The concept of residence used in the SNA is not based on nationality but rather on the notion of economic interest of the entity being considered. Thus, individuals living in a country are generally considered as residents if they have been living in the country for at least 12 months. Enterprises are considered residents where they are engaged in business, provided they have at least one productive establishment that they plan to operate for a long period of time.

Valuation Concepts in the SNA[4]

Two broad systems of valuation are distinguished in the SNA: based on *current* and *constant prices.* In each system, several sets of prices may be used; for example, output is frequently valued both at *basic prices* (excluding all taxes, less subsidies on products) and at *purchaser's prices* (at prices paid by the final purchaser, including taxes less subsidies on products). The price used depends on how the taxes and subsidies on products and transport charges are treated.

- The *basic price* is what the producer receives *minus* any taxes due *plus* any subsidies on the output. It excludes transport charges.
- The *producer's price* is the price the producer receives *minus* any value-added tax (VAT) or similar other *deductible* taxes. It also excludes transport charges.
- The *purchaser's price* is the price the buyer pays, excluding any deductible VAT or similar taxes. Unlike the previous two notions, the purchaser's price includes transport charges.

The preferred method of valuation in the SNA is at basic prices, especially when a VAT is involved. If it is not feasible to use basic prices, producer prices are generally substituted. Purchasers' prices are used when intermediate consumption is valued.

Applying the SNA to Poland

The Polish Central Statistical Office (GUS) has published national account data derived in accordance with the 1993 SNA.[5] Since the GUS's use of the 1993 SNA is in the early stages, the data reproduced here are for illustrative purposes only.

Table 2.8 summarizes the sequence of accounts for Poland for 1992 for the aggregate economy while Tables 2.9–2.14 present the details of the accounts including the sectoral distribution.

The detailed national accounts cover the production account (Table 2.9), the generation of income account (Table 2.10), the allocation of primary income account (Table 2.11), the secondary distribution of income account (Table 2.12), the use of disposal income account (Table 2.13), and the capital account (Table 2.14). Table 2.15 is a matrix presentation of the system of accounts in Poland for 1992.

The summary table for the economy as a whole (Table 2.8) shows how the various accounts are chained and how the macroeconomic aggregates are derived and linked. It illustrates that the balancing

[4]For further details, see Chapter VI of the SNA, 1993.

[5]*Polish National Accounts by Institutional Sectors*, GUS, April 1994 and April 1995.

item for each account represents a familiar macroeconomic aggregate (e.g., GDP for the Production Account, GNI for the Allocation of Primary Income Account), and that a balancing item of one account in this chain is carried forward to the following account in the sequence. For example GNDI, the balancing item of the Secondary Distribution of Income Account, is also the opening item (on the resource side) of the Use of Income Account.

- *The Production Account (Table 2.9).* This account depicts the sectoral origin of *gross output* (on the resource side) as well as the sectoral use of intermediate inputs. The account shows that, for each sector, the value added is derived as the difference between the value of production (i.e., gross output) and the value of the goods and services used up in the production process (i.e., intermediate inputs). For example, the value added of the nonfinancial corporations in 1992 amounted to Zl 618.9 trillion and is derived as the gross output for the sector (Zl 1,526.8 trillion) minus intermediate consumption (Zl 907.8 trillion). *Gross domestic product* (GDP) (Zl 1,149.4 trillion)—the *balancing item* of this account—is obtained as gross output (Zl 2,435.8 trillion) for the economy as a whole *minus* intermediate consumption (Zl 1,333.2 trillion) *plus* customs and other import-related taxes (Zl 46.8 trillion).[6]
- *Generation of Income Account (Table 2.10)* shows how the value added generated in the Production Account is distributed in terms of compensation of employees, taxes less subsidies on production and imports, and *operating surplus* (the balancing item of this account). The account also shows the sectoral origin (on the uses side) of compensation of employees, taxes, subsidies, and operating surplus. For example, it can be seen from Table 2.10 that the largest wage bill was paid by the nonfinancial corporations (Zl 247.2 trillion) followed by the Government (Zl 95.3 trillion). Interestingly the Households Sector had, in 1992, a larger operating surplus (Zl 255.2 trillion) than the nonfinancial corporations (Zl 199.2 trillion). Also noteworthy is the negative operating surplus of the financial corporations.
- *The Generation of Income Account* is useful in shedding light on how for each sector, the operating surplus is derived from the value added. For instance, the value added of the nonfinancial corporations (Zl 618.9 trillion) was used to cover their payments of wages, salaries, and other labor costs (Zl 250.7 trillion), social security contributions (Zl 95.4 trillion), and taxes (Zl 101.4 trillion). Given these uses and the subsidies received (Zl 27.7 trillion), the remainder (Zl 199.2 trillion) represents their operating surplus.
- *Allocation of Primary Income Account (Table 2.11).* This account focuses on the remaining part of the primary distribution of income. Its balancing item, for the economy as a whole, is the *gross national income (GNI)*, which as noted earlier, is the same as the concept of gross national product (GNP) under the 1968 SNA. For each sector, the account depicts the various primary incomes received (on the resources side) and paid (on the uses side). For example, in the case of the households, their resources include their operating surpluses (Zl 255.3 trillion), the wages and salaries received (Zl 389.7 trillion), interest received (Zl 37.0 trillion), and dividend received (Zl 29.1 trillion). Taking into account their payment of interest (Zl 3.5 trillion), the balance of their primary income is Zl 707.4 trillion. It should be noted that the total amount of property income paid is equal to the total amount received. This is also true for each component of property income, e.g., interest income. This identity holds because the system is "closed"—that is, the *rest of the world sector* is included with the *domestic economy* to cover the whole universe of transactors.
- *Secondary Distribution of Income Account (Table 2.12).* This account covers the redistribution of income in the form of transfers. The balancing item is *gross national disposable income (GNDI)*, which can be either consumed or saved.

  The account depicts which sector is the recipient of the transfers (on the resources side) and which effects the transfers (on the uses side). As expected, the general Government and the household sectors are two major players in this account. For the Government sector, on the resources side, the account shows the various taxes received by the Government (e.g., Zl 137.1 trillion in income tax receipt, and Zl 17.0 trillion in excess wage tax) and on the uses side, the various contributors. For instance, income taxes were paid by the nonfinancial corporations (Zl 45.5 trillion), financial corporations (Zl 9.0 trillion), and the households sector (Zl 82.7 trillion).

[6]Note that customs and taxes linked to imports must be added to gross output in order for the GDP to be valued consistently with the expenditure approach. However, since the taxes linked to imports have not been allocated among the sectors, the GDP depicted in the production accounts is not obtained as the sum of value added in each sector but as the sum plus the value of taxes linked to imports.

- *Use of Disposable Income Account (Table 2.13).* This account shows how disposable income is used. The balancing item in this account is *gross saving*. In 1992, of the total disposable income of Zl 1,149.4 trillion, about Zl 957.4 trillion was used for consumption leaving Zl 192.0 trillion in gross savings. It is worth noting that for 1992 the general government in Poland had a negative saving while the households sector accounted for the bulk of saving in the economy. Note also that for the nonfinancial sector there is no final consumption, so that its gross saving is the same as its gross disposable income (Zl 51.5 trillion).
- *Capital Account (Table 2.14)* is the only accumulation account included in the published Polish SNA accounts. It records the changes in assets and liabilities. On the resources side, the account depicts the savings derived in the use of income account and on the uses side, it shows the various types of investment viz. fixed capital formation and changes in inventories. The balancing item of this account is *net lending* (if the result is positive) or *net borrowing* (if the result is negative). Note that while most sectors of the economy were net lenders, the Government and nonfinancial corporations were net borrowers. In the case of the Government, it had a negative saving as mentioned earlier and hence was in no position to be a net lender, while in the case of the nonfinancial corporations, as is sometimes the case, their investment exceeded their savings.
- *Matrix Presentation of the System of Accounts (Table 2.15).* This matrix shows the relationships between the various accounts and sectors. The *Rest of the World* column records transaction between residents and nonresidents from the nonresident point of view (that is why, for this sector, the resources and uses were reversed). For instance, exports which are part of the domestic economy's resources are shown as uses in the matrix. In particular, a negative balance for the rest of the world sector means a surplus on current transaction for Poland. Note that in the matrix, the accounts have been made to overlap so as to show in a single line the balancing item of one account and the starting balance of the following account. Also note that the goods and services columns record the counterparts to the transactions in goods and services by the sectors, including the rest of the world. In this way, the rows of the matrix are balanced. In other words, the goods and services account show the equality between the supply of goods and services and their usage, that is, the total gross output plus imports plus taxes net of subsidies are equal to the sum of intermediate consumption, exports, final consumption, investment (fixed capital formation and changes in inventories). In conclusion, the matrix highlights the three approaches to GDP discussed earlier, namely, the GDP as (i) the sum of value added (production approach); (ii) the sum of income generated by the production process (the income approach); and (iii) the sum of final expenditure (the expenditure approach).

Differences Between the 1993 and 1968 SNA Systems

The System of National Accounts (SNA) was extensively revised in 1993. The 1993 version has several important new features.[7] (It is assumed that national authorities will begin converting their national accounts to the new system in the near future.)

- First, the accounting structure has been reworked to provide a more integrated sequence of accounts. The 1993 SNA is based on institutional sectors and includes current accounts, accumulation accounts, and (new in 1993) balance sheets as well as more detailed information on sectoral transactions.
- Second, although gross domestic product is still an important measure in the 1993 system, more emphasis has been given to identifying and providing details of other key economic aggregates and balancing items such as income flows. The 1993 system also presents a series of income accounts that provide greater insight into the generation, distribution, and uses of incomes.
- Third, in keeping with the development of more sophisticated financial instruments and derivatives, the 1993 accounts provide more information on the types of assets and liabilities each institutional sector employs.
- Fourth, as far as possible, the 1993 SNA is consistent with other international statistical standards—for example, the IMF's *Balance of Payments Manual*. Future revisions of the manuals related to monetary statistics and government finance statistics are expected to be undertaken with a view to maximizing consistency with the 1993 SNA.
- Finally, the 1993 system specifically recognizes the development of satellite accounts that augment the SNA accounts, such as those for environmental statistics.

[7]For a more complete description of the differences between the 1968 and 1993 SNA, see Annex I of the 1993 *SNA*.

Table 2.7.
SNA: Integrated Economic Accounts

Accounts	Purpose	Balancing Item[1]	Main Aggregate[2] Gross	Net
Current accounts				
Production account	Records production of goods and services	Value added	Domestic product GDP	NDP
Income accounts				
Primary distribution[3]	Shows how income generated by production is distributed to institutional sectors[4]	Balance of primary incomes	National income GNI	NNI
Secondary distribution	Covers redistribution in the form of transfers in cash and in kind	Disposable income	National disposable income GNDI	NNDI
Use of income	Shows how disposable income is used to undertake final consumption expenditure	Saving	National saving S	Sn
Accumulation accounts				
Capital account	Records transactions related to the acquisition and disposal of *nonfinancial* assets and to capital transfers involving the redistribution of wealth	Net lending/net borrowing		
Financial accounts	Records acquisition and disposal of *financial* assets and liabilities through transactions	Net lending/net borrowing		
Other changes in assets accounts	Cover changes in assets, liabilities, and net worth due to factors *other* than transactions (e.g., valuation changes)	Changes in net worth		
Balance sheets[5]				
Opening balance sheets and closing balance sheets	Provide the value of assets, liabilities, and net worth at the beginning and end of the period and a summary of changes in those values			

Sources: *System of National Accounts*, Commission of the European Communities, International Monetary Fund, Organization for Economic Cooperation and Development, United Nations, and the World Bank, 1993.

[1]Since each group of transactions does not balance, i.e., total receipts are different from total outlays, a balancing item is used to balance the account and is carried forward to the following account.

[2]Net concepts are net of depreciation.

[3]The sequence of accounts is established for resident transactors called "institutional sectors" in the SNA.

[4]The primary distribution accounts consist of the Generation of Income Account for which operating surplus is the balancing item and the Allocation of Primary Income Account for which GNI is the balancing item.

[5]In most countries, the establishment of balance sheets for the overall economy is severely hampered by lack of information on stocks of real assets.

Table 2.8.
Poland: Sequence of Accounts for 1992
(In trillions of zlotys)

Uses		Resources	
		Production Account	
Intermediate consumption	1,333.2	Output	2,435.8
Value added (GDP)	**1,149.4**	Customs levies and taxes linked to imports	46.8
		Generation of Income Account	
Compensation of employees	540.8	**Value added (GDP)**	**1,149.4**
Taxes on production and imports	160.8		
Subsidies	−27.7		
Operating surplus	**475.6**		
		Allocation of Primary Income Account	
Property income (payable)	229.0	**Operating surplus**	**475.6**
Interest income paid	184.6	Compensation of employees	540.8
Payments to employees out of profits	5.0	Taxes on production and imports	160.8
Distributed income of corporations	39.3	Subsidies	−27.7
Gross national income (GNI)	**1,095.0**		
		Secondary Distribution of Income	
		Gross national income (GNI)	**1,095.0**
Current taxes on income	168.0	Current taxes on income	168.0
Social security and other social transfers	220.2	Social security and other social transfers	220.2
Other current transfers	169.0	Other current transfers	208.9
		Property Income (received)	174.5
Gross disposable income (GNDI)	**1,134.9**		
		Use of Income Account	
		Gross disposable income (GNDI)	**1,134.9**
Final consumption expenditures	957.4		
Individual consumption expenditure	870.2		
Collective consumption expenditure	87.3		
Gross saving	**177.5**		
		Capital Account	
		Gross saving	**177.5**
Capital transfers	15.8	Capital transfers	15.8
Gross capital formation	174.4		
Tangible fixed assets	190.7		
Intangible fixed assets	2.3		
Changes in inventories	−18.6		
Net lending (+) or net borrowing (–)	**3.1**		

Sources: *Polish National Accounts by Institutional Sectors, 1991–92; Experimental Compilation–1994,* Research Center for Economic and Statistical Studies of the Polish Central Statistical Office and the Polish Academy of Sciences, and the Polish Central Statistical Office (GUS).

Table 2.9.
Poland: Production Account, 1992
(In trillions of zlotys, at current prices)

Uses									Resources							
Sectors												Sectors				
Nonprofit institutions	Households	General government	Financial corporations	Nonfinancial corporations	National economy	ROW[1]	Total	Transactions and Balancing Items	Total	ROW[1]	National economy	Nonfinancial corporations	Financial corporations	General government	Households	Nonprofit institutions
								Gross output	**2,435.8**		**2,435.8**	**1,526.8**	**39.9**	**259.1**	**596.2**	**13.8**
5.2	294.4	91.8	34.0	907.8	1,333.2		1,333.2	Intermediate consumption								
								Customs and other taxes linked to imports	46.8		46.8					
8.6	**301.8**	**167.3**	**5.9**	**619.0**	**1,149.4**		**1,149.4**	**Gross domestic product (GDP)**								

Sources: *Polish National Accounts by Institutional Sectors, 1991–92; Experimental Compilation—1994,* Research Center for Economic and Statistical Studies of the Polish Central Statistical Office and the Polish Academy of Sciences, and the Polish Central Statistical Office (GUS).

[1]Rest of the world.

Table 2.10.
Poland: Generation of Income Account, 1992
(In trillions of zlotys, at current prices)

Uses									Resources							
Sectors													Sectors			
Nonprofit institutions	Households	General government	Financial corporations	Nonfinancial corporations	National economy	ROW[1]	Total	Transactions and Balancing Items	Total	ROW[1]	National economy	Nonfinancial corporations	Financial corporations	General government	Households	Nonprofit institutions
								Gross domestic product (GDP)	1,149.4		1,149.4	619.0	6.9	167.3	301.8	8.6
3.5	24.5	102.9	8.0	250.7	389.7		389.7	Compensation to employees								
3.0	24.5	95.3	8.0	247.2	378.1		378.1	1. Wages and salaries								
0.5		7.6		3.5	11.6		11.6	2. Other labor costs								
0.8	9.8	41.2	3.9	95.4	151.1		151.1	Social security contributions								
0.2	12.2		0.2	73.6	133.0		133.0	Taxes less subsidies								
0.2	12.2		0.2	101.4	160.8		160.8	1. Taxes								
	8.6			85.6	94.1		94.1	1.1 Turnover tax								
					46.8		46.8	1.2 Customs and taxes linked to imports								
0.2	3.7		0.2	15.8	19.8		19.8	1.3 Taxes on production								
				−27.7	−27.7		−27.7	2. Subsidies								
4.2	**256.2**	**23.2**	**−16.2**	**199.2**	**476.6**		**476.6**	**Operating surplus**								

Sources: *Polish National Accounts by Institutional Sectors, 1991–92; Experimental Compilation—1994,* Research Center for Economic and Statistical Studies of the Polish Central Statistical Office and the Polish Academy of Sciences, and the Polish Central Statistical Office (GUS).
[1]Rest of the world.

Table 2.11.
Poland: Allocation of Income Account, 1992
(In trillions of zlotys, at current prices)

Uses: Sectors: Nonprofit institutions	Uses: Sectors: Households	Uses: Sectors: General government	Uses: Sectors: Financial corporations	Uses: Sectors: Non-financial corporations	Uses: National economy	Uses: ROW[1]	Uses: Total	Transactions and Balancing Items	Resources: Total	Resources: ROW[1]	Resources: National economy	Resources: Sectors: Non-financial corporations	Resources: Sectors: Financial corporations	Resources: Sectors: General government	Resources: Sectors: Households	Resources: Sectors: Nonprofit institutions
								Operating surplus	**475.6**		**475.6**	**199.2**	**–6.2**	**23.2**	**255.2**	**4.2**
								Compensation to employees	389.7		389.7				389.7	
								Social security contributions						151.1		
								Taxes less subsidies	133.0		133.0			133.0		
2.6	3.5	67.3	60.1	95.4	229.0	9.4	238.4	Property income	238.4	63.8	174.5	14.4	71.8	17.7	66.1	4.5
2.6	3.5	67.1	58.6	52.8	184.6	8.3	192.9	1. Interest income	192.9	63.8	129.0	13.7	71.8	2.0	37.0	4.5
		0.2	1.6	42.6	44.3	1.2	45.5	2. Dividend	45.5		45.5	0.7		15.7	29.1	
								2.1 Dividend received	45.5		45.5	0.7		15.7	29.1	
		0.2	1.6	42.6	44.3	1.2	45.5	2.2 Dividend paid								
			0.8	4.2	5.0		5.0	Payments to employees out of profits	5.0		5.0				5.0	
		0.2	0.8	38.3	39.3	1.2	40.5	Distributed income of corporations	40.5		40.5	0.7		15.7	24.1	
6.0	**707.4**	**257.8**	**5.5**	**118.2**	**1,095.0**	**54.4**	**1,149.4**	**Primary income, gross**								

Sources: *Polish National Accounts by Institutional Sectors, 1991–92; Experimental Compilation–1994,* Research Center for Economic and Statistical Studies of the Polish Central Statistical Office and the Polish Academy of Sciences, and the Polish Central Statistical Office (GUS).

[1]Rest of the world.

Table 2.12.
Poland: Secondary Distribution of Income Account, 1992
(In trillions of zlotys, at current prices)

	Uses							
	Sectors							
Transactions and Balancing Items	Nonprofit institutions	Households	General government	Financial corporations	Nonfinancial corporations	National economy	Rest of the world	Total
Primary Income, gross								
Taxes on income and wealth		88.6		19.7	59.7	168.0		168.0
Taxes on income		82.7		9.0	45.4	137.1		137.1
Other taxes		5.9		10.7	14.2	30.9		30.9
Excess wage tax				2.7	14.2	17.0		17.0
Farm		2.4				2.4		2.4
Households		3.6				3.6		3.6
Profit of banks				8.0		8.0		8.0
Social transfers	9.7	109.9	244.2	15.7	9.7	352.6	113.4	466.0
Social security	9.7	5.2	205.3			220.2		220.2
Benefits			191.2			191.2		191.2
Transfers	9.7		14.1			23.8		23.8
Contributions		5.2				5.2		5.2
Other transfers		104.7	38.9	15.7	9.7	169.0	113.4	245.8
Abroad		73.5				73.5		186.9
Administrative dues		10.6				10.6		10.6
Insurance		11.6	0.1	15.1	3.0	29.8		29.8
Premium		11.6	0.1	0.2	3.0	14.9		14.9
Claims				14.9		14.9		14.9
Other transfers		9.0	2.2	0.6	6.7	18.6		18.6
Operations with banks			36.5			36.5		36.5
Disposable income, gross	**14.9**	**812.4**	**234.3**	**21.7**	**51.5**	**1,134.9**	**14.5**	**1,149.4**

Sources: *Polish National Accounts by Institutional Sectors, 1991–92; Experimental Compilation—1994,* Research Center for Economic and Statistical Studies of the Polish Central Statistical Office and the Polish Academy of Sciences, and the Polish Central Statistical Office (GUS).

Resources							
Sectors							
Nonprofit institutions	Households	General government	Financial corporations	Nonfinancial corporations	National economy	Rest of the world	Total
6.0	**707.4**	**257.8**	**5.5**	**118.2**	**1,095.0**	**54.4**	**1,149.4**
		168.0			168.0		168.0
		137.1			137.1		137.1
		30.9			30.9		30.9
		17.0			17.0		17.0
		2.4			2.4		2.4
		3.6			3.6		3.6
		8.0			8.0		8.0
18.6	303.5	52.7	51.5	2.8	429.1	73.5	502.6
	215.0	5.2			220.2		220.2
	191.2				191.2		191.2
	23.8				23.8		23.8
	5.2				5.2		5.2
18.6	88.5	47.5	51.5	2.8	208.9	73.5	282.4
	76.6	36.8			113.4	73.5	186.9
		10.6			10.6		10.6
	11.9	0.2	15.0	2.8	29.8		29.8
			14.9		14.9		14.9
	11.9	0.2	0.1	2.8	14.9		14.9
18.6					18.6		18.6
			36.5		36.5		36.5

Table 2.13.
Poland: Use of Disposable Income Account, 1992
(In trillions of zlotys, at current prices)

Uses									Resources							
Sectors												Sectors				
Nonprofit institutions	Households	General government	Financial corporations	Nonfinancial corporations	National economy	ROW[1]	Total	Transactions and Balancing Items	Total	ROW[1]	National economy	Nonfinancial corporations	Financial corporations	General government	Households	Nonprofit institutions
								Disposable income, gross	**1,149.4**	**14.5**	**1,134.9**	**51.5**	**21.7**	**234.3**	**812.4**	**14.9**
9.7	686.9	260.8			957.4			Final consumption								
9.7	686.9	173.5			870.2			1. Individual								
		87.3			87.3			2. Collective								
5.2	**125.5**	**–26.5**	**21.7**	**51.5**	**177.5**	**14.5**	**192.0**	**Gross saving**								

Sources: *Polish National Accounts by Institutional Sectors, 1991–92; Experimental Compilation—1994,* Research Center for Economic and Statistical Studies of the Polish Central Statistical Office and the Polish Academy of Sciences, and the Polish Central Statistical Office (GUS).

[1]Rest of the world.

Table 2.14.
Poland: Capital Account, 1992
(In trillions of zlotys, at current prices)

Uses									Resources							
Sectors												Sectors				
Nonprofit institutions	Households	General government	Financial corporations	Nonfinancial corporations	National economy	ROW[1]	Total	Transactions and Balancing Items	Total	ROW[1]	National economy	Nonfinancial corporations	Financial corporations	General government	Households	Nonprofit institutions
								Gross saving	**192.0**	**14.5**	**177.5**	**51.5**	**21.7**	**–26.5**	**125.5**	**5.2**
						17.6		Current external balance								
		15.8			15.8		15.8	Capital transfers			15.8	15.8				
	28.1	27.2	7.2	111.9	174.4		174.4	Gross capital formation								
	33.2	27.2	7.2	123.1	190.7		190.7	1. Tangible fixed assets								
				2.3	2.3		2.3	2. Intangible fixed assets								
	–5.1			–13.5	–18.6		–18.6	3. Changes in inventories								
5.2	**97.4**	**–69.5**	**14.5**	**–44.5**	**3.1**	**–3.1**	**0.0**	**Net lending (+) or net borrowing (–)**								

Sources: *Polish National Accounts by Institutional Sectors, 1991–92; Experimental Compilation–1994,* Research Center for Economic and Statistical Studies of the Polish Central Statistical Office and the Polish Academy of Sciences, and the Polish Central Statistical Office (GUS).
[1]Rest of the world.

Table 2.15.
Poland: Matrix Presentation of the 1992 SNA
(In trillions of zlotys, at current prices)

Accounts	Uses: Sectors: Nonprofit institutions	Households	General government	Financial corporations	Nonfinancial corporations	National economy	Rest of the world	Goods and services (resources)	Total
Production and external account of goods and services									
Imports of goods and services								254.8	254.8
Exports of goods and services							272.4		272.4
Gross output							2,435.8		2,435.8
Customs and taxes linked to imports								46.8	46.8
Intermediate consumption	5.2	294.4	91.8	34.0	907.8	1,333.2			1,333.2
Gross domestic product (GDP)	8.6	301.8	167.3	5.9	619.0	1,149.4			1,149.4
External balance of goods and services							–17.6		–17.6
Generation of income account									
Compensation to employees	4.2	34.3	144.1	12.0	346.1	540.8			540.8
Taxes less subsidies	0.2	12.2		0.2	73.6	133.0			133.0
Gross operating surplus	4.2	255.2	23.2	–6.2	199.2	475.6			475.6
Allocation of primary income account									
Property income	2.6	3.5	67.3	60.1	95.4	229.0	9.4		238.4
Balance of primary income	6.0	707.4	257.8	5.5	116.2	1,095.0	54.4		1,194.4
Secondary distribution of income account									
Current taxes on income and wealth		88.6		19.7	59.7	168.0			168.0
Social transfers	9.7	109.9	244.2	15.7	9.7	352.6	113.4		466.0
Gross disposable income	14.9	812.4	234.3	21.7	51.5	134.9	14.5		1,149.4
Use of income account									
Final consumption expenditures	9.7	686.9	260.8			957.4			957.4
Gross saving	5.2	125.5	–26.5	21.7	51.5	177.5	14.5		192.0
Capital account									
Current external balance							–17.6		–17.6
Capital transfers			15.8						
Gross capital formation		28.1	27.2	72.1	11.9	174.4			174.4
Net lending (+) or borrowing (–)	5.2	97.4	–69.5	14.5	–44.5	3.1	–3.1		00

Sources: *Polish National Accounts by Institutional Sectors, 1991–92; Experimental Compilation—1994,* Research Center for Economic and Statistical Studies of the Polish Central Statistical Office and the Polish Academy of Sciences, and the Polish Central Statistical Office (GUS).

Resources								
Sectors								
Nonprofit institutions	Households	General government	Financial corporations	Nonfinancial corporations	National economy	Rest of the world	Goods and services (uses)	Total
						254.8		254.8
							272.4	272.4
	13.8	596.2	259.1	39.9	1,526.8	2,435.8		2,435.8
					46.8			46.8
							1,333.2	1,333.2
8.6	301.8	167.3	5.9	619.0	1,149.4			1,149.4
						–17.6		–17.6
	389.7	151.1			540.8			540.8
		133.0			133.0			133.0
4.2	255.2	23.2	–6.2	199.2	475.6			475.6
4.5	66.1	17.7	71.8	14.4	174.5	63.8		238.4
6.0	707.4	257.8	5.5	118.2	1,095.0	54.4		1,149.4
		168.0			168.0			168.0
18.6	303.5	52.7	51.5	2.8	429.1	73.5		502.6
14.9	812.4	234.3	21.7	51.5	1,34.9	14.5		1,149.4
						957.4		957.4
5.2	125.5	–26.5	21.7	51.5	177.5	14.5		192.0
				15.8	15.8			
				174.4	174.4			

CHAPTER

3 Fiscal Accounting and Analysis

Fiscal developments and policies play a central role in determining overall economic developments and policies. Fiscal policy directly affects an economy's use of aggregate resources and level of aggregate demand. Together with monetary and exchange rate policies, it also influences the balance of payments, the debt levels, and the rates of inflation and economic growth. Policies that deal with taxation, public spending, and borrowing affect the behavior of producers and consumers and influence the distribution of income and wealth in the economy. Frequently, large macroeconomic imbalances, both internal and external, can be traced to a fiscal imbalance that policy has failed to correct.

In order to assess the overall fiscal performance of an economy in the context of stabilization and structural reform, it is essential to have a firm grasp of the basic principles of fiscal accounting and analysis. This chapter is devoted to an exposition of this basic framework of fiscal accounting and analysis.

The first part of this chapter opens with a discussion of key concepts set out in the IMF's *Manual on Government Finance Statistics* (*GFS*).[1] The *GFS* provides an internationally accepted framework for presenting data on a government's fiscal operations. This framework is designed to facilitate the analysis of government transactions with respect to income, outlays, capital accumulation, and financing. Subsequent sections focus on the definition of the government sector, the measurement of government operations, and some basic concepts employed in the classification and accounting treatment of government operations. Main classifications of revenues and expenditures are also outlined, and the concept of the conventional overall deficit is discussed.

The second part discusses the main analytical issues in fiscal analysis, including the notions of government saving and investment, alternative measures of fiscal imbalance, alternative methods of financing a fiscal deficit and their macroeconomic implications, and the sustainability of the fiscal policy. A more detailed analysis of the methods of assessing developments in government revenues and expenditures is provided also. The third part of this chapter contains background information on the fiscal sector in Poland, including a brief description of the structure of the fiscal sector, coverage of recent fiscal developments, tax and expenditure policies, and the financing of the deficit. The last section contains exercises and issues for discussion.

Fiscal Accounting

Defining the Government Sector

The *GFS Manual* identifies several layers of government: (i) the central government; (ii) the state or regional government; (iii) local government; and (iv) any supranational authority. For most countries, the fiscal operations of the government sector cover, at a minimum, the *central government*, which formulates national budgets. But in many countries, fiscal operations are also performed by local and regional governments. The term *general government* includes all levels of government: central, state, provincial, and local.[2] In order to emphasize the separation between the functions of the government and the monetary sectors, government finance statistics exclude from both definitions any banking or monetary transactions the government performs. In particular, all functions of the monetary authorities, irrespective of the institutions that carry them out, are treated as activities of the monetary rather than the govern-

[1]The GFS accounting framework, which was developed to assist in the compilation of fiscal accounts, is set out in *A Manual on Government Finance Statistics* (Washington: International Monetary Fund, 1986).

[2]In the states of the former Soviet Union, the governments of autonomous republics, oblasts, rayons, and gorads are considered local. The budgetary operations of the general government are recorded in state budgets that cover the central government (republican) and local budgets. For an exhaustive survey of GFS methodology issues in countries of the former Soviet Union, see Marie Montanjees, "GFS in the Countries of the Former Soviet Union: Compilation and Methodological Issues," IMF Working Paper 95/2 (Washington: International Monetary Fund, 1995).

ment sector. In order to distinguish fiscal policy from monetary policy and reconcile monetary and financial statistics with government finance statistics, analysis must separate the activities of these two sectors. Chart 3.1 presents some criteria for differentiating among the sectors.[3]

The broadest level of government is the *public sector*, which includes the general government and nonfinancial public enterprises such as publicly owned railways and airlines or public utilities. Some of the central government's revenues and expenditures typically reflect transfers from or to local governments and public enterprises. Such transfers have to be netted out so that "double counting" is not an issue when aggregates for the different levels of government operations are compiled. The process of netting out and combining accounts at different levels of the government is referred to as *consolidation*.

At each level of government, there are three groups of operations: budgetary, extrabudgetary, and social security. Budgetary operations are, by definition, covered in the budget. Extrabudgetary operations, which are carried out outside the budget, raise resources through compulsory levies and provide nonmarket goods and services. For example, an extrabudgetary fund is often established to raise revenue through special taxes on fuel and then uses these resources to maintain roads.

Social security schemes are a special category of extrabudgetary operations. In transition economies, these schemes typically comprise a pension fund, an employment fund, and a social insurance fund that covers disability and welfare programs.

Irrespective of how the government sector is defined, actual budgetary practices in many countries often lead to seriously distorted measurements of government operations. Two of the most important distortions arise from off-budget or extrabudgetary accounts and the use of counterpart funds. In some countries, particularly the economies in transition, governments set up off-budget or extrabudgetary accounts to conduct what would otherwise be budgetary operations. The extensive use of extrabudgetary funds (particularly if they are not consolidated with fiscal operations) distorts the fiscal position, reduces flexibility in fiscal management by earmarking revenues for specific purposes, and, most importantly, leads to a loss of control over funds channeled through these accounts.[4] To remedy this situation, many countries have set aside funds within the budgetary framework to replace the extrabudgetary accounts. In this way, governments maintain the necessary control, accountability, and scrutiny.

Counterpart funds are another source of fiscal distortions in many transition economies. Counterpart funds are the domestic currency equivalent of foreign loans or grants (including commodity grants). These funds are often a source of financing for the deficit and of credit (on-lending) to institutions and enterprises. Often, the loans are not recorded in the budget and thus escape parliamentary scrutiny, distorting the overall fiscal position and generating interest subsidies.[5] Not only must these counterpart funds be properly reflected in any measure of the budget, but they also must not become an indirect source of subsidized credit for ailing enterprises.

Measuring Government Operations

Government finance statistics compiled in accordance with GFS standards record transactions on a *cash* or *payment basis* rather than on the *accrual basis* used in the national income and product accounts, the monetary accounts, and the balance of payments that make up the System of National Accounts (SNA). Receipts and payments recorded on a cash basis are documented as of the time of monetary settlement, while transactions recorded using the accrual method reflect the point at which a claim or liability arises or becomes due.

Recording government transactions on a cash basis provides analysts with a basis for comparison with the monetary accounts and thus makes measuring the impact of government operations on the monetary aggregates easier. From the standpoint of economic analysis, such a comparison is particularly important when the difference between those transactions recorded on a cash basis (government finance statistics) and those recorded on an accrual basis (monetary accounts) stems from *payments arrears*. Arrears reflect a government's inability to meet its expenditure commitments—often interest payments—on time and result in serious inconsistencies between the accrual and cash deficits (see below). The accrual deficit, which shows the government's net use of resources, reflects the government's full interest obligations (both domestic and foreign), while the cash deficit reflects actual interest payments. A government with a cash deficit

[3]For an elaboration of these criteria, see *GFS Manual*, Chapter 1.

[4]There are two legitimate uses of off-budget accounts: as *trust funds* (money held on behalf of nongovernment entities) and *advance* or *suspense accounts* (funds held against future payments).

[5]The distortion results from the failure to record these funds above the line under "net lending" (thereby understating the extent of the deficit) and to account for the interest received and paid on these "counterpart" accounts as revenues and expenditures.

Chart 3.1. Criteria Determining the Borderline Between the General Government Sector and Other Sectors

	Other Sectors		General Government Sector		
Nonfinancial corporate and quasi-corporate enterprise sector	**Private Enterprise** No majority ownership or control by government	**Public Enterprise** Majority owned and/or controlled by government and selling goods and services to the public on a large scale or incorporated	**Departmental Enterprise** Ancillary or selling to the public on a small scale	Sale of goods and services regulatory in nature (passports)	Sales incidental to other government functions (museum postcards)
Financial institutions sector	Monetary Authorities Subsector	All	None		
	Deposit Money Banks Subsector	All bodies accepting demand deposits, including demand deposit liabilities accepted by government	None		
	Insurance Companies and Pension Funds Subsector	All except social security schemes and pension funds invested entirely with employer	Social Security Schemes	Government employee pension funds invested entirely with the employing government	
	Other Financial Institutions Subsector	Bodies with the authority to choose the form of assets *and* liabilities or accepting time or savings deposits	Lending bodies with only government funds. Savings bodies with liabilities other than time or savings deposits and proceeds automatically channeled to government		
Private nonprofit institutions serving households sector	Nonprofit institutions not both mainly financed and effectively controlled by government		Nonprofit institutions mainly financed and effectively controlled by government		
Rest of the world	International organizations not collecting taxes in the country	Transactions of supranational authorities collecting taxes in the country	Transit account counterpart for transactions of supranational authorities collecting taxes in the country		

Source: IMF, *A Manual on Government Finance Statistics* (Washington, 1986).

that is smaller than the accrual deficit is typically behind on its interest payments and other payment obligations.

The GFS Framework

The GFS framework is designed to provide comprehensive coverage of the government's transactions with the rest of the economy and the world and measures primarily government receipts, payments, and unpaid obligations. Chart 3.2 illustrates the classification of various government transactions within the GFS framework. The main principles underlying this framework are discussed below.

- *Revenues, receipts, payments, and expenditures.* To assess the government's overall fiscal position and the resultant macroeconomic impact, analysts must make a clear distinction between revenues and expenditures. In this respect, it is important to remember that while all revenues are receipts, all receipts are not revenues. Revenues consist only of those receipts that do not give rise to an obligation of repayment. Receipts from loans to the government are not revenues, because the loans must be repaid. Similarly, not all payments are expenditures. For example, a loan repayment is not an expenditure, because it arises out of an obligation incurred when the loan was received. Interest payments, however, are an expenditure item.
- *Gross and net.* As a general principle, revenues and expenditures are shown on a *gross basis*, so that the statistics reflect the full magnitude and impact of the government's revenue-raising operations—and the disposition of revenues. Thus, school fees are not counted as an offsetting item to the cost of providing education, nor are the costs of collecting taxes deducted from tax revenues as "negative revenues." The main exception to this rule is lending and borrowing; in this case, the rapid flows from and to the government make net lending the only meaningful item.
- *Requited and unrequited transactions.* Required transactions are those in which money is paid or received in exchange for goods or services. Unrequited transactions are those in which payment is made or received but nothing is received or given in return. Transfers and grants are examples of unrequited transactions.
- *Tax and nontax revenue.* Revenue includes all nonrepayable receipts except grants. Revenues are divided between current and capital receipts (which include only receipts from the sale of capital assets). Taxes are defined as compulsory and unrequited receipts collected by the government for public purposes. Tax revenues (shown net of refunds of earlier overpayment) include compulsory social security contributions and profits transferred to the government by its fiscal monopolies. Nontax revenues include receipts from property income, fees and charges, fines, and operating surpluses of public enterprises.
- *Grants.* Grants are unrequited receipts from other governments or international institutions. The *GFS Manual* groups grants together with revenues as transactions that reduce the deficit rather than with deficit financing items.[6] Nevertheless, for purposes of fiscal analysis and budgetary planning, it is necessary to recognize that grants differ from revenues in a fundamental way. Because grants are not predictable or sustainable, expenditures planned and incurred on the assumption that they will be available can seriously distort fiscal planning and force a severe adjustment in the future. Despite the *GFS* convention of recording grants above the line, it is often preferable, in analytical presentations of the fiscal accounts, to treat them as a financing item.
- *Government net lending.* Net lending (loans minus repayments) comprises government lending undertaken to achieve public policy objectives rather than to manage government liquidity.[7] Examples of such lending include subsidized loans to farmers, students, or small businesses. Net lending is grouped with expenditures rather than with financing under *GFS* guidelines.[8] This treatment reflects the asymmetry between the reasons for government lending and those that motivate its borrowing. Fluctuations in the government's holdings of currency and deposits, or changes in the cash balance, are treated as financing rather than as net lending.
- *The recapitalization of banks.* In some countries, banks that are fully or partly owned by the gov-

[6]In GFS terminology, grants are unrequited, nonrepayable, noncompulsory government receipts. However, the *GFS* places grants in a line by themselves, separate from revenues. This treatment recognizes that the government has little control over the amount or sustainability of grants, as it does over other receipts.

[7]Loans made by the government to a foreign government for public policy purposes are also included in net lending and thus affect the size of the deficit. The borrowing country, however, treats the loan as foreign borrowing and includes it below the line.

[8]It is important here to distinguish between incurring debt and merely guaranteeing it. Debt liability is included in the deficit (under net lending), while guaranteed debt is not included as a government transaction even though it constitutes a contingent liability of the government.

Chart 3.2. Analytical Framework for Classification of Government Operations

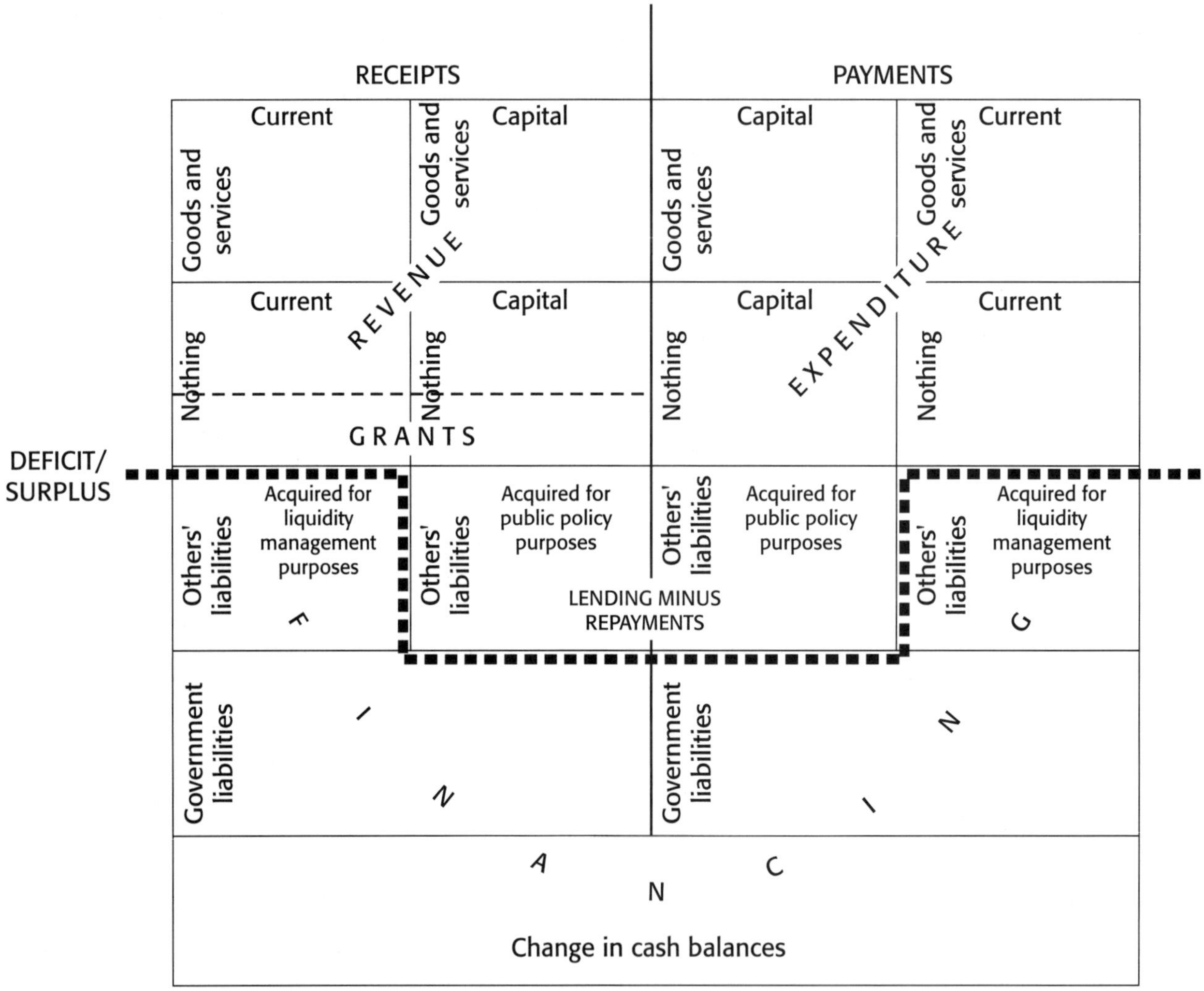

Source: IMF, *A Manual on Government Finance Statistics* (Washington, 1986), p. 101.

ernment have been facing large losses and are now undercapitalized. In such cases, governments may inject capital into the banks and in some cases take over their debts. As noted earlier, the GFS framework is cash based and therefore does not treat the government's noncash assumption of debt as an expenditure at the time the debt is assumed. However, future cash interest payments are included as expenditures and cash amortization payments as negative financing. In other words, according to GFS methodology, only the interest payments on the assumed debt affect the size of the fiscal balance.

- *Privatization receipts*. The *GFS Manual* recommends treating the proceeds of the sales of equity in public sector assets as *negative net lending*. This is to be distinguished from sales of government physical assets that are recorded in nontax capital revenue. The rationale behind this thinking is that privatization proceeds are sales of government equity in enterprises acquired earlier, either through transfers or capitalization. This treatment results in a one-time reduction in the fiscal deficit. While they are formally treated as an above-the-line item, it is often useful to record privatization receipts below the line in analytical presentations of the fiscal accounts, along with other transactions that affect the government's net financial position. The one-time reduction in the fiscal deficit is offset by deficits in future years, reflecting the loss of government revenue from the enterprise's remitted profits. These future deficits, however, can be offset exactly if the government uses the proceeds from the sale of enterprises to purchase other assets or to retire a portion of its own debt. Under such a scenario, the government and the private sector have simply exchanged assets without affecting the demands for real resources. However, if the government uses the proceeds to raise current expenditures, to cut taxes, or both, the deficit in the year of the sale will be unchanged, while future deficits will be larger, and the fiscal policy stance will be affected by privatization. The United Kingdom, which has had significant privatization receipts in recent years, has shown the fiscal deficit in the macroeconomic accounts both inclusive and exclusive of these receipts. This practice is useful because it clarifies the analysis by recognizing that privatization receipts represent an exchange of assets.[9]

[9]See Ke-Young Chu and Richard Hemming, eds., *Public Expenditure Handbook* (Washington: International Monetary Fund, 1991).

- *Central bank profits*. The profits of the central bank that are actually transferred to the government are treated as revenue. However, it should be noted both that these profits should not include unrealized profits stemming from the revaluation of holdings of foreign exchange or gold reserves and that they should cover the entire operations of the central bank, and not just its selected operations (for instance, sales of foreign exchange or gold).

Classifying Revenues and Expenditures

Government transactions are classified into broad categories under "revenues" and "expenditures." The primary classifications are economic, including total, current, and capital revenues and expenditures. Within these categories, taxes are broken down according to the type of activity on which they are imposed, and expenditures according to their purpose—defense and education, for example. The economic classifications are relatively more important for purposes of fiscal analysis. The main categories of taxes and the economic classifications are given in Tables 3.8 and 3.9, respectively. A more extensive presentation of the GFS fiscal data for Poland is shown in Table 3.7.

Conventional Fiscal Deficit[10]

In terms of the *cash flow* of government operations, total receipts are always equal to total payments, and therefore the government's fiscal accounts are always, in one sense, in balance. However, for analytical and policy purposes, it is more useful to focus on the difference between government revenues and grants, and government expenditures, including net lending. The conventional concept of the fiscal deficit does precisely this, defining the fiscal deficit as *the difference between total revenues and total expenditures*:

$$\text{Conventional fiscal deficit} = \text{Total revenue and grants} - \text{Total expenditures and net lending.}$$

[10]For a discussion of the intertemporal shortcomings of the conventional deficit, see Mario I. Blejer and Adrienne Cheasty, "The Measurement of Fiscal Deficits: Analytical and Methodological Issues," *Journal of Economic Literature*, Vol. 29 (December 1991).

A government deficit thus represents the portion of expenditure and net lending that exceeds receipts from revenue and grants. The government covers the deficit by borrowing and/or by running down its liquidity holdings. This conventional concept of the fiscal deficit is of central importance to fiscal analysis because it offers a comprehensive picture of the government's overall financial position and of the resulting impact on monetary conditions, domestic demand, and the balance of payments. This concept of the fiscal deficit, while the most common, suffers from a number of shortcomings when used as a measure of the impact on aggregate demand, the allocation of resources in the economy, and on the distribution of income. First, the same deficit level may have substantially different macroeconomic effects depending on the associated structure of taxation and expenditure. It has long been established that changes in taxes affect macroeconomic aggregates differently from equal changes in expenditures. Second, different ways of financing a given fiscal deficit clearly have different macroeconomic effects. As explained below, central bank financing of the fiscal deficit has substantially different macroeconomic effects from, say, nonbank financing or foreign financing.

Fiscal Analysis

Government Saving-Investment Gap

As with other sectors, two key relationships define the fiscal sector's resource balance and the ways in which the balance is financed.

The saving-investment gap of the government sector is broadly equivalent to the overall fiscal deficit. That is,

$$\begin{array}{c}\textit{Government}\\ \textit{saving} - \textit{Investment}\\ \textit{gap}\end{array} = \textit{Overall fiscal balance}.$$

If total government expenditure (E_g) is defined as the sum of current government expenditures (C_g) and government investment (I_g), it follows that:

$$S_g = R_g - C_g \tag{3.1}$$

and $(S_g - I_g) = R_g - E_g$.[11]

The government sector's resource balance can also be written as

$$S_g - I_g = R_g - C_g - I_g. \tag{3.2}$$

The government has a limited number of ways to finance this gap. It can obtain net foreign borrowing (NFB_g); it can borrow from the domestic banking system (ΔNDC_g); or it can borrow from the nonbank private sector (NB). Therefore, if F_g is total net financing available to the government sector (in other words, the financing needed to cover its gap), then

$$F_g = NFB_g + \Delta NDC_g + NB. \tag{3.3}$$

Thus, the government financing gap will be covered ex post, so that

$$(S_g - I_g) + F_g = 0. \tag{3.4}$$

Measures of the Fiscal Imbalance[12]

Although the GFS concept of the overall deficit is widely used, there is no single or best measure of the fiscal deficit. Alternative concepts of the deficit defined according to different analytical criteria can also be useful, depending on the purpose at hand. The overall deficit measured as a proportion of GDP is often used as a summary measure of fiscal performance and is perhaps the most widely accepted measure of a country's fiscal situation. But even this conventional measure should be supplemented by some or all of the other measures discussed in this section. The summary measures should take into consideration structural aspects of fiscal policy, such as those involving taxes and expenditures.

The choice of an appropriate concept of the deficit is based on several factors: (i) the type of imbalance involved; (ii) coverage (central government, general government or public sector); (iii) accounting method (cash or accrual); and (iv) the status of any contingent liability. Chart 3.3 summarizes the factors involved and the analytical distinctions possible in assessing the fiscal deficit. The various measures of fiscal deficits are discussed below.

- *The public sector borrowing requirement* is the conventional concept of a fiscal deficit de-

[11]Identifying the government saving-investment balance with the overall fiscal position assumes that the definition and coverage of government is identical in both cases. Moreover, the GFS definition of government deficit includes "net lending," whereas the saving-investment gap of the government sector excludes it. It should also be noted that the identification of the overall fiscal position of the government with its resource balance is a broad approximation. Strictly speaking, government revenues should include only current receipts, not all revenues (R_g). In particular, it should exclude capital revenues. Generally, capital revenues are likely to be minimal. The discussion here abstracts from this distinction by treating all revenues as current revenues.

[12]For an in-depth treatment of the subject, see Mario I. Blejer and Adrienne Cheasty, eds., *How to Measure the Fiscal Deficit* (Washington: International Monetary Fund, 1993).

fined for the entire public sector. It is also the most comprehensive standard measure of the fiscal deficit as it includes the net claim on financial resources by the entire public sector. The comprehensive deficit concept can be applied at each level of government. The central government borrowing requirement and the general government borrowing requirement are subsets of the public sector borrowing requirement, which can in fact be derived from the general government and the public enterprise sector borrowing requirements, with appropriate netting out of transfers among the sectors.

- *The current fiscal deficit (current account deficit)* is defined as current revenue *minus* current expenditure. It is often used as a measure of government saving and therefore as a measure of the government's contribution to the economy's total saving. It can be written as

  Current fiscal balance = *Government saving* = *Total current revenues* − *Total current expenditures.*

  There are, however, limits to the usefulness of this concept in practical fiscal analysis. The concept hinges on the distinction between capital and current expenditures and revenues. Capital expenditures include purchases of assets that are expected to be used in production for a period of more than one year and capital transfers; all other expenditures are classified as current. This distinction and the conventions for classifying expenditures as current or capital are inherently arbitrary.[13] More importantly, the underlying assumption that all government investment spending contributes to growth and is therefore desirable is questionable in view of the many instances of highly wasteful public investment projects. Moreover, spending on investment to the detriment of expenditure on maintenance of the existing capital stock may in fact misallocate resources and ultimately reduce (rather than raise) the rate of economic growth.

Thus, while attractive at first glance, the current fiscal deficit is not a very useful indicator. It also is not helpful in analyzing the impact of fiscal developments on either the external or the domestic macroeconomic balance.

- *The primary or noninterest deficit* accurately measures the effects of current discretionary budgetary policy by excluding interest payments from the conventional measure of the deficit.[14] This type of deficit indicates how the *current* fiscal actions of the government affect the government's net debt and therefore is important in assessing the sustainability of government deficit. It can be written as

  Primary fiscal deficit = *Conventional fiscal deficit* − *Interest payments.*

- *The operational deficit* is the conventional deficit less the inflation-induced portion of interest payments or, equivalently, the primary deficit plus the real component of interest payments. Inflation reduces the real value of the outstanding (nominal) stock of public debt, although creditors are compensated through higher nominal interest rates. This compensation, which is often referred to as the "*monetary correction*," represents a return *of* capital and not a return *on* capital. In other words, a part of the government's interest payments on its debt is actually amortization (repayment of principal), and, if this amount is not removed from the interest payments above the line, the deficit will be overstated. The concept of operational deficit overcomes this problem. This concept is particularly important in countries with high inflation and large public debt because it measures the extent to which fiscal policy in a given year affects the *real* stock of public debt.

  In an inflationary environment, the evolution of real public debt provides a more accurate perspective on the sustainability of fiscal policy than the evolution of nominal public debt. In countries with high inflation, the conventional and operational deficit measures show large differences, and trends in the two measures may diverge markedly.

  The relationships can be expressed as

Operational deficit = *Conventional deficit* − *Inflation component of interest payments*

or

Operational deficit = *Primary deficit* + *Real component of interest payments.*

[13]Such conventions also differ sharply among countries, making intercountry comparisons of public investment quite difficult, even for the major industrial countries.

[14]Generally, total interest payments are subtracted from total expenditures to calculate the primary balance. However, conceptually, only the *net* interest payments by the government (net of interest receipts) should be subtracted.

Chart 3.3. Measuring and Monitoring the Fiscal Deficit

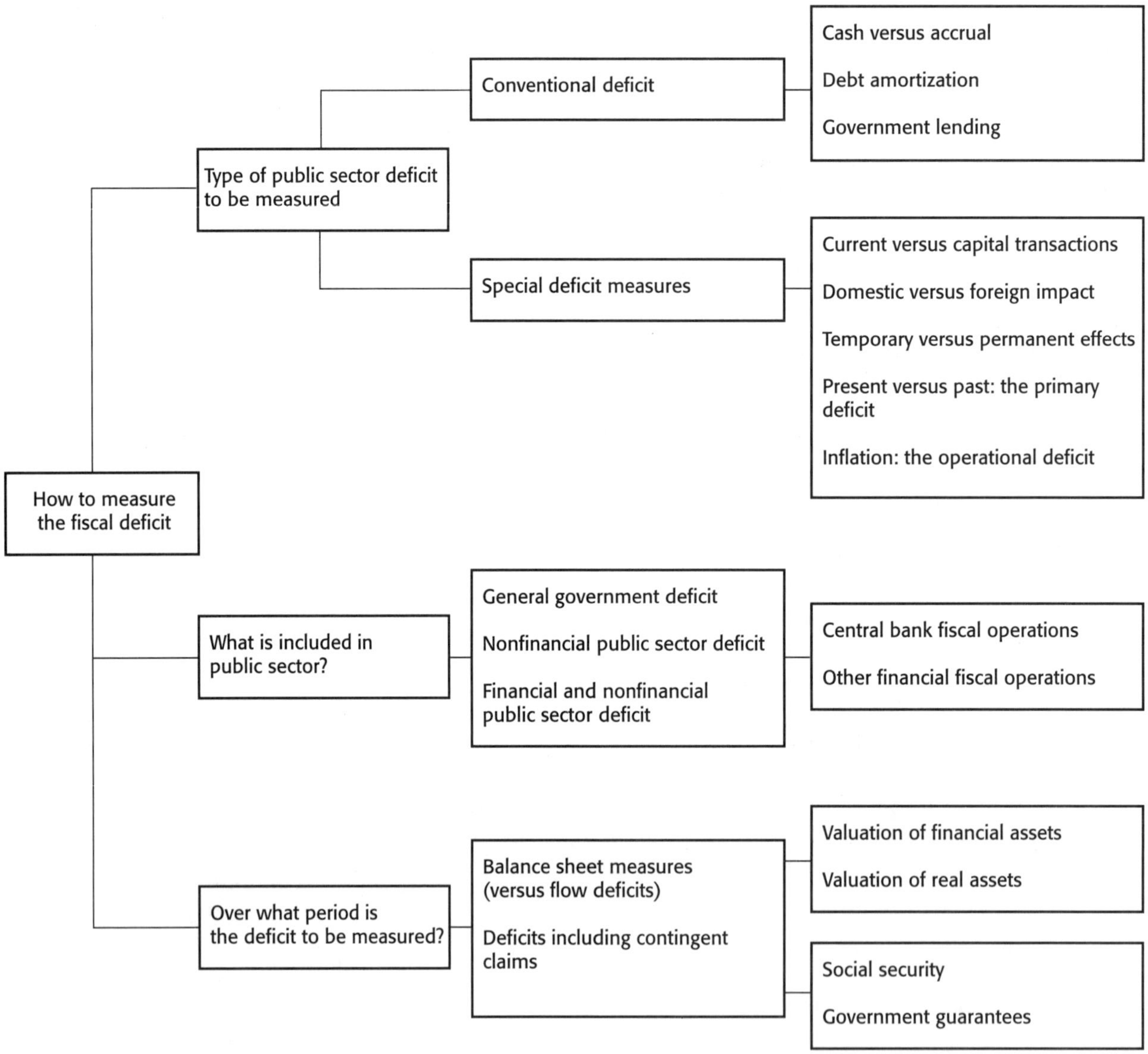

Source: M. Blejer and A. Cheasty, 1992, "How to Measure the Fiscal Deficit," *Finance Development*, Vol. 29 (September).

Financing the Deficit

The macroeconomic impact of the government deficit depends largely on the way the deficit is financed. As previously indicated, there are four ways of financing a deficit: (i) borrowing from the central bank, or "monetizing" the deficit; (ii) borrowing from the rest of the banking system; (iii) borrowing from the domestic nonbank sector; and (iv) borrowing abroad, or running down foreign exchange reserves.

In a broad sense, each form of financing is associated with a major macroeconomic imbalance: excessive money creation with inflation; excessive foreign borrowing with an external debt problem; depletion of reserves with an exchange rate crisis; and excessive domestic borrowing with high real interest rates—and possibly with explosive growth in public debt from the dynamic interactions between interest payments, deficits, and debt.[15] However, the links between these alternative methods of financing and their consequences can be far more complex.[16]

- *Borrowing from the central bank (monetizing the deficit)*. Government borrowing from the central bank is equivalent to the creation of high-powered money. Creating money at a rate that exceeds demand at the current price level creates excess cash balances and eventually drives up the overall price level.[17] In many transition economies, a high proportion of government deficits are monetized and are therefore the principal source of inflation. A government's ability to control real resources by printing money is sometimes known as *seigniorage*.[18] As discussed in Box 3.1, the notion of seigniorage is closely linked to that of the "inflation tax." In fact, seigniorage is equal to the inflation tax whenever the public keeps its demand for real cash balances constant. Seigniorage can be decomposed into pure seigniorage and an inflation tax component. It should be noted that:
    - Seigniorage accrues not just to the government; banks also "collect" part of the seigniorage. However, in many countries, banks "redistribute" their share of the seigniorage by making loans at below market interest rates. In this case, borrowers will also get a portion of the seigniorage.
    - The inflation tax "paid" by the public is significantly higher than that "collected" by the government. Put differently, the cost inflicted on the public by the government's policy aimed at covering part of the deficit through an inflation tax is considerably more than the real resources appropriated by the government. In this sense, the inflation tax is highly inefficient.
    - As inflation accelerates, the demand for real cash balances is likely to be reduced as the public adjusts to the higher inflation including by substituting the heavily "taxed" national currency by foreign currency (e.g., U.S. dollars).
    - A reduction in the real cash balances in response to higher inflation amounts to a shrinkage in the base of the inflation tax. Such an erosion in the base implies that, in order for the government to "collect" the same revenue from the inflation tax, a higher inflation rate ("tax rate") must prevail.
    - Revenue from seigniorage follows an inverted U-shaped curve. As inflation increases, so will the revenue from seigniorage but up to a maximum, beyond which any increase in inflation will lead to a reduction in revenues.
    - In most industrial countries, the maximum seigniorage has been estimated in the range of 1 percent of GDP to 2 percent of GDP while in some developing countries and transition economies, the maximum has fluctuated in the range of 5 percent of GDP to 10 percent of GDP.
- *Borrowing from the rest of the banking system.* Unlike borrowing from the central bank, borrowing from deposit money banks does not

[15]This discussion draws on Stanley Fischer and William Easterly, "The Economics of the Government Budget Constraint," *The World Bank Research Observer*, July 1990.

[16]In practice, reconciling fiscal and monetary data on financing gives rise to a number of problems, for several reasons, including (i) timing; (ii) the definition of government; (iii) the treatment of noncash transactions such as debt assumption by the government that is not reflected but is covered in monetary statistics; (iv) discrepancies in coverage between bank and nonbank financing; and (v) deficiencies in data.

[17]For an influential early treatment of the subject, see Phillip Cagan, "The Monetary Dynamics of Hyperinflation" in Milton Friedman, *Studies in the Quantity Theory of Money* (Chicago: University of Chicago Press, 1956).

[18]Strictly speaking, seigniorage is the difference between the value the government obtains (the face value of money) minus what it costs to create money, or the intrinsic value of money. In the case of paper money, the latter is negligible. For a further discussion of seigniorage, see Olivier Blanchard and Stanley Fischer, *Lectures on Macroeconomics* (Cambridge: The MIT Press, 1990); Pierre-Richard Agénor and Peter J. Montiel, *Development Macroeconomics* (Princeton University Press, 1996), pp. 111–26; and Oleh Havrylyshyn, Marcus Miller, and William Perraudin, "Deficits, Inflation, and Political Economy of Ukraine," *Economic Policy: A European Forum*, Vol. 9, October 1994.

Box 3.1.
The Inflation Tax and Seigniorage: Some Implications

A government can finance spending by raising tax revenue from the public, by borrowing, or simply by printing money. Revenue raised through the printing of money is called *seigniorage*. It arises because of the government's monopoly power to supply fiat or paper money to the economy. Since the cost to the government of printing a currency note is negligible, but it acquires purchasing power over resources equivalent to the face value of the banknote, it gains revenue simply by providing money to the economy. In a modern economy, banks also create money and hence also get "seigniorage." Thus, seigniorage can broadly be defined as the total amount of real resources appropriated by those that issue the money stock in an economy. Formally, seigniorage (S) in this case is given by:

$$S = \frac{\dot{M}}{P} \text{ or } S = \mu m \quad (1)$$

where $\mu = \dot{M}/M$ or the percentage growth in nominal money stock. Seigniorage is thus defined as the change in *nominal* money balances held by the public ($\dot{M}$) expressed in terms of the price level (P) or equivalently, the percentage growth rate of nominal money stock (μ) times the real money stock. $m = \frac{(M)}{P}$[1]

The seigniorage received by the government (S_g) will, of course, be much smaller and will only reflect the government issuance of reserve money or high-powered money (H):

$$S_g = \frac{\dot{H}}{P} \text{ or } S_g = \beta \cdot \frac{H}{P} \quad (2)$$

where $\beta = \dot{H}/H$, that is, the percentage growth in reserve money.

Seigniorage (S) can be decomposed into a "pure seigniorage" component and an "inflation tax" component.[2]

$$S = \dot{m} + \pi * m. \quad (3)$$

S = *Change in real cash balances* + *Inflation rate* * *Stock of real cash balances*.

$$S = \textit{Pure seigniorage} + \textit{Inflation tax}.^3 \quad (4)$$

- The pure seigniorage component is the *change in real cash balances* ($\dot{m}$). It comes about because of real growth in the economy or a favorable shift in the demand for money.
- The inflation tax component is equal to the inflation rate which acts in this case as the "tax rate" (π) times the stock of real cash balances held by the public m (which constitute the tax base). In the absence of inflation, the inflation tax will obviously be zero, but seigniorage will still be collected unless there is no growth in real cash balances.

[1]For any variable x, $\dot{x}$ denotes dx/dt or the change over a given period of time.
[2]It can be seen that the rate of change in real cash balances is equal to

$$\left(\frac{\dot{M}}{P}\right) = \frac{M}{P}\left(\frac{\dot{M}}{M} - \frac{\dot{P}}{P}\right), \text{ hence}$$

$$\frac{\dot{M}}{P} = \left(\frac{\dot{M}}{P}\right) + \frac{\dot{P}}{P} \cdot \frac{M}{P} \text{ or if } \frac{\dot{P}}{P} = \pi,\ S = \dot{m} + \pi m, \textit{ where } m = \left(\frac{M}{P}\right).$$

[3]For discrete data, the equivalent formula for equation 3 above is:

$$S_t = \Delta m_t + \Delta P_t/P_t \bullet m_{t-1}, \text{ where for any variabler } x_t, \Delta x_t \text{ is defined as } \Delta x_t = x_t - x_{t-1}.$$

Also note that seigniorage as a ratio of GDP (s_t) is defined as

$$s_t = \Delta M_t/GDP_t, \text{ where } GDP_t \text{ is } \textit{nominal} \text{ GDP.}$$

automatically lead to the creation of high-powered money. If the central bank accommodates the extra demand for credit from the deposit money banks by supplying them with additional reserves, then this type of borrowing is similar to borrowing from the central bank. But if the central bank does not accommodate the extra demand for credit, the deposit money banks will be forced to reduce credit to the private sector in order to meet the higher demand for government credit. This phenomenon, which is referred to as the *crowding out* of private spending, takes place principally through interest rate increases.

- *Nonbank borrowing.* A nonmonetary way of financing the deficit is by the issuing of domestic public debt.[19] Nonbank borrowing allows governments to sustain, in the short run, a deficit without increasing the monetary base or depleting international reserves. Because of this, it is often considered an effective way to avoid both inflation and external crises. However, nonbank borrowing carries its own dangers if used too often. First, bond financing of the deficit, while it postpones inflation, may lead to significantly higher inflation in the future if the stock of government debt is not kept in check.[20] Second, like bank borrowing, borrowing from the public directly crowds out the private sector, putting upward pressures on domestic interest rates (Box 3.2). Not only do high real interest rates hurt economic growth, but issuing public debt at such rates adds to the cost of future debt servicing and thus to future fiscal deficits. If real interest rates exceed rates of economic growth, debt service can grow explosively, making public debt unsustainable.

  In countries experiencing high inflation, the value of government bonds erodes rapidly, and voluntary demand for such bonds is limited. Governments are often tempted to coerce (directly or indirectly) banks and even the public to hold these bonds, but such actions, and even past episodes of confiscation, can severely damage the credibility of governments for years to come. In such cases, the government must undertake a patient process of building up trust and credibility that is grounded in the sustained pursuit of noninflationary macroeconomic policies and financial stability.

- *External borrowing.* Governments can finance deficits abroad by issuing bonds to nonresidents or by running down foreign exchange reserves. There is, however, a limit to using reserves to finance a deficit. If the private sector expects that this limit is about to be reached, the result can be capital flight and an exchange rate depreciation that adds to inflation pressures. The debt crisis of the 1980s was triggered by the virtual exhaustion of reserves in Mexico in August 1982, which followed a loss of fiscal control that was reflected in large and unsustainable fiscal deficits in the early 1980s.

  Financing the deficit with foreign borrowing and running down reserves tend initially to appreciate the exchange rate, damaging the competitiveness of the traded goods sector. For many developing (and some transition) economies, overborrowing in the past and a lack of creditworthiness severely limit this source of financing for the present. Even when available, foreign borrowing from commercial sources carries interest rates that can be prohibitively high.

If fiscal accounts are presented on an accrual basis, another form of financing enters the picture—payments arrears. In many transition economies, governments have incurred large payments arrears, resulting in cash deficits that are sig-

> Box 3.2.
> **Debt Neutrality**
>
> According to the debt neutrality (or Ricardian equivalence) hypothesis, borrowing is no more than deferred taxation.[1] Specifically, for a given government expenditure, a reduction in current taxes would clearly raise the budget deficit and hence borrowing. Insofar as the private sector recognizes that increased government borrowing today means higher taxes in the future, under this hypothesis, it increases private saving in order to provide for increases in taxes in the future. The Ricardian equivalence hypothesis in its pure form stipulates that a shift from tax financing to debt financing would not change *total national saving*, as the initial reduction in government saving will be fully and exactly offset by an increase in private sector saving. Thus, a tax cut financed by government borrowing does not reduce the tax burden; it only postpones it.
>
> The debt neutrality hypothesis gets little support from available empirical evidence in either industrial countries or developing countries. While in industrial countries the evidence has been inconclusive, in developing countries, the hypothesis finds no support.[2]
>
> [1]This is also sometimes referred to as the Barro-Ricardo debt neutrality theorem. See Robert J. Barro, "The Ricardian Approach to Budget Deficits," *Journal of Economic Perspectives*, Vol. 3 (Spring 1989).
>
> [2]In industrial countries, there seems to be a tendency for a partial but not a full offset of a decrease in government savings.

[19]In many developing and transition economies, the banking system intermediates purchases of government debt. Government borrowing from the banking system that is refinanced by the central bank cannot be considered nonmonetary financing.

[20]See Thomas Sargent and Neil Wallace, "Some Unpleasant Monetarist Arithmetic," *Federal Reserve Bank of Minneapolis Quarterly Review*, Fall 1981.

nificantly lower than deficits measured on an accrual basis. When the government clears the arrears, however, the accrual deficit will be smaller than the cash deficit. Arrears are also a coercive form of financing a deficit and should be avoided as far as possible (Box 3.3).

The Sustainability of Fiscal Policy

In recent years, the issue of the sustainability of fiscal policy has attracted considerable attention. When can one say that the stance of fiscal policy is unsustainable? How can one devise an operational indicator to guide policymakers? While there is no generally accepted definition of what constitutes a sustainable fiscal policy, there is a broad agreement that fiscal policy is not sustainable if the present and prospective fiscal stance results in a persistent and rapid increase in the public debt-to-GDP ratio. Thus a key indicator of sustainability is based on the *size* and *growth rate* of the debt-to-GDP ratio. Indeed, as the experience of many countries has shown, persistently high debt-to-GDP ratios are costly and will eventually become unsustainable, in the sense of requiring policy revisions. High debt ratios are costly because they tend to put pressure on real interest rates and increase the debt service component of the deficit, thereby reducing the scope for fiscal maneuver and policy flexibility.[21] They are unsustainable because at some point, financial markets will alter their expectations as they realize that present policies are not credible and will have to be revised. This changed expectation will make it increasingly difficult—and eventually impossible—for the government to sell its debt. In fact, the market will realize that the higher the outstanding debt-to-GDP ratio, the more difficult it becomes for the government to meet the budget constraint through fiscal retrenchment (i.e., through higher primary surpluses), hence the higher is the risk for the monetization of the deficit or debt repudiation and restructuring.

The above discussion suggests that one approach to fiscal sustainability is to define a sustainable fiscal policy stance as one that does not lead to an increase in the debt-to-GDP ratio, that is, one that stabilizes the debt-to-GDP ratio under reasonable rates of growth, interest rates, and inflation. While this criterion does provide a simple indicator of sustainability, it suffers from two main shortcomings. First, economic theory generally provides little guidance about an optimum or desirable debt-to-GDP ratio.[22] Second, it turns out that stabilizing the debt-to-GDP ratio can impose too stringent a condition on policy. A less restrictive requirement has been developed based on the notion of *solvency*. Solvency, a necessary condition for fiscal sustainability,[23] requires only that debt-to-GDP ratios grow at a rate below the real interest rate minus the real growth rate of GDP. Equivalently, the nominal stock of debt must grow at a rate below that of the nominal interest rate.[24]

To see how the notion of solvency has been useful in the development of an operational indicator of sustainability, consider the government's budget constraint. It can be shown that the *temporal* budget constraint can be written in terms of GDP as

$$\textit{Rate of growth of the debt-to-GDP ratio} = \textit{Primary balance} + \left[\textit{Real interest rate} - \textit{Real growth rate}\right] * \left[\textit{Debt-to-GDP ratio in the previous period}\right] - \textit{Seigniorage}$$

or

$$\dot{d} = p_d + (r - g) * d - s \qquad (3.5)$$

where

$\dot{d}$ = rate of change in the debt-to-GDP ratio in the current period
d = debt-to-GDP ratio in the previous period
p_d = primary balance in GDP terms[25]
r = real interest rate
g = real growth of GDP
s = seigniorage in GDP terms (broadly defined).

Note that the temporal budget constraint of the government (equation 3.5) implies that:

- The change in the debt-to-GDP ratio is determined by the primary balance, seigniorage, and the growth term, or *built-in momentum* of the debt-to-GDP ratio. When interest rates exceed

[21]Rising debt-to-GDP ratios affect real interest rates through two main channels of transmission: crowding out effects and portfolio (or risk premium) effects. For more details, see Paul R. Masson, "The Sustainability of Fiscal Deficits," *Staff Papers*, International Monetary Fund, Vol. 32 (December 1985).

[22]Clearly, policymakers are not indifferent to the long-term level at which public debt is stabilized. In many countries, official, medium-term targets are set for public debt.

[23]It is necessary and not sufficient because solvency is consistent with many kinds of primary surpluses/seigniorage levels, all of which are not feasible.

[24]See Willem H. Buiter, "The Arithmetic of Solvency," *Principles of Budgetary and Financial Policy* (Cambridge: The MIT Press, 1990).

[25]Please note that a primary deficit implies a $p_d>0$ while a primary surplus implies a $p_d<0$.

Box 3.3.
Expenditure Arrears

Government expenditure arrears, which indicate delays in government payments to suppliers or creditors, have become an important fiscal issue in many transition economies. Arrears can lead to underestimates of spending and of the size of the fiscal problem facing a country. Since arrears are a form of forced deficit financing, the government's borrowing requirement is also understated, leading to a distorted picture of the sources of credit expansion in the economy. While deficit financing can allow the government to absorb more of the economy's resources than would otherwise be possible, this initial effect is offset as the rest of the economy responds by raising suppliers' prices or holding back payments for taxes and fees. Ultimately, expenditure arrears raise the cost of providing government services.

The accumulation of government arrears may also have a serious adverse impact on the private sector's confidence in the soundness of government finances. Private consumers and investors may anticipate an increase in the tax rate, higher inflation, or a general worsening of the financial situation in the medium term. Arrears may accumulate throughout the economy as a result of government arrears, with severe consequences for the stability of the financial system and prospects for economic growth. Late payments for government wages and transfers are likely to have an impact on aggregate demand that needs to be taken into account in a proper economic analysis of the government deficit.

Arrears are often caused by an unrealistic, overly optimistic revenue forecast or a lack of proper mechanisms for monitoring and controlling government spending. A well-functioning Treasury can therefore play an important role in preventing the emergence of payment arrears.

Adapted from Ke-Young Chu and Richard Hemming, eds., *Public Expenditure Handbook* (Washington: International Monetary Fund, 1991).

the growth rate, the debt ratio will tend to rise by feeding on itself, since interest payments add more to public debt than growth adds to GDP, unless $(p_d - s)$ is kept negative. This latter condition will be automatically satisfied whenever the government is running a primary surplus $(p_d < 0)$. However, in the presence of a primary deficit $(p_d > 0)$, the primary deficit would have to be kept below what can be financed by seigniorage. Put differently, when interest rates exceed the growth rate, it becomes impossible for the government to run a permanent primary deficit in excess of revenues that can be raised through seigniorage. Further, since the amount of seigniorage is limited, it eventually becomes necessary for the government to run a primary surplus. The more the policy adjustment is delayed, however, the higher the debt-to-GDP ratio will be and the lower the room to maneuver for the government.

- If, on the other hand, the real interest rate is lower than the growth rate, then the country could grow out of its debt. This means essentially that the country can bear a higher level of debt-to-GDP ratio and can afford to run a primary deficit permanently in excess of the desirable level of seigniorage. It does not, however, mean that there is no constraint on the debt-to-GDP ratio. Indeed, if the country increased its borrowing substantially, it would risk raising interest rates to a point where they exceed growth rates. This would make unsustainable what had been sustainable policies.
- Whether fiscal policy is sustainable depends not only on factors that the fiscal authorities control, such as revenue and spending programs, but also on other factors, such as the interest rate on government obligations, the long-run growth rate of the economy, and demographic trends.
- The proper measure of debt for the government budget identity is *net* rather than gross debt, because it corresponds most closely to the overall, or general, government deficit. Net debt comes close to measuring the net worth of the government (assets minus liabilities), although it records financial assets at book value and may not adjust for unfunded liabilities and nonfinancial assets.
- The government budget identity can be used to calculate budget targets that would achieve specific debt objectives, such as stabilizing or making specific reductions in the debt-to-GDP ratio. It can easily be shown that stabilizing the debt-to-GDP ratio requires that the ratio of the deficit to GDP, inclusive of interest payments on the debt, not exceed the initial debt-to-GDP ratio multiplied by nominal GDP growth.

In terms of the *intertemporal* budget constraint

$$\begin{matrix}\textit{Debt stock}\\ \textit{in terms}\\ \textit{of GDP}\end{matrix} = \begin{bmatrix}\textit{PDV of expected}\\ \textit{future primary}\\ \textit{balances in terms}\\ \textit{of GDP}\end{bmatrix} + \begin{bmatrix}\textit{PDV of expected}\\ \textit{future}\\ \textit{seigniorage in}\\ \textit{terms of GDP}\end{bmatrix} \quad (3.6)$$

where *PDV* is the present discounted value using as the discount rate the difference between real interest and real growth.

Solvency can be defined as a situation in which the government is in a position to meet its obligations fully (i.e., to service the outstanding public debt *fully*).[26] Assessing the solvency of a government involves not only considerations pertaining to current revenues and expenditures but also expectations of future revenues and expenditures. The starting point in assessing solvency has traditionally been the balance sheet of the public sector, i.e., a summary of government assets and liabilities. Government assets include the current stock of assets (both domestic and foreign) as well as anticipated future revenues (i.e., the present value of future revenues). Government liabilities include current obligations as well as the present value of future expenditures. In this way the balance sheet of the public sector becomes a forward-looking balance sheet integrating both the short-term and long-term fiscal performance. Using the above expanded notion of assets and liabilities, one can define the government's (or more generally the public sector's) net worth as the difference between assets and liability. If the net worth is positive (i.e., assets exceed liabilities), then the government (public sector) is said to be solvent. Otherwise, the government is regarded as insolvent; that is, without an increase in its assets (current or future), it is not able to meet its obligations.

Thus, if the government adheres to the budget constraint above (equation 3.6), then the initial debt stock ratio must be matched by the present discounted value of expected future primary balances and seigniorage in terms of GDP.[27]

Some useful indicators of fiscal sustainability have been developed, including the concept of primary gap, net worth, and medium-term tax gap (see Box 3.4).

Analysis of Revenues

Introduction

Any assessment of revenue developments and performance should focus on revenues as a proportion of GDP in light of revenues-to-GDP ratios in comparable economies. When fiscal deficits need to be reduced, the economic cost of raising taxes must be weighed against the costs of reducing public spending. As a general rule, both will be required. In the short term, most governments are tempted to rely on ad hoc increases in revenues, which are administratively and politically convenient. However, this approach often leads to complex, inefficient, and highly distortionary tax systems that not only fail to bring in sufficient revenue, but also damage incentives to work and save, thereby reducing economic growth. In assessing the efficiency of a tax system and determining the scope for necessary reforms, analysts find the concepts of tax *elasticity* and tax *buoyancy* useful.

Tax Elasticity and Buoyancy

The *elasticity* of a tax is defined as the relative change in revenues from that tax under a given tax system (which remains unchanged) compared with the relative change in the tax base. Elasticity provides a tax system with built-in flexibility. It can be written as

$$\textit{Elasticity of tax revenue} = \frac{\textit{Percent change in tax revenues (under an unchanged tax system)}}{\textit{Percentage change in the tax base}}.$$

If GDP is taken as a proxy for the tax base, then elasticity with respect to GDP is

$$Elasticity = \frac{\Delta AT/AT}{\Delta GDP/GDP}. \tag{3.7}$$

where

AT = is the tax receipts from an unchanged tax systems.[28]

Δ = refers to the change during a period.

A tax system is *elastic* when it has an elasticity value greater than one, suggesting that tax revenues are increasing at a higher rate than GDP without new taxes or increases in tax rates, that is, with no discretionary change in tax policy. Elasticity is desirable in a tax system and should be encouraged in countries where government expenditures tend to increase more rapidly than GDP. The tax system is likely to be elastic with respect to GDP when taxes are levied on growing economic

[26]See Pablo E. Guidotti and Manmohan S. Kumar, *Domestic Public Debt of Externally Indebted Countries*, IMF Occasional Paper No. 80 (Washington: International Monetary Fund, June 1991).

[27]This condition is obtained from the intertemporal budget constraint by imposing the so-called *transversality* or *terminal* condition that the public debt ratio grows at a rate less than the interest rate. In other words, debt should not be serviced indefinately by borrowing (i.e., *Ponzi* games are assumed away by this condition). It should be noted that imposing an intertemporal budget constraint, even with a no-Ponzi game assumption, in itself does not imply that the debt ratio will stabilize, nor does it help point to the optimum level of debt-to-GDP; it simply imposes an upper bound on the growth path of the debt-to-GDP ratio.

[28]AT is usually a data series that is not observed. It is often derived from the tax revenue series T by adjusting for the effects of changes in the tax system that occurred during the period under consideration. The resulting data series shows the revenues that would have been collected if all tax rates, exemptions, brackets, and other elements of the tax system had remained constant over the period.

Box 3.4.
Measures of Sustainability

The indicators of fiscal sustainability presented below aim at assessing the magnitude of the required adjustment, to ensure solvency and measure the size of the permanent fiscal adjustment necessary to stabilize the debt-to-GDP ratio.[1] They assume that the permanent level of seignorage is negligible.

- *Positive net worth.* This requires that government net worth be non-negative, that is, the present discounted value of the primary fiscal balance be larger than or equal to the debt stock. A measure of the needed fiscal adjustment to ensure sustainability under this approach is the difference between the initial debt-to-GDP ratio and PDV of the primary balance.[2]
- *Primary gap.*[3] The primary gap is equal to the present discounted value of the primary balance that would stabilize the initial debt-to-GDP ratio *minus* the *actual* primary balance. If the gap is positive, then fiscal retrenchment will be necessary for the debt-to-GDP ratio to be stabilized. This measure is useful and requires minimal information—the actual primary balance, initial debt-to-GDP ratio, real interest rates, and output growth. This indicator is equivalent to the positive net worth approach when the initial debt is stabilized.
- *Medium-term tax gap.*[3] This indicator measures the required adjustment in the tax ratio needed to stabilize the outstanding public debt-to-GDP ratio, given the projected path of noninterest expenditures and transfers (in terms of GDP), real interest, and growth rates.

[1]Based on Jocelyn Horne, "Indicators of Fiscal Sustainability," IMF Working Paper 91/5 (Washington: International Monetary Fund, January 1991).

[2]The PDV of a variable can be approximated by the value of the variable divided by the discount rate, so that *PDV* (x,i) is x/i where i is the discount rate.

[3]See also Olivier Jean Blanchard, "Suggestions for New Set of Fiscal Indicators," OECD Working Paper, April 1990.

sectors; when tax rates are progressive, and are ad valorem rather than specific; and when taxes are collected promptly. This last point is especially important during periods of high inflation, when an unduly long lag between the assessment and collection of taxes erodes the real value of tax revenues.

An elastic tax system is useful from the point of view of economic growth, which generally calls for a sustained rise in spending on social and economic infrastructure and maintenance. If these increases in expenditures are not accompanied by rising revenues, they can lead to undue reliance on deficit financing, either external (with consequences for the external debt burden) or domestic. With an elastic tax system, there is usually no need for the frequent and unanticipated tax increases that can adversely affect work and reduce confidence in the government.

Elasticities are calculated not only for overall tax revenues, but also for individual taxes. For example, ad valorem taxes are generally more elastic than specific taxes. Individual income taxes are another example of a relatively elastic tax.

The *buoyancy* of a tax is defined as the increase in the revenue collected compared with the relative increase in GDP. The change in revenue includes any effects of changes in the tax system, including discretionary changes in the tax structure. The algebraic expression of the formula for tax buoyancy is

$$Buoyancy = \frac{\Delta T/T}{\Delta GDP/GDP}. \tag{3.8}$$

In the case of buoyancy, the ΔT measures the change in *actual* tax revenues over the period, but in the elasticity formula, ΔAT measures the change in tax revenues adjusted for the estimated impact of changes in the tax system over the period (i.e., excluding the impact of all discretionary changes). If the changes in the tax system are revenue enhancing, then buoyancy will exceed elasticity, because the actual tax revenue will exceed the amount that would have been generated in the absence of changes in the tax system.

Assessing a Tax System

Analysts engaged in considering a country's tax system will want also to consider the appropriateness of that system and explore possible directions for reforming it. While the primary objective of taxation is to generate revenue, it has often been used to correct market failures and to help redistribute incomes. Given these objectives, a number of criteria have been developed to assess how well a tax system works. The Tanzi Diagnostic Test (summarized in Box 3.5) can be a useful guide to evaluating a country's tax system.[29]

Tax Effort Analysis

Generating adequate revenues in the most efficient manner is one of the essential functions of a tax system. More specifically, a tax system needs to transfer economic resources from private users to the government in an orderly and noninflationary way. This criterion, *revenue productivity*, can be assessed for any tax system using a methodology known as tax effort analysis.[30]

The question underlying the assessment of a system's revenue productivity is whether the government can raise the level of tax revenues if necessary with few adverse effects. In this context, a commonly used indicator of tax performance is the ratio of tax revenue to GDP, or the *actual tax ratio*. International comparisons of such tax-GDP ratios are used to make broad statements regarding the efforts a government makes to raise tax revenues. However, using the actual tax ratio to judge these efforts can be misleading, because the actual tax ratio ignores the *taxable capacity* of a country by assuming that the GDP is the appropriate indicator of this capacity.

Taxable capacity is defined as the level of tax revenue that would result if tax bases were taxed at some average intensity. The amount of tax revenue actually collected as a proportion of the taxable capacity therefore indicates tax effort. Taxable capacity, of course, is not a precise concept, but it nevertheless provides broad guidance in assessing tax effort. Three major factors that can determine capacity have been identified: (i) the degree of openness of an economy; (ii) the level of development and income; and (iii) the composition of income.

Tax effort analysis, while useful in assessing tax performance, has obvious limitations. It is not a normative measure, in that a country with below-average "tax effort" may nevertheless find the tax ratio appropriate in light of national preferences. Tax effort analysis is also purely static in nature, because it does not take into account rapid changes in the tax ratios and tax efforts unless it assesses tax effort over time. In the dynamic sense, the elasticity of tax revenue with respect to GDP is often regarded as a more useful indicator.

Box 3.5.
The Tanzi Diagnostic Test for Revenue Productivity

Vito Tanzi has proposed eight qualitative diagnostic tests to help assess the "revenue productivity" of a given tax system. These tests are as follows:

1. *Concentration index:* Does a large share of total tax revenue come from relatively few taxes and tax rates?
2. *Dispersion index:* Are there very few, if any, low-revenue-yielding, nuisance taxes?
3. *Erosion index:* Are actual tax bases as close as possible to potential ones?
4. *Collection lags index:* Are tax payments made by taxpayers without much time lag and close to the time when they should be made?
5. *Specificity index:* Does the tax system depend upon as few taxes as possible with specific rates?
6. *Objectivity index:* Are most taxes levied on objectively measured bases?
7. *Enforcement index:* Is the tax system enforced fully and effectively?
8. *Cost of collection index:* Is the fiscal cost of collecting taxes as low as possible?

A positive answer to all these questions simultaneously, according to Tanzi, should entitle a country's tax system to high marks for revenue productivity.

Source: Vito Tanzi, "Tax System and Policy Objectives in Developing Countries: General Principles and Diagnostic Tests," unpublished IMF paper, November 28, 1983.

Analyzing Expenditures[31]

Introduction

Public expenditure represents the cost of the government's activities, which involve the provision of

[29]For a more detailed analysis of tax policy, see Parthasarathi Shome, ed., *Tax Policy Handbook* (Washington: International Monetary Fund, 1995).

[30]For a detailed review and discussion of the "tax effort" approach, see Chelliah Raja, Hessel Baas, and Margaret Kelly, "Tax Ratios and Tax Effort in Developing Countries, 1969–71," *Staff Papers*, International Monetary Fund, Vol. 22 (March 1975), pp. 187–205.

[31]This section draws heavily on Ke-Young Chu, "Public Expenditure Policy: An Overview of Macroeconomic and Structural Issues," *Fiscal Adjustment in Eastern and Southern Africa* (Washington: International Monetary Fund, 1994).

goods and services, production, and income transfers. The government provides two types of goods and services: those that can be consumed directly by the population, individually or collectively (such as public passenger transportation and national parks), and those that enhance the productivity of factors of production (such as industrial ports). Many expenditures, including those for infrastructure such as highways, combine the two. Some public expenditures—pensions and unemployment compensation, for example—represent direct transfers to households and business enterprises. The next sections discuss the main categories of public expenditures, with particular emphasis on subsidies, the role of the state, macroeconomic implications of public expenditures, and the interaction of macroeconomic and structural aspects of public expenditures.

It is important to evaluate the level and composition of public expenditure in an appropriate analytical framework. Such a framework should be systematic, containing five elements:

- An aggregate spending level and deficit that are consistent with the macroeconomic framework;
- Judicious use of the private sector in the delivery of certain goods and services (even when public financing is necessary, public spending should be concentrated first on programs that provide public goods, externalities, and benefits to those falling within the social safety net—things that the private market is not providing or that are underprovided);
- Spending that is allocated on the basis of outcomes within and across programs;
- Careful analysis of capital and current spending within a program or a sector to ensure a balanced allocation for each; and
- A similarly careful analysis of budgetary institutions, to ensure that incentives and rules help to control aggregate spending, and facilitate efficiency and equity in the composition of spending.[32]

Adjustment strategies often require a substantial degree of fiscal retrenchment. The adverse effects of higher rates for existing taxes and a lack of alternative revenue sources may dictate that a substantial share of this retrenchment be achieved through expenditure cuts. In transition economies facing increasingly tight resource constraints, adjustment programs have to focus on spending priorities. Governments seeking to reform spending must identify areas in which markets can effectively substitute for public sector involvement and consider how scarce government sector resources can best be utilized in those areas where public sector involvement is considered appropriate.

Types of Public Expenditures

The main economic categories of public expenditures are wages and salaries, goods and services, subsidies, and capital expenditures.[33]

- *Wages and salaries*. Government policies on civil service employment and pay have a major impact on the efficiency of government expenditures. Low pay and inadequate salary differentials for skilled and technical staff may discourage workers and contribute to low productivity in the government sector. At the same time, the widespread practice of using the public sector as employer of last resort may substantially increase wage costs. Recent reforms in several countries have sought to reduce the government wage bill through a variety of measures, including a civil service census and the elimination of "phantom" workers; the elimination of vacancies and temporary positions; hiring freezes; the suspension of employment guarantees; voluntary retirement programs; wage cuts, caps, and freezes; and the most difficult measure, layoffs. Attempts have also been made in some countries to increase salary differentials in favor of senior staff.
- *Goods and services*. This category represents a significant portion of current spending in most countries and accounts for the administrative and overhead costs of running the government. Although substantial economies are often possible under this heading, it is important to ensure that cuts in goods and services do not compromise the efficient delivery of government services. An important part of current spending on goods and services goes for the *operation and maintenance* of capital stock. Inadequate spending on operations (whether supplies or personnel costs) can lead to low levels of effectiveness in areas such as education and health. Similarly, inadequate spending on maintenance can lead to the rapid deterioration of physical capital. Pursu-

[32]For a detailed exposition of these principles of public expenditure analysis, see Sanjay Pradhan, *Evaluating Broad Allocations of Public Spending: A Methodological and Data Framework for Public Expenditure Reviews* (Washington: World Bank, 1995).

[33]In addition, interest payments and transfers play an important role.

ing a policy that focuses on creating new capacity while allowing existing infrastructure to deteriorate can be costly and counterproductive. In some cases, if the rate of depreciation on existing assets is measured accurately, net investment may be negative. Similarly, across-the-board cuts in materials, supplies, and services in macroeconomic adjustment programs should be avoided in order not to undermine the programs' effectiveness.

- *Subsidies.*[34] Subsidies are defined as any government assistance to producers or consumers for which the government receives no compensation in return. Subsidies can take many different forms, including (i) direct payments to producers or consumers (cash grants); (ii) loans at interest rates below the government borrowing rate and with government guarantees (credit subsidies); (iii) reductions in specific tax liabilities (tax subsidies); (iv) the provision of goods and services at below market values (in-kind subsidies); (v) government purchases of goods and services at above-market prices (procurement subsidies); (vi) implicit payments through government regulatory actions that alter market prices or access (regulatory subsidies); and (vii) maintenance of overvalued currencies (exchange rate subsidies).

Whether explicit (direct) or implicit (indirect), subsidies are a major drain on government budgets in many transition economies. Subsidies are explicit if they are fully reflected in the budget as expenditures, and implicit if they are not. Implicit subsidies may arise as a result of administered prices that are set at levels below or above free market values—for example, for energy—or may support unrealistic interest rates and overvalued exchange rates. Since a significant portion of government subsidies are implicit, budgets do not fully reflect their range and value. Subsidies also affect resource allocation by reducing the flexibility of the economy, and are often an obstacle to structural adjustment. One example of the distortions that subsidies can cause is the pricing of energy products below market levels, leading to wasteful energy consumption.

Any assessment of subsidies should take account of the following:

- *Effectiveness.* Not all subsidies are bad, but only those that meet given policy goals by transferring a minimum of resources with a minimum of distortions to the incentive system can be called effective. Effective subsidies are also well targeted—that is, they do not spill over into groups and activities for which they are not intended.
- *Duration.* How long subsidy programs last is a serious concern because people change their behavior in order to be included in these programs and may resist being excluded even when their circumstances change. It is this behavior that makes many subsidies ineffective over time. While some subsidies should be limited from the outset, effectively implementing a subsidy program requires regular periodic reassessments of the rationale behind the subsidy, and, if needed, revision, retargeting, or termination of the program.
- *Transparency.* The size of a subsidy program and the implied financing requirement should be made explicit in public budgets. Transparency is desirable from both public and private perspectives in order to identify clearly the benefits and costs of individual programs. As a general rule, governments should aim to identify subsidy expenditures and financing explicitly in public budgets and should to the extent possible provide them as cash grants, rather than as procurement, tax, interest, or regulatory supports. Only cash grants provide both government and beneficiary with a clear and explicit picture of the amounts involved. In turn, this transparency provides a basis for judging the affordability and desirability of subsidies.
- *Financing.* Subsidies should always be financed through the budget. Attempting to solve financing problems either with extrabudgetary instruments such as government marketing boards, parastatal agencies, and specific extrabudgetary funds, or through the central bank is dangerous. Such methods frequently reduce transparency and lead to reductions in producer prices, with adverse effects on producer incentives.
- *Selecting a pragmatic approach.* Subsidy programs must be consistent with a government's institutional and administrative ca-

[34]This section is adapted from Gerd Schwartz and Benedict Clements, "Note on Subsidies: Evaluation and Impact," IMF Seminar on Fiscal Adjustment in Eastern and Southern Africa, September–October 1994. For a further discussion of the issues relating to subsidies, see Benedict Clements, Rejane Hugounenq, and Gerd Schwartz, "Government Subsidies: Concepts, International Trends, and Reform Options," IMF Working Paper 95/91 (Washington: International Monetary Fund, September 1995). See also "Social Safety Nets for Economic Transition: Options and Recent Experiences," IMF Paper on Policy Analysis and Assessment 95/3 (Washington: International Monetary Fund, February 1995).

pabilities. Implicit (indirect) subsidies may be more difficult to control effectively than explicit (direct) subsidies. To simplify administrative burdens, subsidy programs should be made as explicit as possible.

- *Spending on social insurance.* Expenditures aimed at protecting the poorer sections of society, including pensions for the elderly and unemployment insurance, constitute a major part of budgetary spending in many countries. Under central planning, public enterprises were responsible either directly or indirectly for a significant part of social insurance expenditures. As these enterprises are reformed during the transition and their social responsibilities reduced or eliminated, there is an urgent need for governments to establish adequate social safety nets (see Box 3.6).
- *Capital expenditures.* Growth-oriented adjustment requires productive government investment, combined with policies to correct distortions in relative factor and commodity prices. However, it is important to ensure that the investment program is well designed and that projects are economically sound, because the cost of poorly designed or inefficiently implemented projects can be high. Emphasis should be given to government investment that complements and supports rather than competes with market-determined activities. Education, health, urban services, and rural infrastructure are priority areas for government involvement.

Box 3.6.
Social Safety Nets

Many transition economies have begun to put in place social safety nets designed to mitigate the short-term adverse effects of economic reforms on the poor, such as the increases that result from the reductions in subsidies on basic necessities and unemployment caused by the reform of state enterprises and the civil service. Social safety nets need to be tailored to the circumstance of each country, including its administrative framework and formal and informal social support systems.

Major components of social safety nets include:

- Targeted commodity subsidies and cash compensation aimed at protecting people's ability to buy basic foodstuffs during inflationary periods;
- Social security arrangements, including pension and disability insurance and child care allowances, with effective targeting and incentive structures; and
- Unemployment benefits and public works schemes that mitigate the impact of rising joblessness on low-income groups.

The main issues in the design of social safety nets are *targeting* and *incentives*. Social benefits should be limited to those most in need. In the absence of sophisticated means testing, many countries rely on categorical targeting, such as limiting benefits to children or pensioners. In terms of incentives, the fiscal cost of social safety nets is reduced if benefits are phased out as household incomes increase, but this is at the cost of increasing the implicit marginal tax rate facing beneficiaries, and the potential adverse impact on incentives.

Adapted from *Guidelines for Fiscal Adjustment*, IMF Pamphlet Series, No. 49 (Washington: International Monetary Fund, 1995).

Public Expenditure and the Role of the State

Governments often engage in production activities because markets have failed to fill a need. Markets will not provide public goods such as national defense, law enforcement, and national parks, because these goods are consumed collectively and do not enable producers to make profits. Governments compensate for these market failures through public expenditures, regulations, and taxes.

Over the long run, the government can aim at either a limited role or a more extensive role—through taxation, expenditures, and regulations. It is desirable to make the role of the public sector as transparent as possible (see Box 3.7 on quasi-fiscal operations). One could defend more extensive roles for government on the ground of market failures and the need for equity. However, such an expansion can entail direct and indirect economic costs to society. In most transition economies, reducing the excessive role of the state in economic life is both an economic and political objective of the authorities. In many developing countries, however, the relatively low public expenditure-to-GDP ratio may reflect the government's limited financing capacity and distorted prices rather than a limited role for the state.

Public Expenditure Policy Issues

How can productive public expenditures be distinguished from unproductive public expenditures? Three basic issues are important here.

Box 3.7.
Quasi-Fiscal Operations

In many transition economies, central banks and other public financial institutions are involved in activities that give rise to financial transactions affecting the effective size of the fiscal deficit.[1] Some of the main types of quasi-fiscal operations are:

- exchange rate subsidies administered through the exchange system;
- subsidized lending to government, public enterprises, or private entities; and
- unfunded or contingent liabilities such as exchange rate guarantees.

Where these quasi-fiscal operations are significant, their costs need to be included in any comprehensive measure of the public sector deficit, for several reasons. In many countries, central and public sector bank losses are so large that they contribute to financial instability. Their existence also means that the conventional measures of government's fiscal balance are misleading indicators of the role of fiscal operations in the economy. The taxes and subsidies associated with quasi-fiscal operations may have distortionary effects on resource allocation.

Although they are not always easy to quantify precisely, quasi-fiscal operations need to be extracted from the accounts of the central bank and public financial institutions. To the extent possible, quasi-fiscal activities should be transformed into normal budgetary operations—that is, quasi-fiscal taxes and subsidies should be replaced with explicit taxes and subsidies. The long-term objective should be to address the root causes of quasi-fiscal operations such as lending activities that are essentially substitutes for explicit subsidies that otherwise would be in the budget and the lack of a unified exchange system. The legal authority of the central bank may need to be revised to limit the extent to which it can carry out quasi-fiscal operations. Such structural reforms are essential to minimize and eventually eliminate the need for quasi-fiscal operations.

[1]See International Monetary Fund, SM/95/65, April 5, 1995, "Quasi-Fiscal Operations of Public Financial Institutions." Also see *Guidelines for Fiscal Adjustment*, IMF Pamphlet Series, No. 49 (Washington: International Monetary Fund, 1995).

- *The level problem*. How much should the public sector spend? At any given time, a country has a certain capacity to finance public expenditure through taxation and borrowing. Efforts to exceed this limit are counterproductive and lead to macroeconomic and financial imbalances.
- *The efficiency problem*. How can public sector outputs—whether they are roads, educational services, or defense services—be provided efficiently? Efficient provision implies achieving given objectives at minimum costs, including not only financial and administrative expenses, but also the costs of any negative effects public expenditures and their financing may have on private sector production.
- *The mix problem*. What is the appropriate combination of public sector outputs? With aggregate public expenditure limited by its financing capacity, a country needs to find the right mix of public sector production. Any mix of goods or services chosen should reflect the collective interests of the population.

The level problem is mainly a macroeconomic issue, while the efficiency and mix problems are largely structural. In the short run, the financing capacity of many developing countries effectively limits its public spending (see also Box 3.8).

The level and the efficiency problems are largely positive questions. Analysts can look at the macroeconomic implications of aggregate public expenditure or the efficiency of public sector production in a fairly objective manner. The mix problem has both positive and normative aspects: it is possible to prepare a technical analysis of the combination of investments in human and physical capital required to achieve a growth target, but not to compare the relative merits of education and national defense or the geographical distribution of public investments without making a value judgment. In practice, these positive and normative issues are intertwined, making assessment of public expenditure a particularly controversial subject.

The Macroeconomic Implications of Public Expenditure

Public expenditure affects both aggregate supply (or production) and aggregate demand (or spending). Productive public investment—in physical and human capital—increases the return to invest-

> **Box 3.8.**
> **Sequestering Expenditures**
>
> In many transition economies, the authorities have implemented a number of mechanisms to control public spending, in response to revenue shortfalls or limited access to financing. These mechanisms include sequestering, or limiting government spending to levels below those authorized in the budget. Although governments have found this measure useful, it is a short-term emergency step and can have several adverse effects. Since sequestering expenditures often involves an across-the-board cut in spending, it detracts from an efficient allocation of expenditures; it also interferes with elected officials' oversight of spending priorities and the process of rational, long-term planning.

ment in general, encouraging private investment and economic growth. The effects on supply may be fairly immediate, removing a few key infrastructure bottlenecks. In general, however, the returns to public investment are fully realized only in the long term, especially in areas such as education. At the same time, the public sector competes with the private sector for limited resources, and public expenditure (whether financed through taxation or borrowing) crowds out private expenditure, including private investment. Transition economies are often limited in their ability to finance expenditures through either taxation or borrowing. In the short run, they have neither the administrative capacity to raise taxes nor the well-developed domestic capital markets necessary to support public borrowing, and borrowing from the central bank is costly because it is inflationary. In this situation, a government's attempts to spend more may actually exacerbate its financing difficulties by triggering higher inflation, inducing taxpayers to delay tax payments and thus reducing the real value of tax revenue.

An increase in public sector borrowing can raise domestic interest rates, increase the cost of investment and the government's borrowing costs, reduce the country's long-term growth potential, and create a debt burden. Unless the government uses borrowed resources productively, generating the output and income required to raise tax revenues sufficiently to finance future debt repayments and interest, the public sector will have to finance the debt burden by cutting services in the future. With international capital mobility, an increase in domestic interest rates can induce large capital inflows, an exchange rate appreciation, and a deterioration in the country's external competitive position.

Interactions Between Macroeconomic and Structural Relationships

The macroeconomic and structural aspects of public expenditure policy represent two sides of one problem. Public sector programs—such as those for defense, economic services, and social services—cannot be properly designed unless policymakers take into consideration both the need for efficient delivery and the macroeconomic consequences. The efficiency consideration implies that the distribution of public expenditure among outputs cannot be determined independently of the economic composition of expenditure (wages, other goods and services, transfers, and so forth). The design and implementation of sectoral programs need to be integrated into a coherent macroeconomic framework aimed at achieving sustainable economic growth with stable prices, a viable external payments position, and distributional equity.

Fiscal Sector

Fiscal Structure[35]

The fiscal structure in Poland, as in other transition economies, is a byproduct of the dominant and active role of the state in the prereform economy. The tax system came to be dominated by taxes on enterprises, which were often negotiated between the government and each enterprise. Under this system, enterprise taxes were a kind of ex post profit-sharing system for the enterprises and the government. In order to finance the many economic and social functions conducted by parastatal entities, the government used a system of extrabudgetary funds supported by levies on enterprises. The result was a large and complex extrabudgetary sector. Because the state had extensive control over prices of inputs and outputs, it changed the rates of turnover taxes frequently, with a view to clearing markets for commodities. On the expenditure side of the budget, state-administered price controls led to massive outlays for subsidies to both consumers and producers. The state also played a very active role in incomes policy, especially in determining wages in the public

[35]This section is based on *Poland: The Path to a Market Economy*, IMF Occasional Paper No. 113 (Washington: International Monetary Fund, October 1994). For a review of fiscal performance in the states of the former Soviet Union, see "Fiscal Transition in Countries of the Former Soviet Union: An Intermediate Assessment," IMF Working Paper 96/61 (Washington: International Monetary Fund, June 1996).

enterprise sector. With wages nominally fixed at low levels, wages and salaries comprised a relatively small proportion of budget expenditures, while a large proportion of spending was devoted to subsidies and the social welfare system. Since the inception of economic reforms in 1990–91, the Polish authorities have made significant progress in reforming the system of public finances to meet the needs of a market-based economy.

Poland's *state budget* covers the fiscal operations of the central government and the local authorities. It runs on a calendar year basis and must be approved by parliament. In 1993–94, state budget revenues amounted to about 65 percent of general government revenues, and state budget expenditures were about 70 percent of general government expenditure. (The *general government* consists of central and local governments and extrabudgetary funds.)

Local government expenditures, which in recent years have amounted to about one-third of total budgetary expenditures, are financed by certain revenues that accrue directly to these authorities (the bulk of the revenue from the tax on wages, real estate taxes paid by socialized entities, and receipts from turnover and income taxes from the private sector in the area) and by transfers from the central government. Local authorities cannot directly borrow from the banking system. In recent years, the local governments have recorded surpluses, which they are not required to transfer to the central government.

A number of *extrabudgetary funds* are responsible for carrying out spending related to various social, educational, and infrastructural matters. The funds receive transfers from the state budget equal to about 30 percent of their expenditures, as well as revenues from levies and contributions from the private sector. The funds cannot borrow from the banking system. In 1993–94, spending by these funds amounted to over 60 percent of state budget expenditures. These funds are also generally allowed to keep any surpluses.

Tax revenues typically account for over 80 percent of the general government's total revenues. Income and turnover taxes and social security contributions made up over 70 percent of tax revenues in 1994. Other sources of tax revenue include trade taxes, which have recently grown in importance; the wage tax; and the excessive wage tax (EWT), which penalizes enterprises that increase above the average level. The yield from profit taxes has declined in recent years, although this fall has been partially offset by the requirement that state-owned enterprises transfer part of their profits to the government in the form of dividends. These transfers are considered nontax revenues, along with transfers from financial institutions and privatization receipts.

Current expenditures accounted for over 90 percent of total general government expenditures in 1993–94, and subsidies for 12–13 percent of current expenditures. The most important subsidies were those for food, housing, and coal. Although the share of subsidies in total current expenditures has fallen sharply since 1990, other categories of spending have increased rapidly, notably social security benefits, public consumption, and interest payments.

The five largest extrabudgetary funds (the Social Insurance Fund, the Social Insurance Fund for Farmers, the Foreign Debt Servicing Fund, the Central Fund for the Development of Science and Technology, and the Export Development Fund) dominate the financial position of these operations. The Social Insurance Fund is the largest, accounting for about 60 percent of extrabudgetary expenditures in 1994. This fund is responsible for most social security benefits (the Social Insurance Fund for Farmers services the private agricultural sector) that were previously paid through the state budget. Its revenues consist mainly of contributions from enterprises, and spending on pensions makes up the bulk of its expenditures.

The Foreign Debt Servicing Fund was created to take over from the budget the servicing of the government's foreign debt and the disbursement of subsidies to Bank Handlowy for servicing the foreign debt of the banking system. Its main revenue source has been transfers from the state budget. A substantial portion of debt service obligations on external debt have either been rescheduled or gone into arrears, reducing somewhat the fund's commitment to reimbursing the banking system.

Revenues of the Central Fund for the Development of Science and Technology are provided largely by a compulsory levy charged to enterprises. Spending from the fund finances research and development. The Export Development Fund receives the revenues from taxes on foreign trade and finances export subsidies and promotion.

Recent Fiscal Developments

Following a sharp deterioration at the beginning of the 1980s and some corrective measures implemented in the mid-1980s, the general government accounts were in broad balance in 1984–88. In 1989, the general government deficit rose sharply to about 7.4 percent of GDP, reflecting a decline in revenues relative to GDP and, to a lesser extent, the growth of expenditures.

The authorities' efforts at a major fiscal reform met with some success in 1990, most visibly in a reduction in the general government deficit. The deficit was eliminated, and the government accounts recorded a surplus of over 3 percent of GDP. The brunt of the massive fiscal adjustment was borne by expenditures, which fell by over 7 percentage points of GDP. These reductions were achieved mainly through a sharp cut in subsidies on food and energy, but restraints on wages and salaries also contributed to the decline.

The fiscal adjustment achieved in 1990 was sharply reversed in 1991–92, with the general government deficit climbing to over 6.5 percent of GDP. Revenues from enterprise income taxes fell as the sharp drop in output and substantial increases in wages awarded by the Workers' Councils led to large losses in enterprise profitability. Although subsidies continued to be reduced and capital expenditures were contained, all other categories of expenditures increased in relation to GDP. The rise in social expenditures was particularly marked, largely because of the rise in unemployment benefit payments, but also because of significant (and unanticipated) increases in pensions that reflected the number of workers retiring early or claiming disability.

Since 1993, as the economic recovery has gathered steam, substantial progress has been made in reducing the fiscal imbalance. The general government deficit was reduced to about 3 percent of GDP in 1993 and further to about 2 percent of GDP in 1994. The pressures on public finances, however, continued to pose a challenge to the authorities; these pressures stem in part from the effects of the transformation on the most vulnerable sections of the population—those with little or no income, pensioners, and the unemployed—and in part from increasing demands for a variety of public services—a trend that reflects the growing aspirations of the population. At the same time, the tax base has been narrow, and there have been concerns about the equity of the taxation burden.

Developments in Tax Policy

The authorities took some steps toward reforming the tax system (see the Appendix for a summary of the tax system as of 1994).[36] The changes include:

(1) Frequent adjustments in the structure and levels of the turnover tax rates since 1989, with a view toward reducing their number and complexity. Despite these adjustments, the numerous exemptions and lax administration have kept the effective yield of the turnover tax low. In 1991, the average effective tax rate was 5.5 percent, compared with a general turnover tax rate of 20 percent, and half of all turnover tax revenue came from three products: alcohol, fuels, and tobacco.

(2) A revision of the enterprise profits tax to make it less discretionary. Enterprise profits are now taxed at a flat rate of 40 percent. The new regulations also allow accelerated depreciation allowances and generous reserves for bad debts. However, there are still many exemptions—for example, total exemptions for all agricultural activities.

(3) The introduction of a personal income tax (effective January 1, 1992). The new tax is progressive and covers all earned income—wages and salaries, fringe benefits, and rental incomes—as well as pensions. The three tax rates (20 percent, 30 percent, and 40 percent) are indexed to wage growth. The exemption level is high enough to keep low income earners outside the income tax net. Income from certain interest payments and dividends is subject to a tax of 20 percent. Capital gains from the sale of stocks and bonds were exempt for 1992 and 1993 but are now taxed; gains realized on the sale of real estate are taxed at 10 percent. Agricultural incomes and interest on individual savings accounts remain exempt from taxation.

(4) A value-added tax (VAT) was introduced in 1993 to replace the turnover tax. There are three rates—a standard rate of 22 percent, a preferential rate of 7 percent for basic necessities, and a zero rate on exports. Additional excise taxes are levied on alcohol, fuels, and tobacco.

An important factor behind the shortfalls in tax revenues has been the rapid buildup of tax payment arrears by state enterprises. As of early 1993, arrears were estimated at about 2.5–3 percent of GDP. The authorities continue to be concerned about the financial health of the enterprise sector. While a few state-owned enterprises are financially sound, the overall financial position of these firms deteriorated in 1990–92, with the gross profit rate falling from 7.7 percent in 1991 to 6.1 percent in 1992. Another indicator of financial weakness has been the accumulation of interenterprise arrears, which were estimated to be nearly as large as the outstanding stock of bank credit to enterprises at the end of 1991.

Poland, along with the Czech Republic, has pioneered the use of the EWT as an instrument of in-

[36]For further details of changes in the tax system, see Liam P. Ebrill and others, *Poland—The Path to a Market Economy*, IMF Occasional Paper No. 113 (Washington: International Monetary Fund, 1994), Appendix to Chapter II.

comes policy. The wage norm was first defined in terms of the total wage bill for enterprises, and after 1991, in terms of average wages. Although initially the EWT was considered primarily a regulatory device and not a revenue raiser, it eventually became an important source of budgetary revenues, yielding receipts of over 3 percent of GDP in 1991. The EWT was abolished in 1994.

Developments in Expenditure Policy

Total public expenditure remained broadly stable at about 50 percent of GDP in 1991–94, but its structure shifted substantially. The drop in subsidies—especially to state enterprises—was matched by a rise in cash benefits, in particular unemployment benefits and pension outlays. As in other transition economies, public investment has borne a disproportionate share of expenditure cuts.

Poland's greatest difficulties in controlling expenditures have been in the area of social protection and benefits. The social safety net in Poland consists of three basic benefit programs—social insurance, social assistance benefits, and unemployment benefits. The social insurance system operates on a pay-as-you-go basis and is financed through employee and employer contributions; the general rate for employers was raised from 43 percent to 45 percent in February 1992. Unemployment benefits are funded through a 2 percent employer payroll contribution.

After early 1990, pensions were supposed to be revalued at the end of each quarter and brought in line with the increase in average wages for the previous quarter. However, in practice these revaluations have not taken place, and the real value of pensions has continued to erode. The problems with the social protection system included too-generous access to disability pensions and a lack of targeting of family allowances. Reforms in 1992 tried to address some of these problems but did not succeed in containing the rapid rise in social expenditures. Unemployment benefits have been curtailed by restricting recipients to 12 months of benefits and limiting the benefits themselves to a uniform 36 percent of the average wage.

The large and growing pension system presents a potentially important challenge for public finances. Under the present system, transfers from the state budget cover the growing gap between contributions and benefits. The authorities have increasingly been considering reforming the pension system to address a variety of problems, including the overly liberal eligibility criteria, deteriorating dependency ratios, poor compliance with regulations governing contributions by employers and individuals, and weak administration.

Poland has a large number of regional and local authorities, and therefore the issues of fiscal relations between the central and local authorities are important. In 1991, local authorities were granted increased autonomy, and their revenues and expenditures were separated out of the state budget; only transfers from the budget to the local authorities continued to be recorded as an expenditure item. These transfers are now determined by local need and potential revenue in contrast to the past practice of simply adding on predetermined increases each year.

Financing of the Deficit

In view of Poland's relatively high debt level and the difficulties the country has faced in servicing it (a problem that has manifested itself in the buildup of arrears), access to voluntary sources of external financing was limited. As a result, the predominant source of financing the fiscal deficit was the domestic banking system. This situation contributed to inflationary pressures, which would have been worse but for the cushion provided by increased private savings, the bulk of which are deposited with the banking system, and the relatively subdued demand for loans from the nongovernment sector on account of the downturn in economic activity. The authorities' efforts to tap the nonbank domestic sector for financing initially met with only limited success. Since late 1989, the government has issued treasury bills, and in 1991, introduced an auction system. However, these bills were held mostly by the banking system, industry, and the central bank, with the nonbank public purchasing only relatively small amounts.

Exercises and Issues for Discussion

Exercises

1. The illustrative data given below show that the government's cash flow is in balance—total receipts equal to total payments. Reclassify the information in an analytical way to calculate the conventional deficit and the primary deficit. Show where each item below should be classified (e.g., revenue expenditure, net lending, financing).

Cash Flow of the Government
(Billion rubles)

Receipts	**3,000**
Tax receipts	1,000
Bank loan receipts	550
Interest receipts on loans to public enterprises	100
Proceeds from sale of bonds to the public	250
Repayment of principal on loans to public enterprises	300
Loan receipts from abroad	200
Other nontax receipts	400
Grants from abroad	200
Payments	**3,000**
Wages and salaries	1,200
Pensions	200
Purchases of goods and services	650
Interest	100
Loan repayments to the banking system	150
Lending to public enterprises	400
Redemption of maturing bonds	50
Investment	150
Repayment of foreign loans	100

2. On the basis of the information provided below, compute the conventional, primary, and operational deficits in 1994 and 1995 assuming that the debt stock in the beginning of 1994 equals 100 billion rubles.

	1994	1995
Nominal interest rate	5%	15%
Inflation rate	0%	10%
Revenues	200	230
Noninterest expenditures	300	400

What is the size of the "monetary correction"? Why should it be treated as if it were an amortization payment?

3. On the basis of the data in Table 3.1, calculate Poland's primary deficit for the period 1990–94. Analyze and compare the developments in the conventional and primary deficits during the period.

4. Comment on the evolution of the tax-to-GDP ratio during 1990–94. Is it a good measure of the Polish authorities' tax effort? Comment on the structure of revenues and expenditures on the basis of Tables 3.3–3.6.

5. Calculate the buoyancy of total tax revenues for 1991–93. Could you have deduced the buoyancy on the basis of the observed changes in the tax-to-GDP ratios over the period? Is the available information sufficient to calculate the elasticity of tax revenues with respect to GDP? If not, why?

6. On the basis of the tax revenue data, discuss how the Polish tax system fares using the Tanzi Diagnostic Test given in Box 3.5.

7. Assume that the income (GDP) elasticity of demand for base money is about 1.2 and that base money represents 20 percent of GDP. What will be the level of seigniorage that can be obtained from the economy without adding to inflation (i.e., pure seigniorage) if the growth rate is estimated at 7 percent? What will happen if the financing requirements of the government are much larger?

8. With reference to the table below, in both absolute terms and in relation to GDP,

   (a) compute the seigniorage in 1994 and 1995;

   (b) compute the inflation tax in 1994 and 1995;

   (c) explain the sharp increase in the observed inflation tax;

   (d) explain the observed decline in seigniorage; and

   (e) with reference to Box 3.1, show that when the rate of growth of nominal money balances are in line with the rate of inflation, the seigniorage will equal the inflation tax.

(Monetary data in billions of U.S. dollars)

	1993	1994	1995
Money	2,000	2,800	3,500
Prices	1.0	1.50	3.90
GDP	8,000	12,000	26,500

9. (a) Consider a country with a 60 percent public debt-to-GDP ratio in the current year and an expected nominal growth rate of GDP of only 10 percent. What would be the overall fiscal deficit (i.e., inclusive of interest payments) necessary to stabilize the country's debt-to-GDP ratio in the short run, assuming a possible seigniorage level of 1 percent of GDP?

   (b) Suppose now that nominal interest rates are running at 15 percent a year. Why will the country have to target a primary surplus in order to stabilize the debt-to-GDP ratio, in the short run, at its initial level of 60 percent? How large would the surplus have to be?

   (c) Show that if the above fiscal stance is continued over the long run, it will be sustainable assuming that all above parameters (growth rates, interest rates, seigniorage) will not change over time. You can show, for example, that the government net worth will not be negative or equivalently that the primary gap is zero (see Box 3.4).

   (d) Suppose now that the spending plans call for the ratio-to-GDP of noninterest expenditure to stabilize at about 25 percent; what will be the medium-term tax gap given that the country's tax-to-GDP ratio is currently at about 23 percent of GDP? Comment on the magnitude of the required adjustment.

10. Complete the table that follows and show that the higher the initial debt-to-GDP ratio, the higher the required, permanent adjustment will be in order for the fiscal stance to be sustainable.

Issues for Discussion

1. Discuss the pros and cons of treating grants as revenue items in the GFS. Also discuss the rationale for treatment of government loans to public enterprises as "net lending" above the line.

2. Which of the special deficit concepts discussed in this chapter are useful in analyzing not only the Polish fiscal situation but the situation in your own country?

3. How important is it to take account of arrears in assessing the fiscal position? Discuss the rationale for ignoring tax arrears in assessing the fiscal position.

4. It has been argued that borrowing by the government on behalf of public enterprises should be excluded from the deficit because if the enterprises had been private and if they had borrowed the same amounts in the capital market, the fiscal deficit would have been lower while the total amount of borrowing would have been the same. Discuss this in light of the GFS guidelines on net lending by the government.

5. It has been argued that the main government contribution to growth is through public investment. With reference to the discussion on the concept of the government current account balance, give examples where public investment may not contribute to growth and examples of current expenditure that will have significant impact on long-term growth prospects.

6. Governments often find that the monetary impact of foreign exchange intervention by the central bank needs to be sterilized through the sale or purchase of government securities (also by the central bank). These sterilized interventions usually entail costs to the authorities' budget. Explain how these costs arise and how they can affect the assessment of the appropriateness of monetary and fiscal policies.

7. Many transition economies are faced with the problem of financial institutions that have become insolvent because of their bad portfolios and that may require government bailouts. How should the government react to such a contingent liability in the context of its fiscal planning? What fiscal solutions are desirable in the face of such liabilities?

8. In the light of the discussion on alternative ways of financing a fiscal imbalance, explain:

Primary Surplus (P_d)	Real Interest Rates (r)	Real Growth Rates (g)	PDV of Primary Surplus $PDV(P_d)$	Initial Debt Ratio (d)	Net Worth (w)	Sustainable Primary Deficit (P_d^*)	Primary Gap (PG)
1.0	0.15	0.10	20	30	—	—	—
1.0	0.15	0.10	20	40	—	—	—
1.0	0.15	0.10	20	50	—	—	—
1.0	0.15	0.10	20	60	—	—	—
1.0	0.15	0.10	20	70	—	—	—

(a) how nonbank financing of the deficit avoids inflationary consequences of the deficit;

(b) the difficulties in maximizing the use of nonbank deficit financing; and

(c) the consequences of excessive reliance on nonbank financing (selling debt to domestic residents and foreigners, for instance).

9. In forecasting tax revenues, the IMF has often been reluctant to take into account expected revenue gains from planned improvements in tax administration. Is this approach justified?

10. Comment on the sharp rise in social security benefits in Poland during 1989–93. Do you think that the increases can be sustained? Discuss the role of social safety nets in adjustment programs and compare the situation in Poland with that in your own country.

Table 3.1.
General Government Operations[1]
(In trillions of zlotys)

	1990	1991	1992	1993	1994
Revenues	**254.3**	**341.9**	**503.0**	**742.2**	**977.5**
Tax revenues	**210.5**	**285.6**	**418.7**	**608.5**	**831.5**
Personal income tax	17.7	23.3	81.1	140.4	203.1
Social security contributions	43.8	79.0	111.5	146.0	192.4
Enterprise income tax	82.8	59.4	50.6	66.0	70.6
Excess wage tax (Popiwek)	8.8	27.1	17.0	10.0	3.9
VAT, turnover taxes, and excises[2]	37.3	61.2	103.4	177.5	243.0
Customs duties	3.5	17.1	26.8	43.8	75.0
Other	16.6	18.5	28.3	24.8	43.5
Nontax revenue	43.8	54.6	79.5	121.3	140.0
Capital revenue	...	1.7	4.8	12.4	6.0
Expenditure and net lending	**236.1**	**405.8**	**579.2**	**787.2**	**1,019.6**
Current	**218.7**	**366.3**	**535.0**	**729.3**	**961.6**
Wages and salaries	57.3	94.1	135.3	185.4	206.7
Purchases of goods and services	28.7	46.7	70.0	99.9	135.3
Interest payments[3]	2.4	12.6	36.7	53.4	86.9
Subsidies	43.1	41.4	37.1	35.3	42.8
Income transfers	85.8	140.4	229.1	320.7	458.1
Other	1.4	31.1	26.8	34.6	31.8
Capital and net lending	16.7	29.5	39.3	50.9	61.0
Net lending	0.7	10.0	4.9	7.0	-3.0
Overall balance	**18.2**	**-63.9**	**-76.2**	**-45.0**	**-42.1**
Financing	-18.2	63.9	76.2	45.0	42.1
Domestic	-16.2	41.9	81.4	46.6	83.0
Banking system	-16.3	41.2	75.6	35.2	66.8
Nonbank	0.1	0.7	5.8	11.4	16.2
Foreign (net)[4]	-4.1	-0.9	-2.8	-5.9	-43.0
Change in arrears[5]	-2.6	12.9	-6.4	4.3	2.1
Other[6]	4.0	...	4.0	...	...
GDP	**560.3**	**808.8**	**1,149.4**	**1,557.8**	**2,104.1**

Sources: Juha Kahkonen and others, *Poland–Statistical Tables,* IMF Staff Country Report No. 96/20 (Washington: International Monetary Fund, 1996); and Liam P. Ebrill and others, *Poland: The Path to a Market Economy,* Occasional Paper No. 113 (Washington: International Monetary Fund, 1994).

[1]Comprising the state budget, extrabudgetary funds, and local governments.

[2]1993 data include revenues from the VAT, which replaced turnover taxes in July 1993.

[3]Interest obligations on external debt are recorded on a cash basis, interest obligations on domestic debt are recorded on an accrual basis.

[4]Assume net repayment remains unchanged in U.S. dollar terms from previous year.

[5]Includes expenditure arrears of the state budget to banks and nonbanks that were not converted into treasury bills. Excludes external interest payments arrears, which are recorded on a cash basis above the line.

[6]Unallocated financing.

Table 3.2.
General Government Operations[1]
(In percent of GDP)

	1990	1991	1992	1993	1994
Revenues	**45.4**	**42.3**	**43.8**	**47.6**	**46.5**
Tax revenues	37.6	35.3	36.4	39.1	39.5
Personal income tax	3.2	2.9	7.1	9.0	9.7
Social security contributions	7.8	9.8	9.7	9.4	9.1
Enterprise income tax	14.8	7.3	4.4	4.2	3.4
Excess wage tax (Popiwek)	1.6	3.4	1.5	0.6	0.2
VAT, turnover taxes, and excises[2]	6.7	7.6	9.0	11.4	11.5
Customs duties	0.6	2.1	2.3	2.8	3.6
Other	3.0	2.3	2.5	1.6	2.1
Nontax revenue	7.8	6.8	6.9	7.8	6.7
Capital revenue	. . .	0.2	0.4	0.8	0.3
Expenditure and net lending	**42.1**	**50.2**	**50.4**	**50.5**	**48.5**
Current	39.0	45.3	46.5	46.8	45.7
Wages and salaries	10.2	11.6	11.8	11.9	9.8
Purchases of goods and services	5.1	5.8	6.1	6.4	6.4
Interest payments[3]	0.4	1.6	3.2	3.4	4.1
Subsidies	7.7	5.1	3.2	2.3	2.0
Income transfers	15.3	17.4	19.9	20.6	21.8
Other	0.2	3.8	2.3	2.2	1.5
Capital and net lending	3.0	3.6	3.4	3.3	2.9
Net lending	0.1	1.2	0.4	0.4	–0.1
Overall balance	**3.2**	**–7.9**	**–6.6**	**–2.9**	**–2.0**
Financing	–3.2	7.9	6.6	2.9	2.0
Domestic	–2.9	5.2	7.1	3.0	3.9
Banking system	–2.9	5.1	6.6	2.3	3.2
Nonbank	0.0	0.1	0.5	0.7	0.8
Foreign (net)[4]	–0.7	–0.1	–0.2	–0.4	–2.0
Change in arrears[5]	–0.5	1.6	–0.6	0.3	0.1
Other[6]	0.7	. . .	0.3	. . .	. . .
GDP	**560.3**	**808.8**	**1,149.4**	**1,557.8**	**2,104.1**

Sources: Juha Kahkonen and others, *Poland–Statistical Tables,* IMF Staff Country Report No. 96/20 (Washington: International Monetary Fund, 1996); and Liam P. Ebrill and others, *Poland: The Path to a Market Economy,* Occasional Paper No. 113 (Washington: International Monetary Fund, 1994).

[1]Comprising the state budget, extrabudgetary funds, and local governments.

[2]1993 data include revenues from the VAT, which replaced turnover taxes in July 1993.

[3]Interest obligations on external debt are recorded on a cash basis, interest obligations on domestic debt are recorded on an accrual basis.

[4]Assume net repayment remains unchanged in U.S. dollar terms from previous year.

[5]Includes expenditure arrears of the state budget to banks and nonbanks that were not converted into treasury bills. Excludes external interest payments arrears, which are recorded on a cash basis above the line.

[6]Unallocated financing.

Table 3.3.
Summary of the General Government Operations
(In trillions of zlotys)

	1990	1991	1992	1993	1994
State budget					
Revenue	197.1	212.1	308.5	459.0	631.3
Expenditures	193.2	269.4	386.3	503.0	690.7
Balance	**3.9**	**–57.3**	**–77.8**	**–44.0**	**–59.4**
Local authorities					
Revenue	. . .	50.1	64.4	. . .	. . .
Expenditures	. . .	44.8	64.9	. . .	. . .
Balance	**. . .**	**5.3**	**–0.5**	**. . .**	**. . .**
Extrabudgetary funds					
Revenue	108.5	146.0	244.6	331.9	444.4
Expenditures	95.7	150.4	238.4	328.3	440.8
Balance	**12.8**	**–4.4**	**6.2**	**3.6**	**3.6**
Extrabudgetary funds of state budget					
Revenue	13.7	17.2	21.8	25.6	32.1
Expenditures	11.8	15.3	18.0	25.8	31.2
Balance	**1.9**	**1.9**	**3.8**	**–0.2**	**0.9**
Extrabudgetary funds of local authorities					
Revenue	. . .	. . .	32.6	. . .	. . .
Expenditures	. . .	. . .	32.4	. . .	. . .
Balance	**. . .**	**. . .**	**0.2**	**. . .**	**. . .**
Unidentified expenditures	. . .	–0.7	8.3	. . .	. . .
General government					
Revenue	254.1	341.9	503.0	742.2	977.5
Expenditures	235.6	395.8	579.3	787.2	1,019.6
Balance	**18.5**	**–53.9**	**–76.3**	**–45.0**	**–42.1**

Sources: Juha Kahkonen and others, *Poland–Statistical Tables,* IMF Staff Country Report No. 96/20 (Washington: International Monetary Fund, 1996); and Liam P. Ebrill and others, *Poland: The Path to a Market Economy,* Occasional Paper No. 113 (Washington: International Monetary Fund, 1994).

Table 3.4.
Summary of the General Government Operations
(In percent of GDP)

	1990	1991	1992	1993	1994
State budget					
Revenue	35.2	26.2	26.8	29.5	30.0
Expenditures	34.5	33.3	33.6	32.3	32.8
Balance	**0.7**	**–7.1**	**–6.8**	**–2.8**	**–2.8**
Local authorities					
Revenue	. . .	6.2	5.6	. . .	. . .
Expenditures	. . .	5.5	5.6	. . .	. . .
Balance	**. . .**	**0.7**	**0.0**	**. . .**	**. . .**
Extrabudgetary funds					
Revenue	19.4	18.1	21.3	21.3	21.1
Expenditures	17.1	18.6	20.7	21.1	20.9
Balance	**2.3**	**–0.5**	**0.6**	**0.2**	**0.2**
Extrabudgetary funds of state budget					
Revenue	2.4	2.1	1.9	1.6	1.5
Expenditures	2.1	1.9	1.6	1.7	1.5
Balance	**0.3**	**0.2**	**0.3**	**–0.1**	**0.0**
Extrabudgetary funds of local authorities					
Revenue	. . .	. . .	2.8	. . .	. . .
Expenditures	. . .	. . .	2.8	. . .	. . .
Balance	**. . .**	**. . .**	**0.0**	**. . .**	**. . .**
Unidentified expenditures	. . .	–0.1	0.7	. . .	. . .
General government					
Revenue	45.4	42.3	43.8	47.6	46.5
Expenditures	42.0	48.9	50.4	50.5	48.5
Balance	**3.4**	**–6.6**	**–6.6**	**–2.9**	**–2.0**

Sources: Juha Kahkonen and others, *Poland–Statistical Tables,* IMF Staff Country Report No. 96/20 (Washington: International Monetary Fund, 1996); and Liam P. Ebrill and others, *Poland: The Path to a Market Economy,* Occasional Paper No. 113 (Washington: International Monetary Fund, 1994).

Table 3.5.
Summary of the State Budget Operations
(In trillions of zlotys)

	1990	1991	1992	1993	1994
Total revenue	**197.0**	**212.1**	**308.5**	**466.7**	**647.1**
Current revenue	197.0	210.4	303.7	458.9	631.1
Tax revenue	166.8	180.3	273.0	403.3	564.4
Indirect taxes	37.5	61.2	103.1	177.5	268.8
Enterprise income tax	82.8	50.7	50.6	62.6	68.2
From financial institutions	71.6	42.3	39.7	. . .	57.8
From nonfinancial institutions	11.2	8.4	10.9	. . .	10.4
Personal income tax[1]	17.9	19.5	72.3	119.4	173.8
Real estate tax	3.4	. . .	. . .	. . .	. . .
Tax on excessive wages	8.8	27.1	17.0	10.0	4.7
Foreign trade tax[2]	3.7	17.1	26.8	33.8	48.9
Stamp duties	1.3	. . .	. . .	. . .	. . .
Other	11.4	4.7	3.2	. . .	. . .
Nontax revenue	30.2	30.1	30.7	55.6	66.7
Transfers from central bank[3]	9.9	6.6	8.0	14.2	23.6
Dividend	12.8	12.6	8.5	6.9	6.0
Interest	1.3	2.5	0.0	. . .	. . .
Other	6.2	8.4	14.2	34.5	37.1
Capital revenue[4]	. . .	1.7	4.8	7.8	16.0
Total expenditure and net lending	**193.2**	**269.3**	**382.0**	**503.0**	**689.0**
Current expenditure	176.8	251.2	357.7	471.3	652.3
Wages	24.8	45.8	71.7	92.4	130.3
Social security contributions	9.5	15.2	22.3	30.0	36.7
Purchases of goods and services	77.4	86.3	95.7	124.0	172.7
Interest	2.3	12.6	31.3	53.4	86.9
Domestic	5.4	20.3	41.0	68.6	. . .
Foreign	7.1	10.9	12.4	18.3	. . .
Subsidies	43.1	41.4	39.4	36.5	46.2
Transfers to social security funds[5]	19.7	43.2	89.7	124.0	174.0
General transfer to local governments	. . .	6.7	7.6	11.0	5.5
Capital expenditures and capital grants	16.4	18.1	19.5	24.8	31.3
Of which: net lending	4.9	7.0	5.4	. . .	. . .
Change in arrears	. . .	. . .	4.8	6.9	5.4
Overall balance	**3.8**	**–57.2**	**–73.5**	**–36.3**	**–41.9**
GDP	**560.3**	**808.8**	**1,149.4**	**1,557.8**	**2,104.1**

Sources: Juha Kahkonen and others, *Poland–Statistical Tables,* IMF Staff Country Report No. 96/20 (Washington: International Monetary Fund, 1996); and Liam P. Ebrill and others, *Poland: The Path to a Market Economy,* Occasional Paper No. 113 (Washington: International Monetary Fund, 1994).

[1]Before 1992, various wage taxes.

[2]Revenue from customs duties; shared between the central government and the Export Development Fund.

[3]Excluding revenue from foreign currency auctions.

[4]Gross receipts from privatization.

[5]Includes pensions for uniformed persons and family allowances.

Table 3.6.
Summary of the State Budget Operations
(In percent of GDP)

	1990	1991	1992	1993	1994
Total revenue	**35.2**	**26.2**	**26.8**	**30.0**	**30.8**
Current revenue	35.2	26.0	26.4	29.5	30.0
Tax revenue	29.8	22.3	23.8	25.9	26.8
Indirect taxes	6.7	7.6	9.0	11.4	12.8
Enterprise income tax	14.8	6.3	4.4	4.0	3.2
From financial institutions	12.8	5.2	3.5	0.0	2.7
From nonfinancial institutions	2.0	1.0	0.9	0.0	0.5
Personal income tax[1]	3.2	2.4	6.3	7.7	8.3
Real estate tax	0.6	0.0	0.0	0.0	0.0
Tax on excessive wages	1.6	3.4	1.5	0.6	0.2
Foreign trade tax[2]	0.7	2.1	2.3	2.2	2.3
Stamp duties	0.2	0.0	0.0	0.0	0.0
Other	2.0	0.6	0.3	0.0	0.0
Nontax revenue	5.4	3.7	2.7	3.6	3.2
Transfers from central bank[3]	1.8	0.8	0.7	0.9	1.1
Dividend	2.3	1.6	0.7	0.4	0.3
Interest	0.2	0.3	0.0	0.0	0.0
Other	1.1	1.0	1.2	2.2	1.8
Capital revenue[4]	. . .	1.7	4.8	7.8	16.0
Total expenditure and net lending	**34.5**	**33.3**	**33.2**	**32.3**	**32.7**
Current expenditure	31.6	31.1	31.1	30.3	31.0
Wages	4.4	5.7	6.2	5.9	6.2
Social security contributions	1.7	1.9	1.9	1.9	1.7
Purchases of goods and services	13.8	10.7	8.3	8.0	8.2
Interest	0.4	1.6	2.7	3.4	4.1
Domestic	1.0	2.5	3.6	4.4	0.0
Foreign	1.3	1.3	1.1	1.2	0.0
Subsidies	7.7	5.1	3.4	2.3	2.2
Transfers to social security funds[5]	3.5	5.3	7.8	8.0	8.3
General transfer to local governments	0.0	0.8	0.7	0.7	0.3
Capital expenditures and capital grants	2.9	2.2	1.7	1.6	1.5
Of which: net lending	0.9	0.9	0.5	0.0	0.0
Change in arrears	. . .	. . .	0.4	0.4	0.3
Overall balance	**0.7**	**–7.1**	**–6.4**	**–2.3**	**–2.0**

Sources: Juha Kahkonen and others, *Poland–Statistical Tables,* IMF Staff Country Report No. 96/20 (Washington: International Monetary Fund, 1996); and Liam P. Ebrill and others, *Poland: The Path to a Market Economy,* Occasional Paper No. 113 (Washington: International Monetary Fund, 1994).

[1]Before 1992, various wage taxes.

[2]Revenue from customs duties; shared between the central government and the Export Development Fund.

[3]Excluding revenue from foreign currency auctions.

[4]Gross receipts from privatization.

[5]Includes pensions for uniformed persons and family allowances.

Table 3.7.
Summary Table
(Millions of zlotys/year ended December 31)

		1984	1985	1986	1987	1988	1994p[1]
Consolidated central government							
1	Total revenue and grants (A.I)	375	454	542	660	1,101	87,392
2	Total revenue (A.II)	375	454	532	657	1,097	87,392
3	Current revenue (A.III)	375	454	532	657	1,097	87,246
3.1	Tax (A.IV)	356	435	500	617	1,041	78,578
3.2	Nontax (A.V)	19	19	33	40	56	8,668
4	Capital revenue (A.VI)	–	–	–	–	–	146
5	Grants (A.VII)	–	–	10	3	4	–
5.1	Current (A17.1 + A18.1 + A19.1)	–	–	10	3	4	–
5.2	Capital (A17.2 + A18.2 + A19.2)	–	–	–	–	–	–
6	Total expenditure and lending-repayment (C.I)	379	472	546	684	1,169	92,282
7	Total expenditure (C.II)	380	472	542	675	1,146	92,567
8	Current expenditure (C.III)	357	439	501	621	1,077	89,333
9	Capital expenditure (C.IV)	22	33	41	54	69	3,234
10	Lending minus repayment (C.V)	–	–	4	9	23	–285
11	Current account surplus without grants (3–8)	17	15	31	36	19	–2,087
12	Current account surplus with current grants (3+5.1–8)	18	15	41	38	23	–2,087
13	Granted fixed capital formation (C4–A13)	1	2	3	5	17	2,153
14	Granted capital formation (C4+C5–A13–A14)	1	2	3	5	17	2,153
15	Overall deficit/surplus (1–6)	–4	–18	–4	–24	–67	–4,890
16	Financing (D.I or E.I) (=–15)	4	18	4	24	67	4,890
17	Abroad (D.III or E.III)	4	5	12	5	–7	–1,224
18	Domestic (D.II or E.II)	–	13	–8	19	74	6,114
18.1	Nonbank (D.I+D.4+D.5)	1	–2	–1	–3	–1	1,958
18.2	Deposit money banks (D.3)	–1	14	–4	15	63	1,198
18.3	Monetary authorities (D.2)	–	1	–3	7	12	2,958
	Memorandum items:						
19	Government debt end period (F.I or G.I)	. . .	. . .	. . .	. . .	. . .	146,275
24	National currency units/US$ (annual avg.)	.01	.01	.02	.03	.04	2.27
25	Average consumer price index (1990=100)	1.7	1.9	2.2	2.8	4.4	468.4
27	Gross domestic product (GDP)	858	1,045	1,295	1,694	2,963	. . .
28	Mid-year population (millions)	36.91	37.20	37.46	37.66	37.86	. . .
Budgetary central government							
1	Total revenue and grants (A.I)	276	324	372	394	705	61,636
2	Total revenue (A.II)	276	324	371	394	704	61,636
3	Current revenue (A.III)	276	324	371	394	704	61,614
3.1	Tax (A.IV)	263	313	354	376	671	56,438
3.2	Nontax (A.V)	13	11	17	18	34	5,176
4	Capital revenue (A.VI)	–	–	–	–	–	22
5	Grants (A.VII)	–	–	1	–	1	–
5.1	Current (A17.1 +A18.1 + A19.1)	–	–	1	–	1	–
6	Total expenditure and lending-repayment (C.I)	268	330	348	389	683	45,652
7	Total expenditure (C.II)	268	331	348	388	680	46,227
8	Current expenditure (C.III)	247	300	311	338	616	43,451
9	Capital expenditure (C.IV)	22	31	38	50	64	2,776
10	Lending minus repayment (C.V)	–	–	–	1	3	–575

Table 3.7 *(continued)*

		1984	1985	1986	1987	1988	1994p[1]
11	Current account surplus without grants (3–8)	29	24	60	56	88	18,163
12	Current account surplus with current grants (3+5.1–8)	30	24	61	56	89	18,163
13	Granted fixed capital formation (C4–A13)	1	1	2	2	14	1,758
14	Granted capital formation (C4 + C5–A13–A14)	1	1	2	2	14	1,758
15	Overall deficit/surplus (I–6)	9	−6	24	5	22	15,984
16	Financing (D.I or E.I)	16	30	16	9	78	5,764
17	Abroad (D.III or E.III)	4	5	–	–	–	−1,224
18	Domestic (D.II or E.II)	11	25	16	9	78	6,988
18.1	Nonbank (D.I+D.4+D.5)	1	−3	−2	–	2	1,998
18.2	Deposit money banks (D.3)	−1	14	–	–	35	2,032
18.3	Monetary authorities (D.2)	12	14	18	9	41	2,958
	Memorandum item:						
19	Government debt end period (F.I or G.I)	. . .	. . .	. . .	. . .	. . .	146,275
	Central government–social security funds						
1	Total revenue and grants (A.I)	58	75	86	162	235	21,741
2	Total revenue (A.II)	58	75	86	162	235	21,741
3	Current revenue (A.III)	58	75	86	162	235	21,741
3.1	Tax (A.IV)	58	74	85	160	235	21,244
3.2	Nontax (A.V)	1	1	1	1	1	497
6	Total expenditure and lending-repayment (C.I)	60	76	90	153	264	41,726
7	Total expenditure (C.II)	60	76	90	153	264	41,726
8	Current expenditure (C.III)	60	76	90	153	264	41,522
9	Capital expenditure (C.IV)	–	–	–	–	–	204
11	Current account surplus without grants (3–8)	−2	–	−3	9	−29	−19,781
12	Current account surplus with current grants (3+5.1–8)	−2	–	−3	9	−29	−19,781
13	Grants fixed capital formation (C4–A13)	–	–	–	–	–	204
14	Grants capital formation (C4–C5–A13–A14)	–	–	–	–	–	204
15	Overall deficit/surplus (1–6)	−2	–	−3	9	−29	−19,985
16	Financing (D.I or E.I)	−9	−13	−17	−8	−19	−206
18	Domestic (D.II or E.II)	−9	−13	−17	−8	−19	−206
18.2	Deposit money banks (D.3)	–	–	–	–	–	−206
18.3	Monetary authorities (D.2)	−9	−13	−17	−8	−19	–
	Central government–extrabudgetary accounts						
1	Total revenue and grants (A.I)	40	54	83	104	161	4,015
2	Total revenue (A.II)	40	54	75	101	157	4,015
3	Current revenue (A.III)	40	54	75	101	157	3,891
3.1	Tax (A.IV)	35	47	60	80	135	896
3.2	Nontax (A.V)	6	7	15	21	22	2,995
4	Capital revenue (A.VI)	–	–	–	–	–	124
5	Grants (A.VII)	–	–	8	3	4	–
5.1	Current (A17.1+A18.1+A19.1)	–	–	8	3	4	–
6	Total expenditure and lending-repayment (C.I)	51	66	108	142	221	4,904
7	Total expenditure (C.II)	51	66	103	134	201	4,614
8	Current expenditure (C.III)	51	64	100	130	197	4,360
9	Capital expenditure (C.IV)	–	2	3	3	5	254
10	Lending minus repayment (C.V)	–	–	4	8	20	290
11	Current account surplus without grants (3–8)	−10	−9	−25	−29	−40	−469

Table 3.7 *(continued)*

		1984	1985	1986	1987	1988	1994p[1]
12	Current account surplus with current grants (3+5.1–8)	–10	–9	–17	–27	–36	–469
13	Granted fixed capital formation (C4–A13)	–	1	1	3	3	191
14	Granted capital formation (C4+C5–A13–A14)	–	1	1	3	3	191
15	Overall deficit/surplus (1–6)	–11	–12	–24	–38	–60	–889
16	Financing (D.I or E.III)	–2	2	5	23	8	–668
17	Abroad (D.III or E.III)	–	–	12	5	–7	–
18	Domestic (D.III or E.III)	–2	2	–7	18	15	–668
18.1	Nonbank (D.1+D.4+D.5)	1	1	1	–3	–3	–40
18.2	Deposit money banks (D.3)	–	–	–4	16	29	–628
18.3	Monetary authorities (D.2)	–3	1	–4	6	–10	–
A. Revenue and grants							
Consolidated central government							
I	Total revenue and grants (II+VII)	375	454	542	660	1,101	87,392
II	Total revenue (III+VI)	375	454	532	657	1,097	87,392
III	Current revenue (IV+V)	375	454	532	657	1,097	87,246
IV	Tax revenue	356	435	500	617	1,041	78,578
1	Tax on income, profits, capital gains	75	107	138	190	333	24,244
1.1	Individual	–	–	–	–	–	17,403
1.2	Corporate	75	107	138	190	333	6,841
	income tax	72	103	131	178	305	6,841
2	Social security contributions	92	111	133	160	235	21,244
2.2	Employers	88	107	128	156	217	21,244
2.3	Self-employed or nonemployed	4	4	4	5	18	–
3	Taxes on payroll and workforce	32	39	12	9	14	742
	Payroll tax	32	39	12	9	14	–
4	Taxes on property	7	6	15	12	23	3
4.1	Recurrent taxes on immovable property	–	–	8	9	23	–
4.3	Estate, inheritance, and gift taxes	–	–	–	–	–	3
4.6	Other recurrent taxes on property	7	6	8	4	–	–
5	Domestic taxes on goods and services	117	129	159	196	334	24,381
5.1	General sales, turnover, or VAT	117	129	159	196	331	15,213
	Turnover tax	114	124	147	175	296	–
	Value-added tax	–	–	–	–	–	15,213
5.2	Excises	–	–	–	–	–	9,003
5.4	Taxes on specific services	–	–	–	–	–	165
5.6	Other taxes on goods and services	–	–	–	–	2	–
6	Taxes–international trade, transactions	23	31	37	43	68	7,488
6.1	Import duties	11	13	18	25	33	7,488
	6.1 1. Customs duties	–	–	–	–	–	4,889
	6.1 2. Other import charges	11	13	18	25	33	2,599
6.2	Export duties	7	10	10	4	3	–
6.5	Exchange taxes	–	–	1	1	3	–
6.6	Other taxes on international trade and transactions	6	8	9	14	28	–
7	Other taxes	10	11	5	5	34	476
7.3	Other taxes n.e.c.	10	11	5	5	34	476
V	Nontax revenue	19	19	33	40	56	8,668
8	Entrepreneurial and property income	5	7	18	19	17	3,821
8.2	Nonfinancial public enterprises and public financial institutions	4	6	10	9	16	3,417
8.3	Other property income	1	1	8	10	1	404

Table 3.7 *(continued)*

	1984	1985	1986	1987	1988	1994p[1]
9 Adminitrative fees, changes, nonindividual sales	6	7	8	12	21	3,022
10 Fines and forfeits	7	5	5	8	15	725
11 Control to government employees' pension and Welfare Fund	–	–	1	2	–	–
12 Other nontax revenue	1	1	–	–	4	1,100
VI Capital revenue	–	–	–	–	–	146
13 Sales of fixed capital assets	–	–	–	–	–	83
16 Capital transfer from nongovernment sources	–	–	–	–	–	63
VII Grants	–	–	10	3	4	–
17 From abroad	–	–	7	–	–	–
17.1 Current	–	–	7	–	–	–
18 From other levels of national government	–	–	4	3	4	–
18.1 Current	–	–	3	3	4	–
C. Expenditure and lending minus repayments by economic type Consolidated central government						
I Total expenditure and lending-repayment (II+V)	379	472	546	684	1,169	92,282
II Total expenditure (III+IV)	380	472	542	675	1,146	92,567
III Current expenditure	357	439	501	621	1,077	89,333
1 Expenditure on goods and services	67	83	100	131	205	24,266
1.1 Wages and salaries	...	...	...	...	...	12,925
1.3 Other purchases of goods and services	...	...	...	...	...	11,341
2 Interest payments	1	3	2	4	6	8,731
3 Subsidies and other current transfers	289	353	399	487	866	56,336
3.1 Subsidies	114	145	191	223	444	6,604
3.1. 1.3 To nonfinancial public enterprises and department enterprises	85	97	130	142	257	1,956
3.1.2 To financial institutions	9	22	25	33	78	2,545
3.1.4 To other enterprises	21	27	36	48	110	2,103
3.2 Transfers to other levels of national government	78	92	76	90	120	4,984
3.3.4 Transfers to nonprofit institutions and households	97	116	132	173	302	44,684
3.5 Transfers abroad	–	–	–	–	–	64
IV Capital expenditure	22	33	41	54	69	3,234
4 Acquisition of fixed capital assets	1	2	3	5	17	2,236
7 Capital transfers	21	31	38	49	52	998
7.1 Domestic	21	31	38	49	52	998
7.1.1 To other levels of national government	–	–	–	–	–	405
7.1.2 To nonfinancial public enterprises	17	23	25	31	31	–
7.1.4-5 Other domestic capital transfers	4	8	13	18	21	593
V Lending minus repayments	–	–	4	9	23	–285
8 Domestic	–	–	2	3	9	–289
8.2 To nonfinancial public enterprises	–	–	–	1	7	–579
8.3-4 To financial institutions and other	–	–	2	2	2	290
9 Abroad	–	–	2	6	14	4
Memorandum item:						
12 Employer contributions to social security schemes at same level of government (not included above)	...	...	...	...	...	5,679

Table 3.7 *(continued)*

	1984	1985	1986	1987	1988	1994p[1]
D. Financing by type of debt holder						
Consolidated central government						
I Financing (II+III)	4	18	4	24	67	4,890
II Domestic financing	–	13	–8	19	74	6,114
2 From monetary authorities	–	1	–3	7	12	2,958
3 From deposit money banks	–1	14	–4	15	63	1,198
4 Other domestic financing	–	–4	–1	–1	–1	1,958
4.3 From nonfinancial private sector	–	–4	–1	–1	–1	
5 Adjustments	1	1	–	–2	–	–
III Financing abroad	4	5	12	5	–7	–1,224
6 From international development institutions	–	–	–	–	–	367
7 From foreign governments	4	5	12	5	–7	–96
8 Other borrowing abroad	–	–	–	–	–	–1,495
E. Financing by type of debt instrument						
Consolidated central government						
I Financing (=D.I)	4	18	4	24	67	4,890
II Domestic financing (=D.II)	–	13	–8	19	74	6,114
1 Long-term bonds	. . .	. . .	. . .	. . .	. . .	2,090
2 Short-term bonds and bills	. . .	. . .	. . .	. . .	. . .	5,216
3 Long-term loans n.e.c.	. . .	. . .	. . .	. . .	. . .	–321
4 Short-term loans and advanced n.e.c.	. . .	. . .	. . .	. . .	. . .	17
5 Other domestic liabilities	. . .	. . .	. . .	. . .	. . .	–17
6 Changes in cash, deposits, etc.	. . .	. . .	. . .	. . .	. . .	–871
III Financing abroad (=D.III)	4	5	12	5	–7	–1,224
9 Long-term loans n.e.c.	. . .	. . .	. . .	. . .	. . .	–1,151
10 Short-term loans and advanced n.e.c.	. . .	. . .	. . .	. . .	. . .	–73
F. Outstanding debt by type of debt holder						
Consolidated central government						
(at end of fiscal year)						
I Total debt (II+III)	. . .	. . .	. . .	. . .	. . .	146,275
II Domestic debt	. . .	. . .	. . .	. . .	. . .	49,698
2 Monetary authorities	. . .	. . .	. . .	. . .	. . .	18,119
3 Deposit money banks	. . .	. . .	. . .	. . .	. . .	26,824
4 Other domestic debt	. . .	. . .	. . .	. . .	. . .	4,755
III Foreign debt	. . .	. . .	. . .	. . .	. . .	96,577
6 International development institutions	. . .	. . .	. . .	. . .	. . .	2,994
7 Foreign governments	. . .	. . .	. . .	. . .	. . .	71,200
8 Other foreign debt	. . .	. . .	. . .	. . .	. . .	22,383
8.1 Bank loans and advances	. . .	. . .	. . .	. . .	. . .	20,015
8.2 Supplier credits	. . .	. . .	. . .	. . .	. . .	208
8.3 Other foreign debt n.e.c.	. . .	. . .	. . .	. . .	. . .	2,160
G. Outstanding debt by type of debt instrument						
Consolidated central government						
(at end of fiscal year)						
I Total debt (=F.I)	. . .	. . .	. . .	. . .	. . .	146,275
II Domestic debt (=F.II)	. . .	. . .	. . .	. . .	. . .	49,698
1 Long-term bonds	. . .	. . .	. . .	. . .	. . .	26,341
2 Short-term bonds and bills	. . .	. . .	. . .	. . .	. . .	21,435
3 Long-term loans n.e.c.	. . .	. . .	. . .	. . .	. . .	302
4 Short-term loans and advanced n.e.c.	. . .	. . .	. . .	. . .	. . .	1,620

Table 3.7 *(concluded)*

		1984	1985	1986	1987	1988	1994p[1]
III	Foreign debt (=F.III)	...	...	...	...	...	96,577
6	Long-term bonds	...	...	...	...	...	216
8	Long-term loans n.e.c.	...	...	...	...	...	96,153
9	Short-term loans and advanced n.e.c.	...	...	...	...	...	208
L. Local governments							
A.	Revenue and grants						
I	Total revenue and grants (II+VII)	120	154	196	256	442	17,891
II	Total revenue (III–VI)	42	62	120	165	322	12,475
III	Current revenue (IV+V)	42	62	120	165	322	11,981
IV	Tax revenue (1–7)	31	46	100	135	282	6,660
1	Tax on income, profits, capital gains	11	21	31	44	106	3,420
1.1	Individual	4	6	10	15	24	3,054
4	Taxes on property	11	11	12	13	25	2,484
5	Dom. taxes on goods and services	8	11	15	21	55	780
3,6,7	Other taxes	1	2	42	57	96	–24
V	Nontax revenue (8–12)	11	16	20	31	40	5,321
8	Entrepreneur and property income	1	1	1	2	2	225
9.10	Fees, sales, fines	9	14	17	26	25	4,638
12	Other nontax revenue	1	1	2	3	13	458
VI	Capital revenue	–	–	–	–	–	494
VII	Grants	78	92	76	90	120	5,416
18	From other levels of national government	78	92	76	90	120	5,416
C.	Expenditure and lending minus repayments by economic type						
I	Total expenditure and lending-repayment (II+V)	120	150	191	245	414	18,033
II	Total expenditure	120	150	191	245	414	18,003
III	Current expenditure (1–3)	87	106	134	171	274	14,663
1	Expenditure on goods and services	65	81	99	130	202	12,467
1.1–2	Wages and salaries and empirical contributions	38	46	55	70	116	6,253
1.3	Other purchases of goods and services	27	36	44	60	86	6,214
2	Interest payments	–	–	–	–	–	12
3	Subsidies and other current transfers	23	25	35	41	72	2,184
3.2	Transfers to other levels of national government	–	–	3	3	5	56
IV	Capital expenditure (4–7)	32	44	57	74	140	3,340
4,5,6	Stocks, land, capital assets	1	3	3	3	4	3,244
7	Capital transfers	31	41	54	71	136	96
7.1.1	To other levels of national government	–	–	–	–	–	1
V	Lending minus repayments	–	–	–	–	–	30
S.15	DEFICIT/SURPLUS (A.I–C.I)	–	4	4	11	28	–142

Source: IMF, *Government Finance Statistics Yearbook* (Washington: International Monetary Fund, 1995).

[1]Note that 'p' stands for provisional data.

Table 3.8.
Government Revenues and Grants

I. Total revenue and grants (II + VII)

II. Total revenue (III + VI)

III. Current revenue (IV + V)

IV. Tax revenue
- Tax on income, profits, and capital gains
  - Individual
  - Corporate
- Social security contributions
- Taxes on payroll and workforce
- Domestic taxes on goods and services
  - General sales tax or VAT
  - Excises
  - Profit of fiscal monopolies
  - Taxes on specific services
  - Taxes on use of goods
  - Other taxes on goods and services[1]
- Taxes on international trade
  - Import duty
  - Export duty
  - Other taxes on international trade
- Other taxes

V. Nontax revenue[2]

VI. Capital revenue[3]

VII. Grants

Source: IMF, *Government Finance Statistics Manual* (Washington: International Monetary Fund, 1986).

[1]Including business and professional licenses and motor vehicle taxes.

[2]Including property income, administrative fees and charges, and fines.

[3]Including the sales of fixed assets, sales of stocks, land, and other intangible assets and capital transfers.

Table 3.9.
Economic Classification of Government Expenditure and Net Lending

I. Total expenditure and net lending (II + V)

II. Total expenditure (III + IV)

III. Current expenditure
- Expenditure on goods and services
  - Wages and salaries
  - Employer contributions to social security and pension
  - Other purchases of goods and services
- Interest payments
  - Domestic
  - Abroad
- Subsidies and other current transfers
  - Subsidies[1]
    - To nonfinancial public enterprises
    - To financial institutions
  - Transfers
    - To nonprofit institutions, households, and abroad

IV. Capital expenditure
- Acquisition of fixed capital assets
- Purchase of stocks and land
- Capital transfers

V. Lending minus repayments

Source: IMF, *Government Finance Statistics Manual* (Washington: International Monetary Fund, 1986).

[1]Subsidies include all unrequited, nonrepayable transfers on current account to private industries and public enterprises and the cost of covering the cash operating deficits of departmental enterprise sales to the public.

Appendix

Summary of the Tax System in 1994

Poland's public revenue system comprises several taxes accruing partially or totally to the state budget; a number of quasi-tax payments, also accruing to the budget; a payroll tax earmarked for social funds; and a series of taxes and nontax revenues administered and collected locally, accruing to municipalities.[1]

Main Taxes

Personal income tax. Effective January 1, 1992, and levied on all personal incomes (except some agricultural incomes). Withheld at the source for wage income at a rate of 21 percent (for incomes over Zl 1,212,600), 33 percent (for incomes over Zl 90,800,000), and 45 percent (for incomes over Zl 181,600). (Tax rates were raised in 1994 from 20 percent, 30 percent, and 40 percent.) Some deductions are allowed, and joint returns are possible. Proceeds of the tax are divided between the state (85 percent) and local governments (15 percent).

Corporate income tax. Effective January 1, 1989. Levied on all legal entities (whether state-owned, cooperative, or private). Rate 40 percent. Proceeds divided between state budget (95 percent) and local governments (5 percent).

Small taxpayer turnover presumption. Presumptive tax assessed as a proportion of sales if the previous year's turnover is less than Zl 1.2 billion (2.5 percent for trade; 7.5 percent for services; and 5.0 percent for production).

Value-added tax (VAT). Introduced July 5, 1993, to replace turnover tax. Rates: 22 percent (general rate), 7 percent (energy products, construction, some consumption goods), zero (exports and associated services). Exemptions include agricultural goods, some processed goods, and financial services. Revenues accrue entirely to the state budget.

Excises. Introduced with the VAT, and applicable to several vice and luxury goods and to petroleum products.

Customs duties. The tariff code ranges from zero to 40 percent, and there are exemptions and tariff quotas. An across-the-board 6 percent customs surcharge was added in 1993. In 1994, the surcharge was transformed into a 6 percent tax on imports and tariffs.

State Enterprise-Based Taxes and Duties

Tax on excessive wage increases (popiwek) (abolished as of April 1, 1994). Applicable to state-owned enterprises, cooperatives, and joint ventures with state participation of more than 50 percent. Provided for sharply increasing tax rates for wage awards above a given norm.

Dividend tax. Compulsory payment from state enterprises based on the re-evaluated value of "founding organ" contribution to enterprise capital. Rate varies by class and vintage of assets.

Main Local Taxes

Real estate tax. Levied on urban and rural property at a rate established yearly by the Ministry of Finance (but not to exceed 0.1 percent for housing and 2 percent for commercial buildings) on assessed value (which is not yet related to market value).

[1]Drawn from *Poland: Policies for Growth with Equity* (Washington: World Bank, 1994).

CHAPTER

4 Balance of Payments Accounts and Analysis

Measuring and assessing the external position of a country are essential steps in the economic policymaking process. Data on the transactions and financial flows between a country and the rest of the world, which are systematically summarized in the balance of payments, form the basis of any analysis of a country's external position and need for adjustment.

The purpose of this chapter is to introduce the accounting framework and key concepts used in analyzing the balance of payments and external debt. The first part of the chapter describes the framework; the second part of the chapter focuses on the measurement of a country's external position, drawing on the methodology developed in the Fifth Edition of the *Balance of Payments Manual* (hereafter known as the *Manual*).[1] The section also examines important issues in measuring balance of payments transactions in former centrally planned economies. The key concepts used in analyzing the balance of payments and external debt are introduced in following sections as well as the main developments in Poland's balance of payments and the exchange rate of the zloty. Finally, the last part of the chapter presents some exercises and issues for discussion.

Conceptual Framework of the Balance of Payments

Basic Conventions

A country's balance of payments tracks payments to and receipts from nonresidents. According to the *Manual*, the balance of payments is "a statistical statement that systematically summarizes, for a specific time period, the economic transactions of an economy with the rest of the world." Various conventions for recording items in the balance of payments are presented below.

[1]See *Balance of Payments Manual*, Fifth Edition (Washington: International Monetary Fund, 1993).

The Double-Entry Accounting System

The basic convention applied in constructing a balance of payments is the double-entry accounting system. Every transaction recorded using this system is represented by two entries with equal values but opposite signs, a debit (–) and a credit (+). Thus, by convention, certain items are recorded as debits and others as credits, as follows:

Exports of goods and services	Credit	(+)
Imports of goods and services	Debit	(–)
Increase in financial liabilities	Credit	(+)
Increase in financial assets	Debit	(–)
Decrease in liabilities	Debit	(–)
Decrease in assets	Credit	(+)

With double-entry bookkeeping, the sum of all credits should be identical to the sum of all debits, and the overall total should equal zero. In this sense, the balance of payments is always in balance. The example in Box 4.1 illustrates how a shipment of cars exported from Russia to Poland and involving a payment by a Polish importer through the banking system is recorded under the above conventions.

Some key points in balance of payments accounting are:

- *Real and financial transactions*. "Real" flows involve transactions in goods and services (such as imports, exports, travel, and shipping). Such transactions contrast with financial transactions, or changes in levels of financial assets and liabilities (for example, the repayment of principal on an outstanding loan constitutes a reduction in a liability). Transactions in goods and services are recorded in the current account of the balance of payments. Financial transactions are recorded in the capital and financial account of the balance of payments.
- *Transfers*. Unrequited transfers across national borders are one-sided transactions.

Box 4.1.
An Example of Double-Entry Accounting

Russia's Accounts		Poland's Accounts	
Exports	Credit	Imports	Debit
Bank deposits increase	Debit	Decline in bank deposits	Credit

Suppose, for example, that the Japanese government donates to the Kyrgyz Republic buses for public transportation. To deal with such transactions, which involve no financial compensation, the balance of payments methodology includes a category called "transfers." This convention allows one-sided transactions to be converted to standard two-sided transactions. The donated buses are recorded as an import (debit) in the accounts of the Kyrgyz Republic, having been "paid for" by a transfer (credit). More generally, all transfers with an economic value, when no quid pro quo is involved, give rise to a counterentry, either a current or a capital transfer. Current transfers include cash transfers, gifts in kind (such as food and medicines), contributions to international organizations, and remittances sent by workers residing abroad to families back home. Capital transfers may be in cash (investment grants) or in kind (debt forgiveness).

- *Errors and omissions.* In practice, accounts tend not to balance, largely because data are derived from different sources or because some items are underrecorded or not recorded at all. All balance of payments accounts contain the item "net errors and omissions," which reflects errors in estimation and omissions of transactions that should have been recorded. Entries are recorded net because of the possibility that credit errors will offset debit errors—that is, an underestimation of exports may be partly offset by an underestimation of imports. Since credit and debit errors may offset each other, the size of the net residual cannot be taken as an indicator of the relative accuracy of the balance of payments statement. Nonetheless, large and persisting net residuals impede the interpretation and analysis of the balance of payments for an individual country. Analogously, at the level of the world as a whole, recording discrepancies in one country are not offset by under- or overestimation in other countries.[2]
- *Flows and stocks.* The balance of payments accounts record flows in two directions. These flows are distinguished from the stocks associated with a country's international investment position—that is, the value of a country's assets and liabilities vis-à-vis the rest of the world. The former are measured for a specific time period, whereas the latter are recorded at a point in time, often the end of the year. Two stocks discussed in this workshop are the level of international reserves (external assets of a country) and the level of external debt (a liability).

Residency

The concept of residency in the balance of payments is based on the transactor's center of economic interest, not on the transactor's nationality. This practice follows the System of National Ac-

[2]In principle, the external current account balances of all countries should sum to zero, as should the sum of the countries' capital account balances. For a number of years, however, global data on current account balances have shown a large discrepancy in the form of an excess of recorded debits. Conversely, the global capital account has shown a large positive balance or excess of recorded credits (capital inflows). These discrepancies derive from errors, omissions, and asymmetries in countries' treatment of balance of payments statistics. Such discrepancies can undermine the credibility of analyses of global economic developments, hinder the formulation of appropriate policies, and even contribute to protectionist pressures owing to mistaken perceptions of countries' balance of payments situations. In 1987, under a specially set up Working Party, the IMF investigated the causes of this discrepancy and recommended procedures to improve statistical practices in these areas. In 1992, a similar effort was undertaken to assess procedures for the collection of capital account statistics in the light of the growth and complexity of international capital account transactions. See the final *Report of the Working Party on the Statistical Discrepancy in World Current Account Balance* (Washington: International Monetary Fund, 1987) and *Report on the Measurement of International Capital Flows* (Washington: International Monetary Fund, September 1992).

counts (SNA) studied in Chapter 2. The main considerations relating to economic territory are as follows:

Individuals living in a country are generally considered residents if they have resided there for at least 12 months. Nonresidents include visitors (tourists, crews of ships or aircraft, and seasonal workers); border workers (who are considered to be residents of the country in which they live); diplomats and consular representatives; and members of armed forces stationed in a foreign country, irrespective of the duration of their stay.

Enterprises are considered residents of the economy where they are engaged in business, provided they have at least one productive establishment and plan to operate it over a long period of time. Therefore, subsidiaries of foreign-owned companies are considered to be resident in the country in which they are located.

General government, including all agencies of the central, regional, and local governments, together with embassies, consulates, and military establishments located outside the country, are considered to be resident.

Time Periods and the Timing of Recording

In principle, the time period for recording balance of payments flows may be of any length. However, it is usually dictated by practical considerations, especially the frequency of data collection. Many countries prepare balance of payments data annually because firm estimates for some balance of payments transactions are available only once each year. However, since other data (for example, for exports and imports) are often available quarterly and sometimes monthly, some countries prepare quarterly balance of payments data consistent with quarterly estimates of the national accounts.

By convention, both parties to an international transaction record it when there is a legal change of ownership. In principle, both parties record the same transaction simultaneously, according to the principles of accrual accounting (when transactions such as interest payments are due to be settled, not when cash settlements are made). In practice, trade, service, and financial transactions may be recorded at different times by the two parties, so that adjustments need to be made to the original data derived from trade returns, exchange records, or enterprise surveys.

Valuation

A balance of payments transaction should be valued at the market price, which reflects the terms of a specific exchange between a willing buyer and a willing seller. The market price is distinguished from a general price indicator (such as a world market price) for a specific commodity.

In practice, this definition creates difficulties in recording certain transactions, including:

- Barter transactions, which involve a direct exchange of goods for other goods rather than for money;
- Transactions between affiliated enterprises (for example, profit transfers between a subsidiary and the parent company); and
- Transfers, which often do not have a market price.

Proxy measures are used to record these kinds of transactions. For example, bartered goods are valued at market prices.

Exports and imports are shown f.o.b. (free on board), or excluding the cost of transportation beyond national borders. Imports are usually recorded by customs on a c.i.f. basis (including the cost of international insurance and freight). However, in the balance of payments accounts, the insurance and freight components are recorded under "services."

Unit of Account

Since transactions may be settled in any currency, an appropriate unit of account is required for recording balance of payments transactions. Although the national currency can be used, its analytical value loses significance over time as the exchange rate fluctuates. For this reason, balance of payments accounts are often expressed in terms of a stable foreign currency (such as the U.S. dollar or the SDR), facilitating comparisons across countries. The appropriate exchange rate (the market rate prevailing on the transaction date) is used to convert data from the currency used in a transaction into the unit of account currency.[3]

[3]See Chapter VII of the *Balance of Payments Manual* for additional details. In the case of multiple exchange rates, the conversion unit can be either a unitary rate (a weighted average of all official market rates) or the principal rate (used for most economic transactions). When there is a *parallel market rate* for some transactions, this rate can be used for conversions, and the official rate for the remaining transactions.

Box 4.2.
Changes in the 1993 *Balance of Payments Manual*

Area of Change	Manuals: Fourth Edition (1977)	Manuals: Fifth Edition (1993)
Overall	Only a statement on balance of payments *flows*.	An articulated set of accounts encompassing both flows (balance of payments) and stocks (net international investment position).
Services and income	Residual category "Other goods, services, and income."	Separate and clear identification of all goods, services, income, and current transfers, to facilitate compilation of SNA aggregates such as Gross National Disposable Income (GNDI).
	Current and capital transfers not distinguished.	
Current account redefined	Current account included *all* unrequited transfers.	The current account excludes capital transfers.
Capital and financial account redefined	Included only financial transactions, but known as the "capital account."	Redesignation to reflect: (i) "Capital account" (mainly capital transfers); and (ii) "Financial account" that broadly corresponds to "capital account" of the Fourth Edition.
Portfolio investment	Limited list of standard components.	Expanded list to include new money market instruments.
Valuation changes	Included all valuation changes, as well as monetization of gold and allocations of SDRs.	All valuation changes excluded from flow data; instead, they are recorded in stock data.
Exceptional financing	Limited coverage.	Expanded coverage.

Changes in the *Balance of Payments Manual*

Changes in Coverage

Between the publication of the Fourth Edition of the *Manual* (1977) and the Fifth Edition (1993), there were many developments in the field of international trade and finance, including increased trade in services, widespread abolition of capital controls, innovations in new financial instruments, and new approaches to restructuring external debt.

As a result, the methodology for recording transactions in the *Manual* had to be adjusted to accommodate these changes. The Fifth Edition aims to improve the integration of external sector accounting with other macroeconomic accounts, particularly the SNA, and incorporate the changes that have taken place in international transactions (see Box 4.2). Unlike the previous edition, the 1993 *Manual* provides a conceptual framework for presenting the external transactions and international financial position of an economy through a comprehensive measure of external assets and liabilities. Among other important changes, the Fifth Edition:

- Records interest on an accrual rather than a cash basis;
- Redefines the current account to exclude capital transfers, including them instead in the capital and financial account (formerly the capital account), which has been revised to provide more detailed data on these flows;
- Changes the heading "nonfactor services" to "income transactions";
- Expands the classification scheme for service transactions in recognition of their growing importance;

- Expands and restructures the coverage of portfolio investment to reflect the development of new financial instruments such as derivatives and financial futures;
- Extends coverage of emerging forms of exceptional financing transactions such as debt forgiveness and debt/equity swaps; and
- Develops a consistent classification scheme for income and financial assets and liabilities, which relates flows to the overall investment position (stocks).

Throughout, the nomenclature has been revised to describe the increasingly sophisticated composition of international transactions more accurately.

The Net International Investment Position

A country's international investment position is its stock of external financial assets minus its stock of external liabilities. The position at the end of a specific period reflects financial transactions during that period (typically one year), valuation changes from movements in exchange rates and prices, and other adjustments that affect the level of assets and liabilities.

Data on balance of payments flows and the international investment position constitute the complete set of international accounts for an economy. Because data on stocks are often used to determine income receipts, consistent classifications of the income component of the current account, the financial account of the balance of payments, and the international investment position are essential for reconciling stocks and flows and for performing a meaningful analysis of yields and rates of return on external investments.

Standard Classification of the Balance of Payments

Main Components

A coherent structure for classifying balance of payments transactions facilitates the process of adapting the data for various purposes, including analyzing recent trends and developing projections. The *Manual's* standard classification system has two key accounts: the current account and the capital and financial account. Their major components are presented in Box 4.3.

In selecting the standard components, the following criteria have been given the greatest weight. Each item should:

- Exhibit distinctive behavior, that is, its economic influences should be unique;
- Be important in a number of countries;
- Be measurable, requiring regular collection of statistics; and
- Coordinate with other statistical systems (especially the SNA).

(i) Current account

The current account comprises "real" transactions—goods, services, income, and current transfers. Transactions classified under "goods" relate to the movement of merchandise—exports and imports—and generally involve a change of ownership. "Services" can be of many different types. "Income" may be derived from labor (wages paid to employees living in neighboring countries) or from financial assets or liabilities (for example, interest payments on external debt).

Most current account entries show gross debits or credits, but entries in the capital and financial account are typically net. Net entries are shown only as credits or debits, according to the conventions.

(ii) Capital and financial account

Box 4.3 shows the two major categories of the capital and financial account. The main item in the capital account is capital transfers. The financial account has four functional categories.

- *Direct investment*, which is further divided into equity capital, reinvested earnings, and other capital. Direct investment is classified primarily on a directional basis (investment in the domestic economy by residents abroad and by nonresidents).
- *Portfolio investment*, which includes long-term debt and equity securities, money market debt instruments, and tradable financial derivatives, including currency and interest rate swaps.
- *Other investment*, such as trade credits and borrowing, including IMF credit and loans. Although transactions are classified primarily by instrument, they may also be classified according to their maturity structure, which is important in the analysis of indebtedness.
- *Reserve assets* that are available to meet immediate needs. Despite the name, reserve assets in the standard balance of payments accounts are not stocks but changes in gross external assets. These assets include foreign exchange (currency, deposits, and securities), monetary gold, SDRs, and the country's re-

Box 4.3.
Classifications of the Balance of Payments

	Credit	Debit
1. **Current account**	**Credit**	**Debit**
A. **Goods and services**		
Goods	Exports	Imports
Services		
Transportation		
Travel		
Government services		
Other services		
B. **Income**		
Compensation of employees		
Investment income		
Of which:		
interest on external debt		
C. **Current transfers**	**Credit**	**Debit**
2. **Capital and financial account**		
A. **Capital account**		
Capital transfers		
Acquisition/disposal of nonproduced, nonfinancial assets		
B. **Financial account**		
Direct investment, net		
Portfolio investment, net		
Other investment, net		
Loans, trade credits		
Use of IMF credit and loans from the Fund		
Reserve assets		
Monetary gold		
SDRs		
Reserve position in the IMF		
Foreign exchange		
Other claims		

Source: IMF, *Balance of Payments Manual* (Washington: International Monetary Fund, 1993).

serve position in the IMF.[4] Reserve assets are under the effective control of the monetary authorities and can be used either directly (to finance payment imbalances), or indirectly (to regulate imbalances by, for instance, intervening in foreign exchange markets to support the value of the currency). Transactions with the IMF affect both reserve assets and reserve liabilities (see Box 4.4).

According to the Fifth Edition of the *Manual*, reserve asset flows exclude those that are not attributable to transactions. Thus, valuation changes resulting from fluctuations in the exchange rate, and the creation of new reserve assets (the monetization of gold or allocations of SDRs) are not included in the data on flows. These items are reflected in the international investment position (the data on stocks).[5]

Supplementary Information

In the standard presentation of the balance of payments, the financial account does not distin-

[4]Note that nonmonetary gold, possibly including stocks held by the authorities for trading purposes, is treated like any other commodity in the balance of payments.

[5]Many countries may still be following the Fourth Edition of the *Manual*, which included valuation adjustments and SDR allocations in the data on flows, and hence in the balance of payments.

Box 4.4.

How IMF Transactions Affect the Balance of Payments

Three types of transactions with the IMF can directly affect a country's balance of payments accounts:

1. ***Use of IMF resources.*** When a country purchases foreign currency from the IMF (for instance through a stand-by arrangement), it increases its financial assets (the foreign exchange received) but at the same time it incurs a financial liability (its obligation vis-à-vis the IMF). Thus, a use of IMF credit is recorded with a positive sign in the Financial Account under "other investment, loans." Its counterpart is shown with a minus sign as an increase in "reserve assets."
2. ***Changes in special drawing rights (SDRs).*** SDRs are international reserve assets created by the IMF to supplement countries' existing assets. If SDRs are used to acquire foreign exchange, to settle financial imbalances, or to extend loans, the transactions are recorded in the balance of payments under reserve asset flows. According to the Fifth Edition, new allocations of SDRs are not recorded. They affect only stocks (the net international investment position of a country).
3. ***Changing a "reserve tranche position" in the IMF.*** This arises from (i) the payment of part of a member's quota in reserve assets, and (ii) the IMF's net use of the member's currency. Changes in a country's reserve position in the IMF, which include a member's creditor position under any arrangement to lend to the IMF, are assets from the country's perspective. Such shifts are recorded as changes in reserve assets in the financial account.

guish between extraordinary and ordinary transactions. As a result, analytical presentations have been developed to highlight items, such as exceptional financing, that may be particularly important in analyses of the balance of payments. Additional data are often prepared for these presentations. The most important supplementary item—exceptional financing—has become increasingly important in recent years, especially in those countries that have experienced debt servicing problems. The main exceptional financing transactions are as follows:

- *The rescheduling of existing debt*, which involves replacing an existing contract with one that postpones debt service payments. The main balance of payments items affected by rescheduling are interest payments (shown in the current account) and amortization payments (shown in the financial account). Debt restructuring may cover arrears on interest or principal as well as scheduled interest and principal payments.
- *Arrears on debt servicing*, which can be either interest or amortization payments that are past due. Interest arrears are treated as if they have been paid for with a short-term loan—that is, as a scheduled interest payment is recorded as an income debit in the current account, it is offset by a credit in the financial account under short-term liabilities.
- *Debt forgiveness*, or the voluntary cancellation by an official creditor of all or part of a debt specified by a contractual arrangement. It is recorded as an official transfer under the capital account.[6]
- *Equity investment*, especially debt-equity swaps. This type of investment involves the exchange of bank claims on debtors, usually at a discount, for nonresident equity investment in a country.

The next part of the chapter discusses how particular subgroups of transactions—especially exceptional financing—are regrouped for analytical purposes.

[6]If the debt forgiveness represents a write-off of debt by a private creditor, it is recorded not in the balance of payments but in the SNA under "the revaluation account." See *Balance of Payments Manual*, Appendix IV (Washington: International Monetary Fund, 1993).

Box 4.5.
Classification of Data Sources

Source	Description
International trade statistics (ITS)	These statistics measure the quantities and values of goods that add to or subtract from a nation's stock of goods as a result of movement into or out of a country. These data are compiled from forms submitted (by exporters, importers, or their agents) to customs officials or directly to the ITS compiler.
International transactions reporting system (ITRS)	The ITRS measures individual cash transactions that pass through domestic banks and the foreign bank accounts of enterprises, noncash transactions, and stock positions. Statistics are compiled from forms submitted to domestic banks and by enterprises to the compiler.
Enterprise surveys (ES)	These surveys collect aggregate data on enterprise activity.
Collections from persons and households	These data provide information on the circumstances of individuals and household units (for example, migration statistics and surveys of travelers).
Official sources n.i.e. = not included elsewhere	"Official sources n.i.e." are not mentioned elsewhere and include sources that measure the activities of the official sector and those that are by-products of administrative systems.
Partner country and international organization	These sources provide data available from foreign government agencies and international organizations.

Source: IMF, *Balance of Payments Compilation Guide* (Washington: International Monetary Fund, 1995).

Data Sources and Special Issues in Economies in Transition

As indicated in Box 4.5, there are several sources of data for the balance of payments, including the *International Trade Statistics* (*ITS*), the *International Transaction Reporting System* (*ITRS*), *Enterprise Surveys* (*ES*), collections from households based on specialized statistical surveys, and partner country data. In compiling balance of payments statistics, economies in transition have experienced acute difficulties with the coverage and valuation of transactions, in part because the data collected under central planning were not designed for preparing a balance of payments. Also, since the state controlled the external trade sector, there was no need to survey private traders. During the transition phase, new institutions are being put in place to record all transactions according to international standards. In the meantime, estimates of the balance of payments for these economies should be used with caution, since they are based on poor-quality data, especially in terms of coverage. There are three principal issues to consider when analyzing these data: the weakness of the sources, the pervasive problem of underreporting, and the difficulty of accurate valuation.

Weaknesses in Data

Data may be unreliable because the information is not collected properly or does not provide complete coverage. Customs records are often incomplete because border monitoring is not adequate. Enterprise surveys have seen their coverage deteriorate in the initial phases of transition, perhaps reflecting the greater autonomy given to enterprises (statistics for private enterprises and individual traders are especially deficient). The domestic banking system as a source of data is also weak. While data from the banking system are probably more complete than enterprise survey data, they are not necessarily reported to the central bank in a systematic fashion. More importantly, many financial transactions are settled outside the banking system, reducing the comprehensiveness of these data.

Underreporting

The integrity of data can also be compromised if transactions are not fully reported. *Unmeasured capital flight* is a major problem in countries where confidence in the domestic currency is low. If the authorities suspect that trade is not being reported, they can often cross-check data on imports (exports) against data on the exports (imports) of trading partners. Cross-checks can also be made with other domestic data for selected items. (For example, motor vehicle registrations can be used to assess the validity of recorded motor vehicle imports.) *Cross-border transactions* such as enterprise arrears have also been seriously underreported in many countries. The available information usually consists only of arrears notified to banks.

Valuation Problems

Valuation practices vary considerably across countries, especially when it comes to the valuation of barter trade. Although in principle *transaction prices* should be used, some countries use alternative measures such as world market prices, enterprise producer prices (for exports), and domestic wholesale prices (for imports).

Analyzing the External Position[7]

Notions of Balance

Under the double-entry accounting system, the sum of credit items equals the sum of debit items, so that the overall balance is zero. How then is it possible to have imbalances—surpluses or deficits—in the external sector accounts? A surplus or a deficit arises when a given subgroup of external transactions (shown above the line) is distinguished from another subgroup of transactions (shown below the line). If the above-the-line transactions are in deficit, then the below-the-line transactions are in surplus, and vice versa.

One of the primary purposes of the balance of payments accounts is to provide an indication of the need to adjust an external imbalance. The decision on where to draw the dividing line for analytical purposes requires a somewhat subjective judgment concerning the imbalances that best indicate the need for adjustment. One approach involves distinguishing a subgroup of items that are autonomously determined from transactions that are determined by policy.

The *trade balance* is the difference between exports and imports of goods. From an analytical point of view, it is somewhat arbitrary to distinguish goods from services. For example, a unit of foreign exchange earned by a freight company strengthens the balance of payments to the same extent as the foreign exchange earned by exporters of goods. Nonetheless, the trade balance is useful in practice, since it is often a timely indicator of trends in the current account balance. The customs authorities are often able to provide data on trade in goods long before data on trade in services—which takes longer to collect—is available.

The *current account balance*, one of the most useful indicators of an external imbalance, is the difference between credits and debits of goods, services, income, and transfers.[8] As explained below, the current account measures the component of the change in an economy's net foreign asset position attributable to transactions in goods and services.

A current account deficit does not necessarily indicate a need for a policy adjustment, since a deficit may be a temporary imbalance caused by a drop in export prices. But a current account deficit that persists necessitates policy adjustments, since a country cannot continue to finance deficits indefinitely by borrowing abroad or running down international reserves.

The *overall balance* equals the current account balance plus all capital and financial transactions that are not considered to be financing items. In analytical presentations of the balance of payments, changes in net foreign assets of the monetary authorities and nonautonomous financing items are placed below the line. The overall balance is an important indicator of the external payments position. Deficits are usually financed by a decline in net foreign assets that illustrates the extent to which the central bank has been financing payments imbalances (in the case of a fixed exchange rate regime) or regulating imbalances indirectly by intervening in exchange markets (in the case of a floating exchange rate regime).

Analyzing the Current Account

The key relationship between the balance of payments and a country's aggregate income and absorption has been discussed in Chapter 2. Ex post, the current account balance is identical to the economy's resource gap (as measured by the difference

[7]The discussion in this section is based on concepts derived from the *Balance of Payments Manual*, Fourth Edition, since many countries have yet to shift to the Fifth Edition. Moreover, analytical and policy discussions around the world continue to be conducted on the basis of the terminology of the Fourth Edition.

[8]The Fifth Edition of the *Manual* includes only current transfers in this definition (see Box 4.2).

between economywide saving and investment). Thus,

$$S - I = CAB = X - M + Y_f + TR_f. \qquad (4.1)$$

Therefore, any analysis of the current account of the balance of payments must consider how changes in saving and investment come about. As seen from equation 4.1, a change in the current account position (such as an increase in the surplus or a decrease in the deficit) must be matched by an increase in national saving relative to investment. Thus, it is important to understand how any policy measures designed to alter the current account balance (through, for example, exchange rates, tariffs, quotas, or export incentives) affect saving and investment behavior.

The current account also reflects the gap between income and absorption in the economy. Thus,

$$GNDI - A = CAB. \qquad (4.2)$$

As this relationship indicates, improving a country's current account balance requires that resources be released either through a decrease in domestic absorption relative to income or through an increase in national income relative to the rise in absorption. It should be noted, however, that equations 4.1 and 4.2 by themselves do not provide sufficient information for an analysis of the current account, because they do not reflect the various interactions and behavior of agents in the economy. For example, changes in absorption are influenced by changes in disposable income, so that equation 4.2 cannot be used to analyze directly the impact of a change in income on the external current account. The two equations nevertheless incorporate the basic macroeconomic framework in which the current account is embedded.

By definition, the current account balance is always matched by net claims on the rest of the world—in other words, the change in net foreign assets of nonbank entities or nonmonetary financial flows (ΔFI) and the change in net foreign assets of the banking system or monetary financial flows (ΔRES). This relationship, which is summarized below, derives from the balance of payments identity, which states that the sum of all credit items must be offset exactly by the sum of all debit items. Therefore,

$$-CAB = \Delta FI + \Delta RES$$

or

$$CAB + \Delta FI + \Delta RES = 0. \qquad (4.3)$$

Equation 4.3 shows that the net provision of resources to or from the rest of the world—as measured by the current account balance[9]—is matched by a corresponding change in net claims on the rest of the world. For example, a current account surplus is reflected either in an increase in net official or private claims on nonresidents or in the acquisition of reserve assets by the monetary authorities. But a current account deficit implies that the net acquisition of resources from the rest of the world must be paid for by either liquidating the country's foreign assets or by increasing its liabilities to nonresidents. Thus, the balance of payments identity shown in equation 4.3 can be viewed as the budget constraint for the entire economy.

As we have seen above, the current account reflects saving and investment of the government and nongovernment sectors. A given current account balance may be consistent with a number of combinations of private and public saving and investment behavior. For example, a deficit in the current account could stem from a private consumption boom or a sharp rise in investment or it could be brought about by a sharp deterioration in the fiscal position, with or without an improvement in private sector saving. Thus the current account balance per se, while an important indicator, is not, by itself, indicative of the need for policy action and even less of the appropriate policy response. It is nevertheless useful as a warning signal—a "red flag"—that alerts policymakers to the possibility of unsound policy. In all cases, the need for policy response and the choice of the appropriate policy will depend on a closer examination of the source of the imbalance.

The conventional view that a large current account deficit, whether originating in decisions of the private or the public sector, is a cause for concern and appropriate corrective action on the part of the government has recently come under some scrutiny in an influential paper. Max Corden[10] analyzed the validity of the "new view" of the current account, viz. the view that if the current account deficit reflects entirely the decisions of private savers and investors, then it should not call forth any governmental policy response. As Corden noted, while the new view has an apparent plausibility in a world dominated by private capital flows, it needs to be heavily qualified on several counts. A private spending boom financed by capital inflows could be based on unsound judgments and could end abruptly. Private external borrowing can have

[9]Given the definition of the current account balance (CAB) in equation 4.1, it follows that a negative balance is a current account deficit and a positive one is a surplus for the compiling country.

[10]W. Max Corden, "Does the Current Account Matter?" *International Financial Policy: Essays in Honor of Jacques J. Polak* (International Monetary Fund, Netherlands Bank, 1991).

spillover effects on other domestic borrowers, in effect, contaminating all debts by residents and therefore the risks of such contamination need to be watched by the authorities. The changes in the real exchange rate brought about as a result of the current account balance also need to be watched carefully by the authorities because they could reverse themselves and lead to general macroeconomic instability. In sum, the macroeconomic consequences of unsustainable current account imbalances are too severe for the authorities to take a "hands-off" attitude toward such imbalances. As a general rule, therefore, the "new view," sometimes called the "Lawson doctrine," is not valid.

This framework for analyzing the current account balance can be used in many situations independently of the exchange rate regime. For example, if the exchange rate is pegged, then the net demand or supply of foreign exchange at the pegged exchange rate will determine the reserve assets transactions (ΔRES). At the other extreme, under a pure float and with no official intervention, $\Delta RES = 0$, and so $CAB = -\Delta FI$. With a managed float, foreign exchange is bought or sold by the central bank in order to adjust the path of the exchange rate.[11] Under a fixed-exchange regime and little capital mobility, countries can afford to run current account deficits only for a limited time period. If a country continues to run a deficit beyond what can be financed through sustainable capital inflows, sooner or later, expectations about an exchange rate devaluation will trigger a foreign exchange crisis well before international reserves are exhausted.[12] This suggests that in the absence of capital mobility and under an exchange rate peg, the current account must be monitored closely so as to avoid a sudden speculative attack on a currency and a balance of payments crisis.

For a discussion of the issue of how to assess the sustainability of a current account position, see Box 4.6.

Analyzing the Trade Account

Changes in the Structure of Trade

An analysis of trade flows requires information such as the commodity structure, the geographical destination of exports and the origin of imports. A summary of such information is shown for Poland in Tables 4.3 and 4.4. Data on trade flows (desegregated by trading partners) are available in the IMF's *Direction of Trade Statistics*.[13]

With more detailed information on values, prices, and volumes of desegregated trade, analysts can answer questions such as the following:

- Is the change in the terms of trade concentrated in a few commodities that are particularly important or whose prices are prone to wide fluctuations? In this context, it is often useful to have separate data on energy and nonenergy prices, since oil products often have significant weight in imports (or exports, in the case of the oil-producing countries). Agricultural exporters may focus particularly on developments in agricultural prices and the volume of agricultural exports.
- Are the changes in exports and imports concentrated in particular geographical regions? This question is particularly important for the states of the former Soviet Union and members of the now-defunct Council for Mutual Economic Assistance (CMEA), as they integrate themselves fully into the world economy.

Trade Policies

Along with exchange rate policies and the state of domestic and foreign demand, trade flows are affected in an important way by trade policies, comprising tariffs, import or export quotas, import or export subsidies, and other incentives or disincentives to trade. Trade policy strategies are broadly divided into two groups, *outward-oriented* and *inward-oriented*. An outwardly oriented strategy is one based on trade policies that do not discriminate between production for the domestic market and exports or between purchases of domestic goods and foreign goods. This neutral or nondiscriminatory strategy is sometimes referred to as an export-promotion strategy. Evidence suggests that most successful exporting economies (such as those in East Asia) followed

[11]The above analysis draws on "Selected Issues in Balance of Payments Analysis" in the 1993 *Manual*.

[12]See Paul Krugman, "A Model of Balance-of-Payments Crises," *Journal of Money, Credit, and Banking*, Vol. II, No. 3 (August 1979).

[13]The quarterly publication of the IMF, *Direction of Trade Statistics* (DOTS), presents current data on the value of merchandise exports and imports for member countries, disaggregated according to their most important trading partners. Data that are not current are supplemented by estimates. The publication includes world trade and industrial and developing country aggregates, as well as data on individual countries. Data are presented in U.S. dollars, converted at period average exchange rates. The data in the DOTS are an internationally recognized source of statistics on trade and are invaluable in analyzing trade flows.

Box 4.6.
Current Account Sustainability

A current account surplus implies that the country is accumulating net international assets (broadly defined). Conversely, a current account deficit implies that it is running down its foreign assets or accumulating foreign liabilities. Thus, the current account can also be defined as the change in the net international investment position of a country. When this position is negative, the country is a net debtor to the rest of the world. Countries, like individuals, are bound by an intertemporal budget constraint; therefore, if the country is a net debtor, then the economy must run current account surpluses in the future with a present discounted value equal to its initial net debt. This ability to generate future current account surpluses (excluding interest payments) sufficient to repay existing debt is known as *solvency*. Thus, a country is solvent if the present value of future current account surpluses is at least equal to its current external debt.

The notion of solvency, while important, is not easy to assess in practice, because if large enough future current account surpluses are assumed, any path of current account deficits can be consistent with intertemporal solvency. A more restricted notion of sustainability can be defined by assuming a continuation of present policies into the future under an unchanged macroeconomic environment. Thus, the current stance of policies is "sustainable" if its continuation in the future does not violate the solvency or budget constraint. In practice, the notion of current account sustainability is more complex because it reflects the interaction between saving and investment decisions of foreign investors. An alternative way of assessing current account sustainability is to ask whether the current account and the underlying behavior of the government and the private sector, if continued, would entail the need for a drastic shift in policies or a crisis (e.g., an exchange rate collapse or an external debt default). If the answer is yes, the current account deficit is unsustainable. The policy change or the crisis can be triggered by a domestic or external shock, involving a shift in investor confidence, brought about by a change in their perception of the country's ability or willingness to meet its external obligations.[1]

[1]See Gian Maria Milesi-Ferretti and Assaf Razin, "Persistent Current Account Deficits: A Warning Signal?" *International Journal of Finance and Economics*, Vol. 1, No. 3 (July 1996).

broadly neutral trade policies.[14] By contrast, an inwardly oriented trade strategy is one that uses trade and industrial incentives that favor production for the home over the export market.

Measuring the extent to which a trade policy regime—involving numerous tariffs, quotas, and export subsidies—departs from the idea of neutrality is a complex task. Several different indicators of the *bias of a trade regime* have been developed in the literature on the analysis of trade policies (see Box 4.7). Quantitative restrictions on trade and a complex structure of tariffs are still common in many transition economies. Often, however, adequate information to construct indicators of bias in the trade policy regime may not be available, and a rough-and-ready assessment of the neutrality of the regime needs to be made. It is important to take into account the four principal factors that determine the overall structure of incentives for exportables: (i) the degree of any exchange rate overvaluation; (ii) the use of direct controls on trade such as quotas and import licenses; (iii) the effective rate of protection; and (iv) the use of export incentives, including direct and indirect export subsidies.[15]

It is important to understand the extent to which the volume of trade has been affected by policy, both domestic and foreign. Certain domestic policy measures in particular influence the course of trade. Reductions in quotas give enterprises and the private sector increased autonomy to import and export. Changes in taxes on traded goods and services (such as reductions in import duties, the lifting of export taxes, and domestic price liberalization) encourage trade. A stable ex-

[14]For a comprehensive discussion of the issues in assessing a country's trade policies and a synthesis of the literature on the empirical evidence on trade policy regimes, see Vinod Thomas and John Nash, *Best Practices in Trade Policy Reform* (New York: Oxford University Press, 1991); for a brief summary of the book's conclusions, see Vinod Thomas and John Nash, "Reform of Trade Policy: Recent Evidence from Theory and Practice," *The World Bank Research Observer*, Vol. 5, No. 2 (July 1991). For a discussion of the inward vs. outwart-looking strategies, see Jagdish N. Bhagwati, "Export-Promoting Trade Strategy: Issues and Evidence," *The World Bank Research Observer*, Vol. 3, No. 1 (January 1988).

[15]For a fuller discussion of the analytical and policy issues in trade policy, see Max W. Corden, *Protection and Liberalization: A Review of Analytical Issues*," IMF Occasional Paper No. 54 (Washington: International Monetary Fund, 1987), and Sebastian Edwards, "Openness, Trade Liberalization, and Growth in Developing Countries," *Journal of Economic Literature*, Vol. XXXI (September 1993).

Box 4.7.
Measuring Neutrality of Trade Regimes[1]

A widely used measure of the bias in trade regimes is based on the notion of effective protection. The trade bias (t_b) is defined as:[1]

$$t_b = \frac{\text{Average effective rate of protection for importables}}{\text{Average effective rate of protection for exportables}} \quad (1)$$

where the effective rate of protection (ERP) for any good captures the protection accorded to the value added in its production and not to the finished product. It is given by

$$ERP = \frac{v' - v}{v} \quad (2)$$

where

v' = Value added at domestic prices including tariffs or subsidies; and
v = Value added at world prices.[2]

It is important to note that

- A t_b ratio of 1 implies neutrality while a ratio greater than one implies that importables have on average higher protection (nominal or effective, as the case may be) than exportables. This implies a bias in favor of import substitution. A ratio of less than one implies a bias in favor of export promotion.
- The use of any aggregate measure of protection for the economy as a whole can be misleading since the effective rate of protection averaged across different industries can be zero (i.e., implying no protection) while in fact the rates of protection vary widely across industries. Full neutrality of a trade regime must therefore require no significant variation across the tradable goods industries.

[1]This box draws on the discussion of the neutrality of trade regimes in *World Development Report 1987* (Washington: Oxford University Press for the World Bank, 1987).
[2]If v' and v stand for the domestic and world prices of a good, then the same formula as in equation 2 would yield the *nominal rate of protection*, and a simpler indicator of trade orientation can be constructed using nominal rather than effective rates of protection of importables and exportables as shown in equation 2.

change rate regime promotes confidence in an economy's stability.

Policy changes in countries that are primary trading partners can also significantly affect trade. Changes in quantitative trade restrictions and tariff barriers in partner countries encourage exports. Special trade agreements, especially regional trade agreements, facilitate cross-border trade within a specified geographic area.

An important objective in analyzing trade developments is to identify those policy changes that have had a significant impact on trade movements. In macroeconomic analysis, there is a trade-off between obtaining the richer understanding a detailed analysis offers and identifying the main structural trends that are most important for projecting aggregate trade. Merchandise trade flows are influenced by a variety of factors that affect the supply of and demand for traded goods, but macroeconomic analysis focuses primarily on domestic and foreign demand and the relative prices of traded goods, which are in turn affected by changes in the exchange rate. Analyzing demand in the domestic and principal foreign markets throws light on the factors affecting the volumes of imports and exports, respectively. Demand in the domestic economy can also influence a country's exports—for example, by making exporting attractive in a period of slack domestic demand.

The most critical influence on trade flows in the long run may well be price competitiveness, which generally is measured by the real exchange rate or the nominal exchange rate adjusted for changes in relative unit labor costs at home as compared with those in trading partner countries (Box 4.8). In transition and developing economies, where data on

Box 4.8.
Assessing the Exchange Rate[1]

Assessing the appropriateness of a country's exchange rate is a complex undertaking that requires taking into account a number of factors. The following indicators are often considered relevant to this assessment.

1. The real exchange rate

The level of the real exchange rate is frequently used as an indicator of the need for exchange rate adjustment. A measure of the real exchange rate based on the ratio of unit labor costs (wage costs adjusted for the productivity of labor) at home to those in trading partner countries or, in the absence of unit labor cost indexes, an index of relative consumer prices, is the most appropriate real exchange rate indicator. It is common to compare the current real exchange rate with the real exchange rate at some date in the past when the current account was considered to be in a satisfactory condition.

2. Foreign exchange reserves

Falling official reserves can indicate an inappropriate exchange rate. The fall in reserves can reflect either a current account deficit or a movement of funds out of the domestic currency on the capital and financial account, suggesting that residents and foreigners lack confidence in the country's policies. However, because foreign exchange reserves can be augmented by borrowing, and central banks can make reserves look larger than they are, movements in foreign assets may not be a good indicator of the need to adjust the exchange rate.

3. The current account

The size of the present and prospective levels of the current account balance are a major criterion for judging the appropriateness of the exchange rate. Under a fixed exchange rate regime, if projections of the current account deficit show that it cannot be financed by drawing down reserves or through continuous borrowing, a devaluation will eventually be necessary. This criterion suggests that a devaluation may be appropriate even if the current account is not at present in deficit. If, however, a current account deficit is temporary, a devaluation may not be needed. The current account balance may not always be a good indicator because it reacts relatively slowly to changes in the real exchange rate.

4. The parallel market exchange rate

Many countries have parallel or black markets for foreign exchange. The exchange rate prevailing in these markets often provides a reasonable indication of the degree of disequilibrium in the official exchange rate. However, as these markets can be thin and subject to the influence of a few dealers, caution is needed in interpreting this indicator. A very large discount on domestic currency in the parallel market, however, is often an indicator of an overvalued exchange rate.

[1]Based on Stanley Fischer, "Devaluation and Inflation," *The Open Economy*, EDI Series in Economic Development (Washington: Economic Development Institute of the World Bank, 1992).

unit labor costs are generally not available, a real exchange rate based on relative consumer prices often serves as a useful proxy for a cost-based measure of competitiveness. It is useful to compare the prevailing exchange rate with the exchange rate during a period in the past when the trade or the current account was considered to be in broad balance.[16] As noted above, changes in the trade policy regime, including tariffs and quotas, can also have a major influence on trade flows. And in many economies, it is also important to consider nonprice aspects of competitiveness such as quality, timely delivery, and packaging, particularly when exporters are attempting to break into new markets, as they often do in transition economies.

[16]The equilibrium rate may change over time because of changes in economic fundamentals such as the rates of productivity growth, technological progress, terms of trade, and the policy regime (including trade barriers and capital controls).

Services, Income, and Transfers

Service transactions are a heterogeneous group, comprising 11 different categories in the standard presentation of the balance of payments. The major subgroups include transportation and travel (credits reflecting tourist receipts and debits reflecting spending abroad by residents), insurance, financial, and consultancy services.

Income covers both labor income and financial income flows. Labor income refers to earnings of nonresident workers. Financial income (or "investment income, net") represents receipts from and payments on financial assets and liabilities. For indebted countries, interest payments due on external foreign debt often constitute the largest income subitem. This negative item is also one of the two components of debt servicing. The important credit items are *interest earned on foreign exchange reserves* and, for creditor countries, *interest received on loans*.

Changes in *general government current transfers* are largely dependent on decisions made by donor countries and therefore can be less predictable. The main component of private current transfers is usually workers' remittances, which reflect the number of workers living abroad permanently and the incentives for transferring funds, particularly expectations concerning the exchange rate and the taxation of such income.[17]

To the extent that a country modifies its restrictions on service transactions by liberalizing the amounts of foreign exchange provided for foreign travel abroad, it is appropriate to identify the impact of such policy changes.[18]

The Capital and Financial Account and External Debt

As we have seen, a current account deficit must be financed by increases in foreign liabilities or by declines in foreign assets. These financial flows constitute the capital and financial account of the balance of payments.[19] This section examines these flows (excluding movements in net reserve assets).

The capital and financial account records an economy's net foreign borrowing and capital transfers. The nonmonetary financial flows (ΔFI) that make up the account are the sum of foreign direct investment (FDI) and net foreign borrowing (NFB) and, together with monetary financing (ΔRES), equal the current account balance.[20] Thus, the sources of current account financing can be summarized as

$$CAB + FDI + NFB + \Delta RES \equiv 0. \tag{4.4}$$

The financial flows associated with a current account deficit involve a reduction in the net foreign asset position of the economy. Therefore, as discussed above, an important policy issue a current account deficit raises is whether the government can service the associated change in the net foreign investment position without modifying its economic policies—for example, by reducing absorption—or by bringing about changes in interest or exchange rates. In general, servicing the debt is easier if capital inflow is used to increase productive capacity. If a spontaneous financial inflow does not result, the government must adjust its policies to attract private investment or, alternatively, seek borrowing abroad. If it does neither of these things, it will need to draw down its international reserves. If the reserves have been already depleted, the country may be forced to endure an unplanned adjustment in its absorption. It is far better to have a planned, orderly adjustment program that can forestall the haphazard adjustment forced on a country when foreign financing is not available.

Debt Stocks and Debt-Creating Flows

The stock of *gross external debt* can be defined as the amount of outstanding contractual liabilities to nonresidents. The amount of debt outstanding covers only that part of a loan that has actually been disbursed. Any undisbursed loan commitments are not part of gross debt and are not recorded in balance of payments data until disbursement takes place. The term *contractual* is also an important part of the definition of gross debt. Debt instruments such as long-term loans, bonds, short-term loans, and trade credits involve contractual obligations to pay interest (either at a fixed or variable rate) and principal. Incurring these obligations adds to a country's gross debt.

Within the capital and financial account, most flows are *debt creating*. There is therefore a link between the stock of gross debt and the flows recorded in the capital and financial account. The major links are captured in the following equation as

$$D_t = D_{t-1} + B_t - A_t \tag{4.5}$$

where

D_t = Stock of outstanding and disbursed debt at the end of period

B_t = Disbursements of new loans during time period t

A_t = Amortization of debt during time period t.

This equation states that debt at the end of a given year is broadly equal to debt at the end of the previous year, augmented by net debt-creating flows—that is, by new disbursements minus amortization (repayments of principal).

[17]For balance of payments recording purposes, remittances from workers living abroad for more than 12 months (classified under "current transfers") are distinguished from labor income earned by workers living abroad temporarily for less than 12 months (classified under "compensation of employees").

[18]Transportation services will be underestimated to the extent that trade is underestimated; the presence of strict controls on foreign travel may lead to parallel market activity (and hence underrecording); other services may be underreported owing to inadequate surveys.

[19]In countries where the Fourth Edition of the *Manual* is still being used, the major counterpart of the current account may be referred to as the "capital account." The Fifth Edition of the *Manual* recognizes that the term "capital account" is imprecise, since most transactions are purely financial, and thus renames it the "capital and financial account."

[20]See footnote 16 in Chapter 5 on Monetary Accounts and Analysis.

Equation 4.5 can be only a rough approximation, for many reasons. First, debt stocks are subject to valuation adjustments owing to the fact that debt is contracted in various currencies. The stock of debt, measured (for example) in U.S. dollars, may change because the value of debt denominated in another currency (such as the deutsche mark) changes in dollar terms when the dollar depreciates or appreciates against that currency. Second, interest is sometimes capitalized, adding to the stock of debt any unpaid interest obligations (interest arrears). Third, outstanding debt is sometimes canceled or written off.

It is clear from the above discussion that debt-creating flows contained in the capital and financial account of the balance of payments should be viewed in the context of a country's gross external indebtedness.[21]

Indicators of External Debt

When a country borrows abroad, it must "service" the loan by paying interest at a rate specified in the loan contract and by paying back principal (amortization) over an agreed time period. The interest component is found in the current account (under "income, debits"), while amortization is recorded in the capital and financial account. In general, countries that have borrowed heavily abroad in the past must devote a sizable portion of their export receipts to servicing foreign debt, limiting the amount of foreign exchange left for financing imports. In assessing the cost of debt servicing, it is useful to relate these costs to total exports of goods and services.

Measuring the debt burden raises a number of complex issues. Conventionally, the debt burden is calculated as the stock of debt in relation to an index of available resources, such as exports of goods and services or gross domestic product (GDP). But such indices do not capture the impact of debt relief or of lower interest rates on the cost of servicing the debt. Conceptually, analysts should compare the present value of future debt servicing obligations with the present value of future export receipts. This approach requires a certain amount of information and can be sensitive to the discount rate used to calculate the present value. In practice, then, three ratios are used to analyze the debt burden:

- the ratio of scheduled debt service payments to exports of goods and services, which measures the impact of debt servicing obligations on the foreign exchange cash flow;
- the ratio of scheduled (or actual) interest payments to exports of goods and services, which measures the current cost of the debt stock; and
- total outstanding debt as a ratio of GDP (or of exports of goods and services), which reflects the long-term sustainability of the debt burden.

The World Bank's debt reporting system uses critical values of two debt indicators to classify countries according to the severity of their indebtedness: the ratio of the present value of total debt service (*PV*) to GNP, and the ratio of the present value of total debt service to total exports.[22] The indicators are based on the present value concept rather than the value of scheduled debt service in order to account for differences in the terms of the loans. A country is regarded as severely indebted if the present value of total debt service to GNP exceeds 80 percent or if the present value of total debt service to exports exceeds 220 percent.

Although these ratios may be helpful in signaling possible debt problems, the economic circumstances of countries with similar ratios may differ. These ratios should therefore be used with caution and only as a starting point for a country-specific analysis of debt sustainability. A full assessment of a country's debt position must take into account the overall macroeconomic situation and balance of payments prospects. Box 4.9 discusses the sustainability of external debt.

An issue of increasing concern has been the fiscal burden of external debt. In many countries with external debt difficulties, scheduled debt service payments absorb a major proportion of government revenues, reducing the government's room to maneuver in terms of fiscal adjustment. External debt sustainability is therefore closely linked to fiscal sustainability.

[21]Gross debt is defined in terms of *liabilities*. A concept of net debt can be derived by subtracting the stock of external assets from gross liabilities. Although such a notion might be useful in countries that are both debtors and creditors (for instance, Russia), there are a number of practical difficulties in defining net debt. Currently, there is no internationally accepted definition of net debt, largely because (i) it is unclear which assets should offset liabilities—for example, should only official assets be used, or should bank and nonbank assets also be included; (ii) a net debt total would mask important differences in the maturity structure, currency composition, and risk features of liabilities and assets; (iii) debt-reporting systems may not record all gross flows in assets and liabilities; and (iv) linking debt servicing to net debt may disguise the seriousness of a country's debt problem if assets broadly offset liabilities. For example, the quality of credit owed by Russia differs from the quality of credit owed to Russia. It would therefore be difficult to interpret the meaning of net debt service and net debt indicators. For these reasons, in this chapter, "total debt" will always refer to *gross* debt.

[22] See *World Debt Tables, 1994–95*, Vol. 1 (Washington: World Bank, 1994).

Box 4.9.
The Sustainability of External Debt

A country's external position is considered sustainable if the government can be expected to meet its external obligations in full without rescheduling its debt, seeking debt relief, or accumulating arrears over the medium or long term. The key indicators for assessing sustainability are:

- The ratio of scheduled debt service to exports of goods and services;
- The external financing gap that remains after allowing for expected inflows in the form of grant receipts, loan disbursements, and any commercial capital flows; and
- The ratio of the net present value (NPV) of the debt to exports. The NPV is defined as the discounted present value of all future debt service payments due on existing external debt, relative to the discounted value of the export receipts.

A country's external debt position is generally considered sustainable over the projection period if scheduled debt service payments decline to 20–25 percent or less of exports of goods and services, if financing gaps are eliminated, and if the ratio of the NPV of debt-to-exports declines to below 200–250 percent of exports.

The concept of sustainability differs importantly from that of medium-term *external viability*, which precludes recourse to further exceptional financing (such as the use of IMF resources). If exceptional financing is necessary, a country's external position cannot be regarded as viable.

Box 4.10.
Direct Foreign Investment[1]

Foreign direct investment takes place when a firm in one country creates or expands a subsidiary in another. The distinctive feature of this type of capital inflow is that it involves not only a transfer of resources, but also the acquisition of partial or full control. Foreign direct investment is valued by countries not only because it does not create a debt obligation for the receiving country, but also because it is an important vehicle for the transfer of technical and managerial skills from abroad. The benefits of such technology transfers are often seen as outweighing the capital flow itself.

This thinking explains why it is not only developing and transition economies that are keen to implement policies that attract foreign investment flows, but also industrial countries. It should be noted that such investment inflows do give rise to some outward resource transfers when the profits and dividends on the investment are repatriated. However, these flows depend on the profitability of the investment and are not binding like contractual debt service payments. Multinational firms are the main vehicles through which the bulk of foreign direct investment takes place.

[1]For an analysis of the role of foreign direct investment in international capital flows, see Edward M. Graham, "Foreign Direct Investment in the World Economy," IMF Working Paper 95/59 (Washington: International Monetary Fund, 1995).

Direct Foreign Investment and Capital Flows

Direct Foreign Investment

When investors acquire equity in a domestic enterprise, there are no contractual obligations. Because direct *foreign* investment does not add to external debt, it is termed "non-debt-creating" (see Box 4.10). In this sense, it contrasts with all other liabilities of the financial account, which either add to gross debt (in the case of inflows) or subtract from it (in the case of repayments such as amortization).

Within the debt-creating flows, it is useful to isolate *portfolio* investment, which includes debt and equity securities.[23] These are increasingly important to countries that have access to international capital markets, which indicates that foreign investors have confidence in the financial condition of the country issuing these debt instruments. Besides securities, portfolio investment also includes relatively newer money market debt instruments (including tradable financial derivatives) that allow debtors to hedge against exchange rate or interest rate risks.

In addition to examining liabilities by type and maturity of debt instruments, it is also helpful to analyze trends in stocks and flows by institutional sector.[24] In particular, the general government sector and the nongovernment sector (which can be split

[23]An investor acquiring equity securities as portfolio investment will have no significant influence over the operation of enterprises.

[24]The definition of debt does not mention the loan maturity, or loan repayment periods. Some liabilities, such as bridging loans, have very short repayment periods and can exhibit volatile behavior, but flows of long-term liabilities are more predictable. For this reason, stocks and flows of short-term liabilities (which are defined as maturing in less than one year) are usually distinguished from medium and long-term liabilities with repayment periods of more than one year.

between banks and enterprises) are analyzed separately, since they have separate determinants. Government flows are determined mainly by budgetary needs. The net financial flows of the government, as recorded in the balance of payments, should be identical to the external financing flows of the budget (ignoring any valuation adjustments resulting from exchange rate movements, since a country's budget is presented in local currency terms).[25]

Capital Flows

In contrast, flows of private capital respond to yields on assets held domestically and abroad. With the growing integration of world financial markets, and as more economies develop domestic financial market instruments, a growing volume of private capital flows should be seen as normal and desirable. However, in many transition economies, domestic financial market instruments are underdeveloped, and the outflow of private capital (often not recorded in official statistics) reflects a lack of confidence in the domestic economy, especially in the presence of high inflation, a depreciating exchange rate, and the expectation that yields from domestic financial assets will be inferior to the risk-adjusted yields from foreign financial assets (Box 4.11).

Reserves and Financing

Gross and Net Reserve Assets

The use of gross reserves has traditionally been the main source of financing balance of payments deficits and for supporting an exchange rate peg. In today's world of floating exchange rates, however, many countries find other means of financing imbalances, including foreign borrowing or changing domestic policies. Thus, as they are acquired and used, gross reserve assets do not necessarily reflect the size of a payments imbalance. The monetary authorities may also have other motives for holding reserves—for instance, to maintain confidence in the domestic currency and economy, to satisfy domestic legal requirements, or to serve as a basis for foreign borrowing. Analysts should keep these considerations in mind in examining the reasons for changes in reserves. Net foreign assets are calculated as gross foreign assets minus foreign liabilities of the banking system.

Using Reserve Assets to Finance a Deficit

Fundamentally, the appropriateness of using reserve assets to finance a current account deficit rather than adjusting domestic policies depends on the extent to which the deficit is regarded as temporary or reversible. The size of a country's reserve assets and its ability to borrow to supplement these assets limit the extent to which reserves can be used to finance a deficit. In the case of temporary shocks, such as poor harvests, reserves can be a useful shock absorber, allowing for a temporary excess of absorption over income. Reserves can also be used to finance a seasonal swing in the current account balance. If the current account imbalance is expected to persist, however, adjustment measures will be necessary. It is important to note that in practice, it is also difficult to judge ex ante whether a current account deficit is temporary or permanent. It may therefore be prudent to initiate some adjustment measures in conjunction with a drawdown of reserves (Box 4.8). Because reserve levels frequently function as signals to foreign investors indicating the policy and investment climate in the country (including the need for an exchange rate change), an adequate reserve level is important in sustaining investors' confidence.[26]

Recording Changes in Reserve Assets

With any definition of the overall balance, it is important to be clear about which transactions are included above the line and which appear below the line. From an analytical perspective, it is useful to group all autonomous transactions above the line and to place below the line transactions authorities control that can be used to finance autonomous flows. However, there are practical difficulties in distinguishing autonomous and policy-controlled transactions; for instance, two extremes of below-the-line classifications can be distinguished. One includes only movements in gross reserve assets held by the monetary authorities; the other, all transactions of the domestic banking system.

Under the first option, if changes in gross reserve assets are taken as the sole source of financing the

[25]Central governments in many countries often borrow not on their own account but to on-lend to public enterprises.

[26]See Paul Krugman, "A Model of Balance of Payments Crises," *Journal of Money, Credit, and Banking*, Vol. II, No. 3 (August 1979).

Box 4.11.
Capital Flows and the Balance of Payments

In recent years, capital flows have played an increasingly important role in the balance of payments of a number of countries. Capital flows, defined as the increase in net international indebtedness of an economy, are measured by the balance in the capital and financial account of the balance of payments (excluding reserve assets). In recent years, after a period of capital outflows and debt servicing difficulties, a number of developing countries in Asia and Latin America and some transition economies in Europe have begun to experience sizable capital inflows as nonresidents begin to invest in the economy and the flight of resident's capital is reversed. These capital inflows have helped to finance larger current account deficits associated with higher imports and higher economic growth. It also permitted buildup of reserves. Despite these benefits, the sudden surges of these sizable inflows have also caused some concern for economic policymakers, because of the difficulties that large-scale inflows of capital can cause for the management of macroeconomic policy (see next chapter on Monetary Accounts and Analysis). There are four important concerns:

- Capital inflows can be temporary and hence quickly reversed.
- Capital inflows can induce growth in the money supply and cause domestic inflation to rise if the monetary authorities intervene in the foreign exchange market to buy the excess supply of foreign exchange. These inflationary consequences can be avoided if the intervention is sterilized.
- If the monetary authorities do not intervene, the capital inflows can cause the exchange rate of the domestic currency to appreciate.
- Capital inflows can finance a temporary boom in consumption, which will eventually lead to a cutback in absorption in order to service the accumulated debt.[1]

[1]See Guillermo Calvo, Leonardo Leiderman, and Carmen Reinhart, "The Capital Flows Problem: Concepts and Issues," PPAA/93/10 (Washington: International Monetary Fund, 1993); and Guillermo Calvo, Ratna Sahay, and Carlos Végh, "Capital Flows in Central and Eastern Europe: Evidence and Policy Options," IMF Working Paper 95/57 (Washington: International Monetary Fund, 1995).

above-the-line transactions, then any liabilities of the central bank are necessarily classified above the line. However, some central bank liabilities are special, in that they allow gross reserves to be reconstituted. For example, if a central bank decides to use IMF credit (recorded as an increase in liabilities), then gross reserve assets need not be run down. Another example of financing that augments reserves is borrowing abroad from a line of credit available to the central bank. It is therefore usual, in analytical presentations of the balance of payments, to include such reserve-related liabilities below the line. Thus, changes in net foreign assets are grouped below the line.

The second option—which is based on a much broader definition of net foreign assets—includes all transactions of the banking system below the line. However, commercial banks are usually free to choose their foreign asset and liability structure, and such flows are driven largely by market forces (that is, are autonomous transactions). It is only when the central bank has direct and effective control over commercial banks and foreign assets that these assets can be considered for inclusion below the line. Including changes in net foreign assets of the banking system below the line provides a direct link between balance of payments transactions and domestic liquidity creation. Chapter 5 on Monetary Accounts and Analysis provides a fuller discussion of the link between the swings in total net foreign assets and the domestic money supply.

Analytically then, the most useful definition of the overall balance places all transactions that are under the *direct control* of the monetary authorities below the line. These transactions include changes in gross reserve assets held by the monetary authorities, and easily identified fluctuations in central bank liabilities used to finance the balance of payments.

It is important to remember that the overall balance is not necessarily determined by the trade and capital accounts. Indeed, as discussion of the monetary approach to the balance of payments in Chapter 5 makes clear, the opposite may be true. An increase in the demand for a country's currency relative to other currencies may be reflected in an overall balance of payments deficit, in turn causing shifts in the current as well as financial and capital account balances. More generally, the changes in assets and liabilities of the banking system are closely linked to the overall balance of payments, and this link underpins the monetary approach to the balance of payments.[27]

[27]See *Theoretical Aspects of the Design of Fund-Supported Adjustment Programs*, IMF Occasional Paper No. 55 (Washington: International Monetary Fund, 1987).

Reserve Adequacy

Although conventionally, the level of reserves has been assessed in relation to the projected total import bill of goods and services, more recent indicators of reserve adequacy have focused on financial vulnerability.[28] Whichever indicator of foreign exchange adequacy is used, it is important to keep in mind that the nature of the exchange rate regime plays a part in determining the adequacy of the reserve level. Traditionally, as we have seen, the presumption has been that a country with a fixed exchange rate needs larger reserves than a country with a floating exchange rate regime, since reserves are the only cushion against shocks. However, in practice, if confidence in the authorities' ability to maintain supporting policies is high, a country with a fixed exchange rate may not require large reserves to defend its currency. For example, the Polish authorities were able to maintain a fixed exchange rate in the early stages of their reform program in 1991 despite only a moderate level of reserves, because their economic policies commanded a high degree of confidence in financial markets. Even with a managed float, a lack of credible economic policies can quickly lead to capital flight and may deplete reserves, even if the authorities allow the exchange rate to depreciate. Thus, at a fundamental level, the credibility of the authorities' economic policies and the confidence that market participants place in them are key to assessing the adequacy of reserves. Indeed, it is credible policies that allow the authorities to augment reserves by borrowing abroad at favorable terms; such borrowed reserves can potentially provide a major supplement to the country's own reserves. In the case of Poland, the stabilization fund provided by the IMF played an important role in boosting the credibility of policies, although the fund was never used.

Reserves in Relation to Imports

This indicator measures a country's gross international reserves in relation to its monthly import bill (annual import bill/12).[29] Thus,

$$\textit{Gross international reserves coverage in terms of months} = \frac{\textit{Gross international reserves}}{\textit{Monthly import bill}}.$$

A general rule of thumb has been that gross reserves should be equal to at least three months of imports. Countries with six months of import coverage enjoy a relatively comfortable reserve position. However, this rule of thumb evolved during a period when controls on international financial flows were much more extensive than they are today. Therefore, in assessing the appropriateness of the reserve level, analysts should keep in mind a number of factors, including (i) the openness of the capital and financial account; (ii) the stock of highly liquid liabilities; (iii) the country's access to short-term borrowing facilities; and (iv) the seasonality of imports and exports of the country.

The average level of import coverage, based on actual data for a sample of IMF members (excluding those whose external position is considered difficult) was 4.5 months of imports in 1994, appreciably above the three-month rule of thumb. However, the coverage level for the Baltic countries, Russia, and the other states of the former Soviet Union has been considerably lower, falling below the three-month benchmark in many cases.

Broader Concepts of Reserve Adequacy

In recent years, as world capital markets have become increasingly integrated and the size and volatility of private capital flows have risen sharply, the traditional notion of reserve adequacy (three months of import coverage) is being reassessed by policymakers as well as economic analysts. This reassessment has been prompted, in part, by the speed with which even a sizable level of international reserves can be depleted in the face of a crisis in confidence and the associated sudden capital outflow, as was demonstrated in Mexico in late 1994 and early 1995.

The debate on reserve adequacy in a world of volatile capital flows has focused on *indicators of financial vulnerability*. In this context, it has been noted that analysts must consider not only traditional flow variables (such as the external current account balance and the fiscal balance) but also stock variables (such as the ratio of domestic money supply, expressed in foreign currency, to the foreign currency value of international reserves).[30] The rationale be-

[28]Reserves provide an insurance against unforeseen changes in total foreign exchange outflows from the country. Therefore, a measure of expected payments is often considered the appropriate reference base. For example, if debt service payments are expected to be heavy, they can be added to the projected imports of goods and services.

[29]The indicator can also be expressed in terms of weeks of imports, or in extreme cases, days of imports, by adjusting the import bill accordingly.

[30]See Guillermo Calvo, "Capital Flows and Macroeconomic Management: Tequila Lessons," *International Journal of Finance and Economics*, Vol. 3 (July 1996).

hind this thinking is that international reserves are used to back domestic currency in the event of a crisis in confidence. Reserves also need to be considered in the context of the maturity structure of public sector liabilities. An excess of short-term liabilities in foreign currency increases a country's financial vulnerability. The degree of openness of both the economy, as reflected in the ratio of external trade to GDP, and the external capital account is also important. It helps to determine the extent of a country's exposure to risk from volatile capital flows and consequently affects the need for a larger reserve cushion to absorb unanticipated shocks.

In some cases, reserve holdings are related to the variability (variance) and/or volume of foreign exchange transactions. While these measures on their own are not good indicators of reserve adequacy, they are useful in assessing the need for reserves in countries with mature financial systems. A measure of reserve adequacy defined as the *ratio of reserves to the monetary base* has been found useful for countries desiring to shift to a fixed exchange rate in the form of a currency board. The rationale behind this indicator is that if gross international reserves are sufficient to cover base money, they provide a benchmark against which the adequacy of reserves to defend the exchange rate can be measured.

It should be noted that while the three-month import coverage and the monetary base rules tend, on average, to indicate that broadly similar levels of reserves are appropriate for countries with either pegged or managed floating exchange rates, most transition economies find the three-month rule overly demanding.

The quantitative indicators of reserve adequacy discussed above, while they provide useful rules of thumb, are not a substitute for a careful qualitative assessment of a country's macroeconomic situation and policies and of the financial markets' perception of those policies.

Exceptional Financing

By definition, the *overall* balance ex post is always in balance. Therefore, any disequilibrium will necessarily be financed by one of several methods. Besides using reserve assets and/or drawing on the IMF, countries may resort to exceptional financing arrangements to finance external payments imbalances. Exceptional financing arrangements include the following:

- exceptional grants, including debt forgiveness;
- the rescheduling of external debt obligations;
- the accumulation of arrears of principal and interest on foreign debt; and
- debt/equity swaps (exceptional direct investment).

Exceptional financing is not autonomous, since governments are often involved in negotiations to arrange it, especially in debt-burdened countries. Nor is it likely to be repeated year after year in predictable amounts. For these reasons, and since exceptional financing is controlled in part by the government and in part by foreign creditors, it is usual to isolate such transactions below the line in analyzing balance of payments developments—that is, to consider them as a special type of financing that will not be repeated on a regular basis.[31]

Developments in the Balance of Payments and the Exchange Rate

Since the inception of economic reform in 1990, Poland's foreign trade has expanded dramatically, with total foreign trade as a percent of GDP rising from an estimated 18 percent in 1989 to 38 percent in 1994. This expansion is also associated with a shift from trade with markets of the former CMEA to markets in Western Europe and has been accompanied by a gradual widening of the inflows of capital, which accelerated rapidly starting in late 1994. If the large volume of estimated unrecorded trade is taken into account, Poland has registered a surplus in its external current account for most of the period since reform. With steadily rising capital account inflows, Poland has added substantially to its gross official international reserves.

The Current Account

It is important to note that Poland's official balance of payments statistics show a deficit on the current account for 1991–94. However, as noted above, there is substantial evidence that a significant amount of cross-border trade and tourism receipts have gone unrecorded. Foreigners have made millions of visits to—and transactions in—the numerous formal and informal markets on Poland's borders. If reasonable estimates of nonresidents' unrecorded purchases of Polish goods and services are included, the "true" current account shows a sizeable surplus (see Chart 4.1).

[31]For more details about exceptional financing and how exceptional financing transactions are recorded in the balance of payments, see *Balance of Payments Textbook* (Washington: International Monetary Fund, 1996).

These "unofficial" transactions are not captured in the current account, but two types of "official" transactions can provide an idea of the extent of the underreporting. First, the official data classify sales of foreign currency for zloty in the small foreign exchange bureaus (known as *kantors*) as short-term capital inflows. These sales more likely reflect receipts from unrecorded exports and tourism receipts; therefore, they should appear under the current account. Second, private transfers are estimated by the change in the households' foreign exchange deposits. A drop in these deposits (and therefore in net private transfers) during 1991–94 more accurately reflects residents' sales of dollars for zlotys as confidence in the domestic currency returns.

The inflows underlying these items are generated mainly by transactions involving border trade and tourism, as well as workers' remittances and other transfers. Adjusted for these changes, the current account shows estimated surpluses of 2–3 percent of GDP in 1991–92 and again in 1994. Independent information based on surveys of border trade and tourism support this reinterpretation of the official statistics.

The Capital Account

External debt restructuring and macroeconomic uncertainty dominated developments in the capital account during 1991–93. Therefore, medium- to long-term inflows, foreign direct investment, and portfolio inflows were relatively small. Overall, the adjusted capital account deficit was equal to almost 4 percent of GDP in 1991 and still stood at the equivalent of 0.5 percent of GDP in 1993–94. After an increase in foreign direct investment and large portfolio inflows, especially on the short-term account, the capital account is estimated to have turned around sharply in 1995, registering a large surplus. There was a sharp pickup in foreign direct investment, and foreign investors also became interested in the equity and Treasury bill markets, reflecting the virtual disappearance of devaluation risk and attractive interest rate differentials.

Exchange Rate Policy

The Polish authorities' initial choice of a fixed exchange rate was motivated by a desire to provide the economy with a nominal anchor and thus to calm worries about emerging hyperinflation caused by sizable monetary overhang and impending price liberalization. At the same time, the authorities were concerned about maintaining the competitiveness of the

Chart 4.1. Poland: Current and Capital Accounts
(In billions of U.S. dollars)

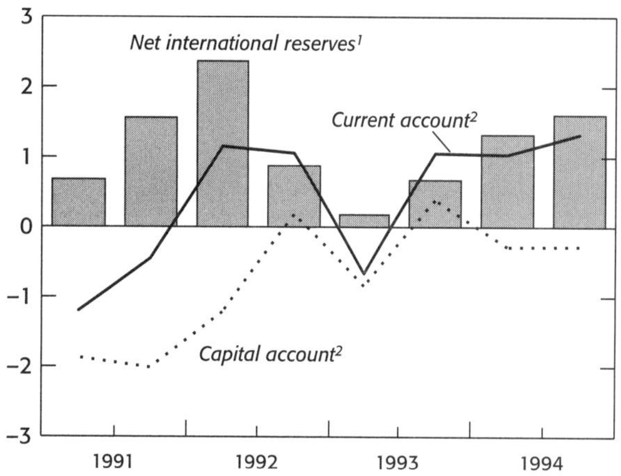

Source: Juha Kahkonen and others, *Poland—Statistical Tables,* IMF Staff Country Report No. 96/20 (Washington: International Monetary Fund, 1996).

[1]Excluding valuation effects.

[2]On a cash basis. Hence, these estimates differ from those in the balance of payments presentation, which are on an accrual basis.

traded goods sector, especially in view of the large external imbalance. They fixed the exchange rate at a level that required devaluing the zloty by over 31 percent in U.S. dollar terms. A parallel market responsive to market forces was allowed to operate alongside the official market.

The authorities initially regarded the exchange rate peg as provisional, but it turned out to be more durable than expected because of fiscal and monetary tightening and firm wage restraint. The increase in official reserves and the availability of the $1 billion Stabilization Fund also helped to underpin the exchange rate for over 18 months.

The peg to the U.S. dollar was changed to a peg to a basket of currencies in May 1991 in recognition of Europe's increasing role in Poland's trade, and the zloty was devalued by over 14 percent against the basket. The authorities soon recognized that because inflation was higher at home than it was among Poland's trading partners, a fixed exchange rate would severely erode the country's competitive position and place intolerable pressures on the balance of payments. The exchange rate regime was therefore changed again in October 1991, this time to a preannounced crawling peg. Under this system, the monetary authorities fix a preannounced path for the exchange rate involving periodic and predictable fluctuations. This system is especially suited to a country that does not wish to abandon the discipline of a fixed exchange rate completely but needs to prevent the erosion of competitiveness in the face of a relatively high domestic inflation rate.

An important issue in implementing a crawling peg regime is determining the *rate of the crawl*, or the rate at which the exchange rate is changed periodically. Matching the rate of depreciation to the projected inflation differential during the period is tantamount to targeting the real exchange rate and is sometimes known as a "passive" crawl. An "active" crawl keeps the rate of depreciation lower than the inflation differential, effectively conceding some loss of competitiveness but still putting downward pressure on the domestic inflation rate. Poland adopted an active crawl in October 1991, setting the rate at 1.8 percent a month, significantly below the projected inflation differential. The corrections were to take place daily rather than monthly to avoid sharp movements in the exchange rate.

As expected, Poland's inflation rate remained higher than the rates in the countries with which it traded, leading to an appreciation of the real exchange rate under the new regime. To maintain the country's competitiveness, in late 1991, the authorities adopted a policy of occasional discrete devaluations. In February 1992, the zloty was devalued by 11 percent and in August 1993, by 7.5 percent. The monthly rate of crawl was also reduced in August 1993, from 1.8 percent to 1.6 percent and later to 1.4 percent. Large capital inflows and associated monetary expansion have raised the exchange rate above its projected level recently, forcing the authorities to move to a managed floating regime that permits the rate to float by ±7 percent on either side of the official rate (see Chart 4.2).

In their efforts to reconcile the objectives of lowering inflation and maintaining competitiveness, the Polish authorities moved from a fixed rate pegged to the U.S. dollar to a rate pegged to a basket, then to a preannounced crawling peg, and finally to a managed float. Their exchange rate policy has broadly succeeded in remaining anti-inflationary while maintaining the external balance.

Exercises and Issues for Discussion

Exercises

1. On the basis of the data in Table 4.11 on international transactions, compile the balance of payments for Transitia in the format of Table 4.12 and according to the Fifth Edition of the *Balance of Payments Methodology*.

2. How is the balance of payments of Transitia affected if (a) an estimated $2 billion in exports have not been reported and (b) if there is an estimated unreported capital outflow of $1 billion?

3. Consider the effect of tariffs on the shoe industry in a country. Suppose that shoes sell for $10 in the world market (and domestically in the absence of any import restrictions) and that the material input—leather—costs $6 in the world market. Assuming for simplicity that no other costs are involved, compute the nominal and effective rates of protection if 20 percent tariff is levied on the import of shoes and no tariff is levied on leather. What would happen if a 10 percent tariff is now levied on leather? How about a 50 percent tariff on leather? As a producer of shoes, would you support the increase in tariff on leather? Would you, as a consumer of shoes? Would it make sense as a matter of policy for the government to increase the tariff on shoes to 50 percent?

4. A Polish exporter of toys initially faces production costs of 1,000 zlotys and an exchange rate of 100 zlotys per U.S. dollar but is able to export at a profit. Assuming domestic cost inflation of 50 percent and zero foreign inflation, calculate the following:

(a) The effect of a pegged exchange rate on exports;

(b) The level of the exchange rate that would restore the real exchange rate; and

(c) Given an exchange rate depreciation of 25 percent, the change in the real exchange rate and the magnitude of the change in productivity the Polish exporter needs to restore the profitability of his exporting activity.

5. Analyze the changing structure of Poland's foreign trade on the basis of Tables 4.1 and 4.2 with a view toward assessing the sustainability of Poland's recent export performance, focusing on:

(a) The extent of trade created rather than diverted in the shift from the old to the new markets;

(b) The impact of growth in partner countries and of foreign protectionism; and

(c) The competitiveness of exports.

6. On the basis of Table 4.5, calculate the terms of trade for Poland during 1990–94 and comment on their evolution.

7. On the basis of Table 4.5, calculate the effect of changes in the volumes of exports and imports and of prices, respectively, on the change in the trade balance in 1993.

8. Using the information provided on Polish exchange rate development (Table 4.6), show graphically how the preannounced crawl can be represented. Confine your graph to the period after August 27, 1993. In particular, show how the graph changes with (i) an increase in the rate of crawl; and (ii) a widening in the margin permitted for fluctuation. Contrast this graph with that of (i) a fixed rate regime; and (ii) a fixed band.

9. Based on the balance of payments table for Poland (Table 4.3), discuss the nature and sources of the imbalance in Poland's external accounts and the way in which this imbalance affects the external debt position of Poland. Like many transition economies, Poland has significant unrecorded cross-border trade. How does the existence of such trade affect your analysis of the balance of payments? Discuss how the current account deficits in 1993 and 1994 were financed, and comment on the differences in financing patterns observed.

10. With reference to Tables 4.9 and 4.10, analyze the external indebtedness of Poland. Construct

Chart 4.2. Poland: Exchange Rate Developments

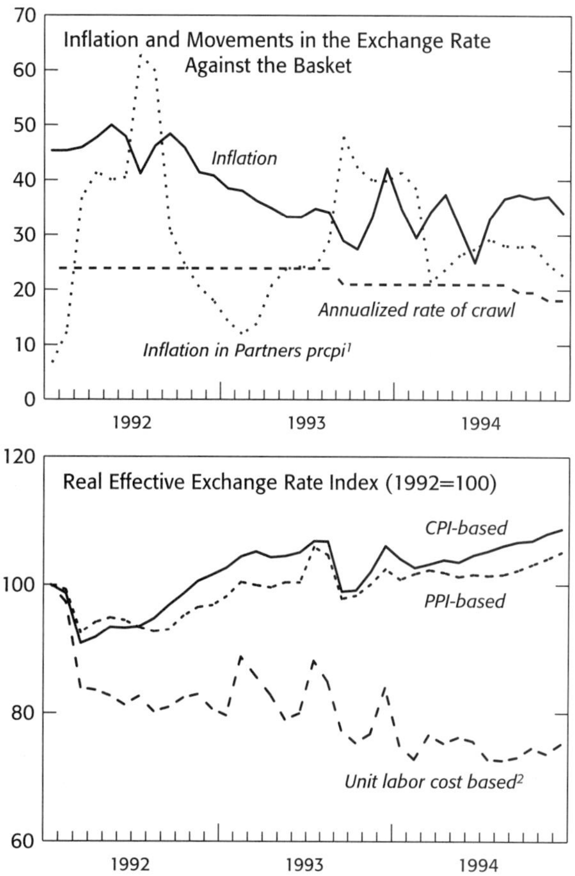

Sources: IMF, Information Notice System; and IMF Institute database.

[1]As measured by the percent change in CPI.

[2]Unit labor cost series calculated by the IMF Institute.

several indicators of external indebtedness discussed in this chapter and comment on their evolution. Comment on the sustainability of Polish external indebtedness.

11. Discuss the evolution of Poland's competitiveness during 1991–94 on the basis of Chart 4.1, which shows the movements in Poland's nominal and real exchange rates (based on consumer and producer prices and unit labor costs) and data given in Table 4.8.

Issues for Discussion

1. Although the balance of payments account is a useful framework for capturing an economy's transactions with the rest of the world, it is desirable to supplement it with other information, such as data on external debt and arrears and foreign direct investment. Discuss why it is essential to use such supplementary information for Poland in order to obtain a full picture of the country's external position. What specific supplementary information would you use?
2. One of the differences between the Fourth and the Fifth Editions of the *Manual* lies in the treatment of valuation changes and new reserve assets created by the monetization of gold and the allocation of SDRs. What is the reasoning behind the exclusion of valuation changes from the balance of payments in the Fifth Edition? How does such a treatment affect the reconciliation of the balance of payments and the monetary accounts?
3. It is sometimes said that a current account surplus is always desirable and a deficit undesirable. Do you agree with this statement? If not, why? Explain your answer with examples from various countries.
4. In cases where a country is subject to internal or external shocks such as a drought or a fall in the price of its main export, the balance of payments outcome—such as a large current account deficit—may not represent the underlying trend. In such cases, how should the underlying current account deficit be estimated? Can you think of other factors affecting the balance of payments that would make it necessary to attempt to estimate the underlying current account?
5. If a country is subject to a terms of trade shock (such as a rise in the price of a major import such as oil or a fall in the price of a major export such as coffee), how should the authorities formulate their policy response? Discuss the factors that need to be taken into account in determining the mix of adjustments and financing and the type of financing that should be used.
6. In recent years, reflecting the increasing integration of world capital markets, the liberalization of controls on the capital account, and policy reforms, many developing and some transition economies are experiencing rising capital inflows. Are such inflows always an unmixed blessing? What difficulties do such inflows raise for the conduct of macroeconomic policy? In particular, should some type of capital inflows be preferred over others and if so, why?
7. This workshop discusses the main issues analysts should consider in assessing reserve adequacy. In view of the liberalization of the capital account in many countries, are the conventional criteria for measuring reserve adequacy still relevant? Why do some countries seem to encounter no difficulties even while holding rather low levels of reserves in relation to their imports?
8. Are the various external debt indicators presented in this chapter sufficient to assess a country's debt situation? Why do countries such as Italy and Ireland, which have rather high debt ratios, seem not to suffer from a "debt problem," while others countries with relatively low ratios have debt servicing difficulties?

Table 4.1.
Commodity Composition of Trade[1]

	1990	1991	1992	1993	1994
		(At current prices, in millions of U.S. dollars)			
Exports f.o.b.	**10,863**	**12,760**	**13,997**	**13,585**	**16,950**
Agriculture	1,825	2,284	2,058	1,386	
Energy and raw materials	1,727	2,169	2,240	1,888	
Manufacturing	7,311	8,307	9,700	10,311	
Imports f.o.b.	**8,649**	**12,709**	**13,485**	**15,878**	**17,786**
Agriculture	1,687	1,767	1,672	1,969	
Non-energy raw materials	448	497	881	997	
Oil and gas	875	2,553	2,261	1,655	
Manufacturing	5,639	7,892	8,671	11,258	
			(In percent of total)		
Exports f.o.b.	**100.0**	**100.0**	**100.0**	**100.0**	**100.0**
Agriculture	16.8	17.9	14.7	10.2	
Energy and raw materials	15.9	17.0	16.0	13.9	
Industrial products	67.3	65.1	69.3	75.9	
Imports f.o.b.	**100.0**	**100.0**	**100.0**	**100.0**	**100.0**
Agriculture	19.5	13.9	12.4	12.4	
Non-energy raw materials	5.2	3.9	6.5	6.3	
Oil and gas	10.1	20.1	16.8	10.4	
Manufacturing	65.2	62.1	64.3	70.9	

Sources: Juha Kahkonen and others, *Poland–Statistical Tables,* IMF Staff Country Report No. 96/20 (Washington: International Monetary Fund, 1996); and Liam P. Ebrill and others, *Poland: The Path to a Market Economy*, Occasional Paper No. 113 (Washington: International Monetary Fund, 1994).

[1]Since there were considerable problems collecting trade statistics during these years, the data indicate broad orders of magnitudes for the various categories of exports and imports.

Table 4.2.
Direction of Trade
(In percent of total)

	1990	1991	1992	1993
Total exports	100.0	100.0	100.0	100.0
1. Non-CMEA countries	75.7	81.2	84.3	81.7
European Union	47.5	55.6	57.9	53.0
Of which: Germany	25.1	29.4	31.3	30.6
Other non-CMEA Europe	16.2	16.1	9.5	8.8
All other countries	12.0	9.5	16.9	19.9
2. Former CMEA	24.3	18.8	15.7	18.3
Of which: former U.S.S.R.	15.3	11.0	9.1	15.7
Total imports	100.0	100.0	100.0	100.0
1. Non-CMEA countries	71.5	79.2	83.5	87.2
European Union	42.5	49.9	50.7	56.4
Of which: Germany	20.1	26.5	23.9	29.5
Other non-CMEA Europe	18.4	16.1	14.4	11.0
All other countries	10.6	13.2	18.4	19.7
2. Former CMEA	28.5	20.8	16.5	12.8
Of which: former U.S.S.R.	19.8	14.1	11.4	11.0

Source: IMF, *Direction of Trade Statistics Yearbook* (Washington: International Monetary Fund, 1994).

Table 4.3.
Balance of Payments[1]
(In millions of U.S. dollars)

	1989	1990	1991	1992	1993	1994
Trade balance	**240**	**2,214**	**51**	**512**	**–2,293**	**–836**
Exports	7,575	10,863	12,760	13,997	13,585	16,950
Imports	7,335	8,649	12,709	13,485	15,878	17,786
Of which: oil and gas exports	–	–	2,553	2,261	1,655	1,278
Unrecorded trade	–	–	277	1,182	1,750	3,211
Nonfactor services (net)	–228	–150	236	344	369	57
Receipts	767	1,327	1,577	1,612	1,846	2,100
Payments	995	1,477	1,341	1,268	1,477	2,043
Interest (net)	–3,087	–3,329	–2,862	–1,740	–1,392	–1,633
Private	382	581	541	527	400	271
Official (including debt converted)	3,469	3,910	3,403	2,267	1,792	1,904
Of which: paid	–	474	885	1,097	827	1,110
Transfers (net)	1,232	1,933	353	528	929	1,182
Private	1,144	1,676	308	230	821	1,025
Official (including debt converted)	88	257	45	298	108	157
Investment income	–	–	–	85	139	222
Transfer of profits	–	–	–	–	–39	–75
Current account balance (excluding unrecorded trade)	**–1,843**	**668**	**–2,222**	**–270**	**–2,287**	**–1,083**
Current account balance (including unrecorded trade)	–1,843	668	–1,972	913	–537	2,128
Capital account	**–1,531**	**–2,350**	**–7,954**	**373**	**1,524**	**2,682**
Medium- and long-term capital (net)	–1,442	–2,526	–6,059	–292	–471	31
Disbursements	226	428	786	562	922	894
Amortization due	1,668	2,954	6,845	854	1,393	863
Of which: paid	–	369	347	443	903	503
Credit extended	–	42	13	–1	11	–11
Direct investment	36	10	117	284	580	542
Short-term capital	–125	–236	–1,254	598	1,095	1,800
Error and omissions	–	360	–713	38	92	738
Valuation adjustment	–	–	–58	–254	217	–418
Overall balance	**–3,374**	**–1,682**	**10,176**	**103**	**–764**	**1,599**
Net reserves, official and banks (–, increase)	–356	–4,442	1,317	–1,613	–634	–2,534
Net reserves (–, increase), official	–200	–2,153	1,201	–485	–173	–1,153
Gross official reserves (–, increase)	–415	–2,417	866	–473	7	–1,747
Liabilities (+, increase)	215	264	335	–12	–180	594
Of which: IMF credit, net	–	500	322	–	–138	594
Change in other NIR of banking system	–156	–2,289	116	–1,128	–461	–1,381
Gross (–, increase)	–	–1,989	250	–1,414	–370	–1,531
Liabilities	–	–300	–134	286	–91	150
Debt relief	382	9,054	4,382	202	–	7,900
Principal (and arrears)	–	–	2,939	202	–	7,205
Interest	–	–	1,443	–	–	695
Change in arrears	3,192	–2,930	4,477	1,309	1,397	–6,965

Source: Juha Kahkonen and others, *Poland–Statistical Tables,* IMF Staff Country Report No. 96/20 (Washington: International Monetary Fund, 1996).

[1]Convertible currency trade on a payments basis from commercial banks.

Table 4.4.
Current Account of Balance of Payments in Convertible and Nonconvertible Currencies[1]
(In millions of U.S. dollars)

	1989	1990	1991	1992	1993	1994
Exports, f.o.b.						
In convertible currencies	7,575	10,863	12,760	13,997	13,585	16,950
In nonconvertible currencies	4,337	4,151	546	47	13	74
Imports, f.o.b.						
In convertible currencies	7,335	8,649	12,709	13,485	15,878	17,786
In nonconvertible currencies	4,122	2,276	368	90	202	133
Trade balance						
In convertible currencies	240	2,214	51	512	−2,293	−836
In nonconvertible currencies	214	1,875	178	−43	−189	−59
Services and unrequited transfers, net						
In convertible currencies	−2,083	−1,546	−2,274	−782	6	−247
Of which: interest payments, net	−3,087	−3,329	−2,863	−1,740	−1,392	−1,633
In nonconvertible currencies	77	125	63	64	38	31
Of which: interest payments, net	−85	−37	15	60	31	29
Current account[1]						
In convertible currencies	−1,843	668	−222	−270	−2,287	−1,083
In nonconvertible currencies	291	2,000	241	21	−151	−28

Source: Juha Kahkonen and others, *Poland–Statistical Tables,* IMF Staff Country Report No. 96/20 (Washington: International Monetary Fund, 1996).

[1]Represents the summation of transactions, expressed in U.S. dollars. Transactions in transferable rubles were converted into U.S. dollars at the cross-commercial rate.

Table 4.5.
External Trade[1]
(Percentage change)

	1990	1991	1992	1993	1994
Exports					
Value (U.S. dollar)	6.2	4.0	−11.5	7.3	21.9
Volume	13.7	−2.4	−2.6	−1.1	18.3
Price (U.S. dollar)	−6.6	6.6	−9.1	8.5	3.0
Imports					
Value (U.S. dollar)	−8.3	61.1	1.0	18.4	14.5
Volume	−7.9	37.8	16.9	18.5	13.4
Price (U.S. dollar)	0.4	13.9	−11.3	—	1.0
Terms of trade	−0.7	−8.8	2.5	8.5	2.0

Source: Juha Kahkonen and others, *Poland–Statistical Tables,* IMF Staff Country Report No. 96/20 (Washington: International Monetary Fund, 1996).

[1]Data may not be consistent with the data provided in Tables 4.1–4.4.

Table 4.6.
Exchange Rate Developments

Period	Exchange Rate Policy	Action	Comments
Before 1990	Multiple exchange rates, adjustable peg to a basket of currencies	Frequent and substantial devaluations	
January 1, 1990	Fixed exchange rate system	Unification of official and black market rates; Devaluation (31.6 percent)	Exchange rate: Zl 9,500 per U.S. dollar
May 17, 1991	Fixed exchange rate system	Devaluation (16.8 percent against the dollar, 14.4 percent against the basket); Shift from a dollar peg to a basket peg	Exchange rate: Zl 11,100 per U.S. dollar. Basket includes: U.S. dollar (45 percent), deutsche mark (35 percent), pound sterling (10 percent), French franc (5 percent), Swiss franc (5 percent)
October 19, 1991	Preannounced crawling peg	Rate of crawl announced: 1.8 percent per month (Zl 9 per day)	
February 25, 1992	Preannounced crawling peg	Devaluation (10.7 percent against the basket); Rate of crawl: 1.8 percent per month (Zl 11 per day)	Exchange rate: Zl 13,360 per U.S. dollar
July 10, 1992	Preannounced crawling peg	Rate of crawl: 1.8 percent per month (Zl 12 per day)	Basket unchanged Technical adjustment made
August 27, 1993	Preannounced crawling peg	Devaluation (7.4 percent against the basket); Rate of crawl reduced: 1.6 percent (Zl 15 per day)	Exchange rate: Zl 23,113 per U.S. dollar
September 13, 1994	Preannounced crawling peg	Rate of crawl reduced: 1.5 percent per month	
November 30, 1994	Preannounced crawling peg	Rate of crawl reduced: 1.4 percent per month	
January 1, 1995	Redenomination	One new zloty equal to 10,000 old zlotys	
February 15, 1995	Preannounced crawling peg	Rate of crawl reduced: 1.2 percent per month	
March 6, 1995	Preannounced crawling peg	Margin in interbank market widened to +/–2 percent around official rate	
May 16, 1995	Float within crawling band	Rate permitted to fluctuate +/–7 percent around mid-rate that continues to crawl at 1.2 percent per month	

Source: Juha Kahkonen and others, *Poland–Statistical Tables,* IMF Staff Country Report No. 96/20 (Washington: International Monetary Fund, 1996).

Table 4.7.
Tariff Structure, as of July 1, 1995[1]
(Percentage rates)

		Trade-Weighted	
	Average	Effective average	Effective average[2]
All commodities	**14.33**	**12.77**	**9.44**
Agricultural products	**25.15**	**24.72**	**21.24**
Animal products	33.06	33.00	31.57
Vegetable products	15.87	15.74	8.28
Fats and oils	16.22	16.22	14.92
Prepared foodstuffs	29.53	28.48	26.62
Industrial products	**12.96**	**11.26**	**7.95**
Mineral products	3.83	2.76	2.30
Chemical products	11.76	10.79	6.83
Plastics	13.37	11.97	9.50
Leather products	11.22	9.50	7.42
Wood products	12.33	12.02	8.99
Wood pulp products	4.30	0.09	0.01
Textile products	16.06	14.87	12.25
Footwear	17.15	17.15	15.68
Stone products	11.66	11.22	8.59
Precious materials	18.57	18.57	14.70
Base metal products	16.38	13.03	10.35
Mechanical and electrical machinery	13.81	11.29	5.44
Transport equipment	22.98	22.96	20.68
Optical products	13.39	10.08	7.12
Arms	33.00	33.00	28.67
Miscellaneous manufactured products	15.84	15.84	12.96
Art	—	—	—

Source: Juha Kahkonen and others, *Poland–Statistical Tables,* IMF Staff Country Report No. 96/20 (Washington: International Monetary Fund, 1996).
[1]Based on CN nomenclature excluding tariff-free quotas.
[2]Including Free Trade Agreements.

Table 4.8.
Effective Exchange Rate
(Quarterly average indices January 1990 = 100)

Real Effective Exchange Rate		Wage Based[1]	Price Based[2]	Nominal Effective Exchange Rate
1990:	I	...	47.9	126.4
	II	...	57.9	125.6
	III	...	60.0	119.3
	IV	...	65.2	113.8
1991:	I	95.6	82.9	115.7
	II	108.0	92.1	116.4
	III	105.6	88.9	106.8
	IV	102.8	93.7	103.5
1992:	I	96.9	96.3	94.9
	II	86.0	92.1	83.8
	III	82.9	92.5	78.7
	IV	85.3	98.6	76.9
1993:	I	90.0	103.8	74.5
	II	85.0	104.0	70.5
	III	85.3	101.0	65.6
	IV	81.4	100.4	60.1
1994:	I	78.6	102.6	56.9
	II	79.3	103.1	53.9
	III	76.7	102.8	50.9
	IV	79.0	105.9	48.8

Source: Juha Kahkonen and others, *Poland–Statistical Tables,* IMF Staff Country Report No. 96/20 (Washington: International Monetary Fund, 1996).

[1]Based on data on unit labor costs in Poland and partner countries.

[2]Nominal effective exchange rate index deflated by seasonally adjusted index of relative prices; a decrease indicates depreciation.

Table 4.9.
Scheduled Debt Service by Creditor
(In millions of U.S. dollars)

	1990	1991	1992	1993	1994
Paris Club/other guaranteed/jumbo					
Interest	2,519	1,940	620	535	577
Principal	2,467	2,907	69	79	40
Former CMEA banks and Russia					
Interest	198	193	133	124	89
Principal	62	114	242	292	156
London Club (including revolving facility)					
Interest	856	1,030	1,140	906	832
Principal	145	3,521	165	157	266
Other commercial creditors					
Interest	249	87	139	119	243
Principal	280	303	378	865	401
World Bank					
Interest	—	17	44	43	61
Principal	—	—	—	—	—
International Monetary Fund					
Interest	25	63	74	49	42
Principal	—	—	—	138	310
Other multilateral institutions					
Interest	2	—	4	11	20
Principal	—	—	—	—	—
Interest on short-term debt	—	70	113	5	40
Total (including IMF)	**6,803**	**10,245**	**3,121**	**3,323**	**3,077**
Interest	3,849	3,400	2,267	1,792	1,904
Principal	2,954	6,845	854	1,531	1,173

Source: Juha Kahkonen and others, *Poland–Statistical Tables,* IMF Staff Country Report No. 96/20 (Washington: International Monetary Fund, 1996).

Table 4.10.
External Reserves and Other Foreign Assets
(In millions of U.S. dollars)

At End of Period	1989	1990	1991	1992	1993	1994
Official external reserves	2,503.2	4,680.3	3,814.0	4,287.3	4,230.8	5,196.7
Gold[1]	189.0	189.0	189.0	189.0	189.0	189.0
Foreign exchange	2,314.2	4,491.3	3,625.0	4,098.3	4,041.8	5,007.7
Other foreign assets in convertible currencies[2]	2,399.9	4,521.6	4,278.9	5,746.4	6,184.5	7,119.7
Foreign assets in nonconvertible currencies	609.1	2,384.5	. . .	. . .	. . .	. . .

Source: Juha Kahkonen and others, *Poland–Statistical Tables,* IMF Staff Country Report No. 96/20 (Washington: International Monetary Fund, 1996).

[1]Gold is valued at US$400 per ounce.

[2]Includes prepaid letters of credit.

Table 4.11.
Transitia: Data on International Transactions Classified by Source[1]
(In millions of transitia dollars)

Description	1993	1994
Data provided by the customs administration		
Exports of goods, f.o.b.	35,538	45,382
Imports of goods, f.o.b.	32,543	36,684
Data provided by carriers		
Import freight payments to nonresident companies	3,320	3,340
Receipt by resident companies		
Export freight	190	200
Foreign tourist transport	575	560
Data derived from the foreign exchange record		
Purchase of foreign exchange from foreign tourists	1,300	1,350
Sale of foreign exchange to residents for travel abroad	2,815	2,880
Purchase of foreign exchange from foreign embassies	250	300
Receipts from abroad, other services	128	127
Payments abroad, other services	1,970	3,431
Remittances received from family members living abroad	80	50
Remittances abroad by foreign nationals working in Eden (for more than one year)	262	256
Data provided by the port authorities		
Receipts for port services provided to nonresidents	530	515
Data provided by the Central Bank of Eden		
Interest received on foreign exchange assets	730	650
IMF charges	140	160
Total change in reserves	−1,796	1,103
Of which: revaluation changes	−198	0
Use of IMF credit	1,369	0
Data provided by commercial banks		
Interest accrued on deposits abroad	40	30
Interest paid to correspondent banks	27	60
Change in foreign assets	1,000	1,500
Change in foreign liabilities	1,991	1,000
Data provided by the central government		
Interest on loans received from abroad	2,210	3,870
Operating expenditures of diplomatic missions abroad	350	400
Grants received from foreign governments	27	28
Drawings on loans received from abroad	5,182	4,800
Repayments on these loans	2,100	1,303
Refinanced debts	0	586
Data provided by nonfinancial public enterprises		
Interest on loans received from abroad	300	820
Drawings on long-term loans from abroad	2,223	1,613
Repayments on these loans	400	300
Data provided by nonfinancial private enterprises		
Interest accrued on deposits abroad	700	600
Dividends distributed to direct investors	1,200	1,400
Interest paid to nonresidents	2,400	1,700
Drawings on long-term loans from abroad	2,390	1,849
Repayments on these loans	285	250
Net change in short-term loans received from abroad	−765	−400
Change in deposits held in foreign banks	1,323	−1,217

[1]Exercise taken from the training material of the IMF's Statistics Department.

Table 4.12.
Transitia: Balance of Payments Statements[1]
(In millions of transitia dollars)

	1993	1994
Current account	**–7,449**	
Balance of trade	**2,995**	
Exports of goods, f.o.b.	35,538	
Imports of goods, f.o.b.	–32,543	
Services (net)	–5,482	
Freight on exports	190	
Passenger services: credit	575	
Port services: credit	530	
Travel expenditure: credit	1,300	
Government services, n.i.e.: credit	250	
Other services: debit	128	
Freight on imports	–3,320	
Travel expenditure: debit	–2,815	
Government services, n.i.e: debit	–350	
Other services: debit	–1,970	
Investment income (net)	–4,807	
Interest received by the Central Bank	730	
Interest received by commercial banks	40	
Interest received by nonfinancial private enterprises	700	
Dividends distributed to direct investors	–1,200	
IMF charges	–140	
Interest paid to correspondent banks	–27	
Interest on loans received by the central government	–2,210	
Interest on loans received by public enterprises	–300	
Interest paid by private enterprises	–2,400	
Current transfers (net)	–155	
Remittances received from family members living abroad	80	
Grants received from foreign governments	27	
Remittances abroad by foreign nationals working in Eden	–262	
Capital account (capital transfers)	**0**	
Financial account (excluding financing items)	5,913	
Direct investment	0	
Portfolio investment	0	
Other investment	5,913	
General government	3,082	
Drawings on loans from abroad	5,182	
Loan repayments	–2,100	
Bank	991	
Foreign assets	–1,000	
Foreign liabilities	1,991	
Other sectors	1,840	
Public enterprises	1,823	
Drawings on long-term loans from abroad	2,223	
Loan repayments	–400	
Private enterprises	17	
Short-term assets: deposits in banks abroad	–1,323	
Short-term liabilities: loans received	–765	
Long-term liabilities	2,105	
Drawings on loans received	2,390	
Loan repayments	–285	
Net errors and omissions	–1,431	
Overall balance	**–2,967**	
Financing	2,967	
Reserve assets	1,598	
Use of IMF credit	1,369	
Exceptional financing	0	
Debt rescheduling	0	

[1]Exercise taken from the training material of the IMF's Statistics Department.

CHAPTER

5 Monetary Accounts and Analysis

Among the main macroeconomic accounts, the monetary accounts play a special role, for a number of reasons. First, in a market economy based on money, the financial system provides intermediation for the resources flowing among the economic sectors. Because the monetary sector serves as a clearinghouse for all financial flows, the monetary accounts provide unique insight into the behavior of these flows, which mirror the flows of real resources among the sectors.

Second, monetary accounts focus on variables (such as money, credit, and foreign assets and liabilities) that play a central role in the macroeconomic analysis of an open economy. Various classical and modern theories have been developed to explain how income, prices, and the balance of payments are determined using these variables. This chapter presents monetary accounting concepts that lie at the heart of the monetary approach to the balance of payments.[1] But the monetary accounting framework is broad and flexible enough to be useful for analyses based on many alternative theories of money, prices, and the balance of payments.

Third, the adjustment programs supported by the IMF use a variety of different instruments and approaches adapted to the situations of individual countries. A central element of the theoretical foundations of these programs is the link between monetary aggregates and fiscal operations (as well, of course, as balance of payments outcomes). A clear understanding of the monetary accounts is therefore indispensable for conducting the kind of monetary analysis underlying IMF-supported adjustment programs.

Finally, the monetary accounts are generally available with little delay. Even in developing and transition economies, where reliable economic data can be scarce, they are among the most reliable of the macroeconomic statistics and are therefore useful to policymakers who need to monitor economic developments. For the same reason, financial aggregates are often used as benchmarks and performance criteria in IMF-supported adjustment programs.

The next sections of this chapter outline the structure of the financial system and review the accounting principles underlying the compilation and presentation of monetary statistics in the IMF's *International Financial Statistics* (IFS). Also, following sections analyze the balance sheets of the monetary authorities and the deposit money banks.[2] In particular, the distinction between the initial creation of base money, which is reflected in the balance sheet of the monetary authorities, and secondary money creation by deposit money banks (in the form of deposits) is discussed. The last part of the chapter discusses the consolidated balance sheet of the banking system (the monetary survey), outlines the rationale for analyzing it, and illustrates the monetary survey's usefulness in assessing the impact of monetary and credit developments on the economy.

Monetary Accounting

The Structure of the Financial System

Financial institutions specialize in channeling financial savings to firms planning to undertake real investment, although they can also provide funds for government institutions. This process, called *financial intermediation*, is accompanied by a transformation of the maturity structure of financial assets. Borrowers gain access to the surplus funds of savers deposited with the banking system through a variety of credit instruments, including stocks, bonds, commercial bills, mortgages, and mutual funds.

The financial system consists of the banking system and nonbank financial institutions such as in-

[1]See *The Monetary Approach to the Balance of Payments* (Washington: International Monetary Fund, 1977). These concepts follow closely those underlying the IMF's *International Financial Statistics*.

[2]*International Financial Statistics* is published monthly by the IMF. It includes monetary and banking statistics on an internationally comparable basis. See "A Guide to Money and Banking Statistics in International Financial Statistics," a draft, IMF, December 1984.

surance companies, mutual funds, pension funds, and money market funds. In many countries, there is a third sector, the unorganized financial sector, which can often be an important part of the financial system. The banking system, which consists of the monetary authorities (MAs) and deposit money banks (DMBs), creates an economy's means of payment, including currency and demand deposits. In the IFS, the widely accepted framework for classifying financial statistics, monetary, and financial data is presented on three levels (see Fig. 5.1). The first level contains the separate balance sheets for the monetary authorities and the DMBs.[3] The second level consolidates the data for the monetary authorities and the DMBs into the *monetary survey*, which provides a statistical measure of money and credit. Finally, the third level consolidates the monetary survey and the balance sheets of other financial institutions (OFIs) into the *financial survey*.

This chapter focuses on the banking system rather than the entire financial system for three reasons. First, empirical evidence shows that the monetary liabilities of the banking sector strongly influence aggregate nominal spending in an economy and thereby affect the final objectives of economic policy—growth, inflation, and the balance of payments. Second, data on the banking sector are usually readily available, even for developing and transition economies, making them invaluable for timely economic analysis and monitoring of financial policies. And, third, in countries where financial markets are not well developed, the banking system typically accounts for the bulk of an economy's financial assets and liabilities, although, as noted above, the unorganized financial sector often plays a major role in financial intermediation in these economies.

Accounting Principles Underlying Monetary Statistics

Stocks versus flows. Monetary statistics are based on balance sheets and therefore are compiled in the form of *stock* data—that is, in terms of outstanding stocks of assets and liabilities at a particular point in time rather than as flow data, which record transactions carried out over a period of time. However, the statistics are analyzed in terms of changes in stocks from one period to the next, or in terms of flows. Since changes in stocks need to be assessed in relation to the amount of liabilities outstanding at the beginning of the period, both stocks and flows are important.

Cash versus accrual. The IFS records transactions on a cash basis (when an obligation is settled rather than when it is incurred). In many countries, banking sector data tend to be recorded on an accrual basis (when a liability is incurred), because the balance sheets of the banking system from which the statistics are derived are constructed in accordance with the rules of business accounting. However, since most transactions of banks are typically carried out immediately in cash, this distinction is of little practical importance.

Currency denomination. Monetary accounts are expressed in local currency. All items denominated in foreign currency are converted into domestic currency at the exchange rate prevailing on the date the balance sheet is compiled (i.e., *end-period exchange rate*), because the balance sheet aggregates are stocks. This is in sharp contrast to the conversion of flow aggregates (e.g., imports or exports), which are converted at an *average* exchange rate for a period.

Consolidation. Unlike aggregation, consolidation involves netting out the transactions between the entities being consolidated. For example, in consolidating the accounts of different deposit money banks, interbank entries (items due from and to other banks) are netted out. Two levels of consolidation are carried out for the monetary survey. First, the balance sheets of all DMBs are consolidated. Second, the balance sheet of the monetary authorities is then consolidated with those of the DMBs to obtain the monetary survey.

Monetary Authorities

The Definition and Role of Monetary Authorities

The term "monetary authorities" is a functional rather than an institutional concept. In most countries, the monetary authorities are represented by the central bank, but the concept can include agencies of the government, such as the treasury, that perform some of the functions of a central bank. The monetary authorities issue currency, hold the country's foreign exchange reserves, borrow for balance of payments purposes, act as banker to the government, oversee the monetary system, and serve as the lender of last resort to the banking system. In many countries, the treasury issues coins and holds

[3]DMBs are often commercial banks but may also be financial institutions, such as savings banks, whose liabilities include appreciable deposits against which checks can be written to settle obligations. For more details, see "A Guide to Money and Banking Statistics in International Financial Statistics," a draft, IMF, December 1984.

Figure 5.1. Scope of the Financial System

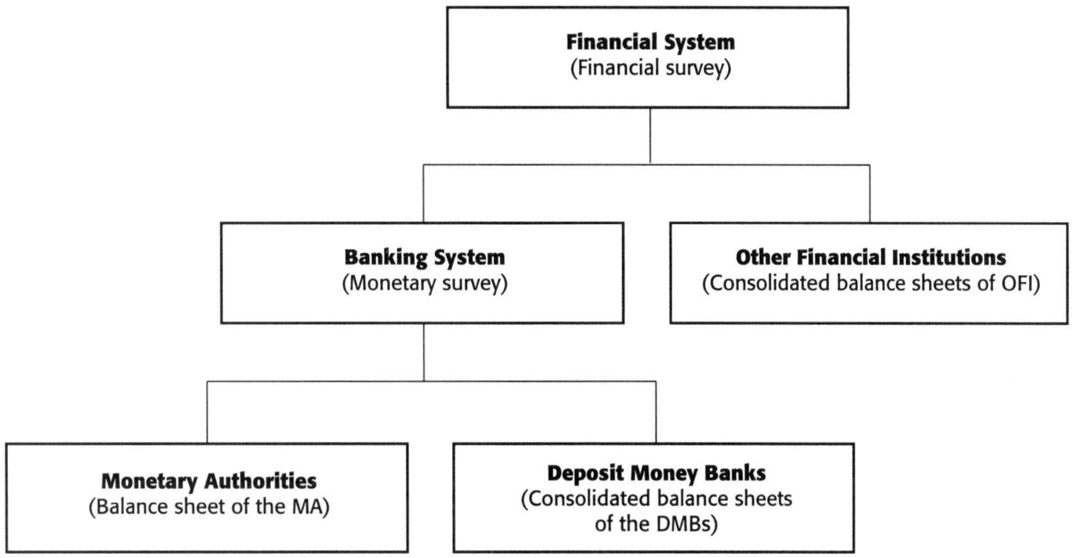

the official reserves. In some countries, a treasury-controlled exchange stabilization fund instead holds the country's official reserves. Under IMF accounting procedures, the monetary functions of the government are grouped with the accounts of the central bank, so that all of the functions of the monetary authorities are presented under one accounting unit.

As noted above, an important function of the monetary authorities is to act as a lender of last resort to the banking system. When financial panic threatens the banking system, the monetary authorities need to take swift action to restore investors' confidence and avoid a systemwide run on the banks. The rationale for using the central bank as a lender of last resort is based on the essentially illiquid nature of the credit system. While debtors can, given time, repay their loans, they cannot do so on demand. But many liabilities, such as bank deposits, have very short maturities, so that if all creditors ask for their assets, some banks may be pushed into default. If one deposit money bank has payment difficulties, the entire system can become illiquid, and because of the many layers of credit and intermediation in the system, the source of the actual default may not be clear. The result of this uncertainty is a systemwide crisis of confidence that leads to a credit "freeze." To prevent financial collapse, the central bank can isolate the problem bank and guarantee payment to its depositors, preventing spillover effects in the credit market. As lender of last resort, the central bank comes into its own when it steps in to prevent illiquidity, either on the part of an individual bank or throughout the banking system.[4]

Because of its unique nature, the balance sheet of monetary authorities has a central place in monetary analysis. The creation of *high-powered money* (also known as *reserve money* or the *monetary base*) is a prerogative of the monetary authorities. The control they exercise over the amount of high-powered money in the economy is the main route through which the monetary authorities control the money supply and obtain seigniorage. Since the central bank creates reserve money whenever it acquires assets and pays for them by creating liabilities, an analysis of its balance sheet is key to understanding the process of money creation. The monetary authorities' operations, such as open market purchases or sales of government securities, their lending to government as well as to the deposit money banks, and their purchases and sales of foreign exchange—known as foreign exchange intervention—all affect the amount of reserve money. By virtue of being the monopoly supplier of

[4]For a comprehensive discussion of the role and objectives of a central bank, see Stanley Fischer, "Modern Central Banking," *The Future of Central Banking*, Chapter 2, The Tercentenary Symposium of the Bank of England, Forrest Capie, Charles Goodhard, Stanley Fischer, and Norbert Schnadt (Cambridge, Massachusetts: Cambridge University Press, 1994). See also Stanley Fischer, "Central Banking: The Challenges Ahead," Statement at the 25th Anniversary Symposium of the Monetary Authority of Singapore, May 10, 1996.

Box 5.1.
Typical Balance Sheet of the Monetary Authorities

Assets	Liabilities
Foreign Assets	**Reserve Money**
Gold	Of which:
Foreign exchange	Currency outside banks
Reserve position in the Fund	Deposit money banks' cash in vault
Holdings of SDRs	Deposit money banks' deposits
Foreign correspondent banks	Private sector demand deposits
Foreign investments	Public sector demand deposits other than government
	Nonmonetary financial institutions' deposits
Claims on Government	**Time, Savings, and Foreign Currency Deposits**
Treasury bills	
Other government securities	
Loans and advances	
Other claims	**Bonds**
Claims on Nonfinancial Public Enterprises	**Import and Other Restricted Deposits**
Loans and advances	
Bills and securities	
Other claims	**Foreign Liabilities**
	Deposits of foreign central banks
	Swap facilities
	Use of IMF credit
	Other foreign debts
	Government Deposits
Claims on Private Sector	**Capital Accounts**
	Capital
	Reserves
Claims on Deposit Money Banks	**Unclassified Liabilities**
Rediscounts and secured advances	
Loans and overdrafts	
Other claims	
Claims on Nonmonetary Financial Institutions	
Rediscounts and secured advances	
Loans and overdrafts	
Other claims	
Unclassified Assets	

reserve money, the monetary authorities are the undisputed arbiter of monetary policy and monetary conditions in the economy.

The Balance Sheet of Monetary Authorities

A typical balance sheet of the monetary authorities is shown in Box 5.1, and an analytical summary table presented in Box 5.2. While most of the items in the monetary authorities' balance sheet are self-explanatory, it is important to highlight the key features of some of the main items as those features appear in the analytical version.

Net foreign assets include the domestic currency value of (i) the net official international reserves (on the asset side, including gold, foreign exchange, the country's reserve position in the IMF, and holdings of SDRs; on the liability side, including short-term liabilities to foreign monetary authorities—that is, deposits of foreign central banks, swap facilities, overdrafts, and some medium- and long-term foreign debt, such as a country's use of IMF

Box 5.2.
Analytical Balance Sheet of the Monetary Authorities

Assets	Liabilities
Net foreign assets (NFA*)	**Reserve money (RM)**
Net domestic assets (NDA*)	Currency issued (CY*)
	Held in banks
Domestic credit (net) (NDC*)	Held outside banks (CY)
Claims on the government (net) (NCG*)	Deposits of deposit money banks
Claims on the DMBs (CDMB*)	
Claims on other domestic economic sectors (CPS*)	
Other items (net) (OIN*)	

credit); and (ii) any other foreign assets and liabilities of the monetary authorities not included in the definition of official reserves (for the treatment of IMF transactions, see Box 5.4). While in many countries the net foreign assets of the monetary authorities are equated with the net official international reserves, the definition of net foreign assets is broader than the definition of net official international reserves. For example, in some transition economies, net foreign assets include monetary authorities' holdings of foreign assets that are not regarded as available if a balance of payments problem develops (i.e., should not be included as net official international reserves). Such holdings include foreign currency that cannot be converted and claims arising from bilateral payments agreements. By definition, these assets can be used only for official settlements with specific countries.

Claims on the government[5] *(net)* are direct loans and government securities held by the monetary authorities. They are shown net of government deposits, because the government has easier access to credit than do other sectors (including overdraft facilities at the central bank), so that its expenditures are not usually constrained by its deposits or cash balances. Moreover, it is the monetary authorities' net credit to government that corresponds to the creation of high-powered money. Claims on deposit money banks include all direct credits to DMBs, as well as bills of exchange for discount from the DMBs accepted by the central bank. The central bank interest rate on loans to banks is called the discount rate. Both the amount of central bank lending to deposit money banks and the discount rate can be important instruments of monetary policy. These claims are gross claims, since DMBs' deposits in the monetary authorities' accounts are not netted out. These deposits play a key role in monetary policy.

Claims on the private sector are in general likely to be insignificant; typically it is the business of the deposit money banks, not the central bank, to make loans to households and enterprises. Note, however, that this category also includes the monetary authorities' claims on other financial institutions and public enterprises.

Other items (net) is a residual category that is usually shown on a net basis. In Box 5.2, it is shown on the asset side. Other items (net) include the physical assets of the central bank (on the asset side); capital and reserves (as a liability); profits or losses of the central bank; valuation adjustments to the net foreign asset position resulting from developments such as changes in the exchange rate and including any unrealized profits or losses resulting from these changes; and any other items that have not been classified elsewhere.

Reserve money is the main liability of the monetary authorities, and it plays a central role in monetary analysis and policy. Reserve money includes mainly currency that has been issued and is held both in banks (cash in vault) and outside banks (currency in circulation), plus bank and nonbank deposits with the monetary authorities. It excludes the deposits of the government and nonresidents with the monetary authorities; these are netted against claims on the government and foreign assets, respectively. Deposits of other domestic sectors (such as private individuals or firms) with the monetary authorities are included, as well as foreign currency deposits by residents. This treatment

[5]The concept of "government" used in the monetary authorities' accounts is often at variance with the concept that is used in other macroeconomic accounts. It is important, especially in the case of the fiscal accounts, to ensure that the reconciliation of the two accounts is based on the same concept of government.

is based on the fact that the central bank, in essence, has the power to create money simply by writing a check against itself. When it makes payments to domestic residents (for instance, for a government bond it purchases from them) by writing checks against itself, the resident can deposit the checks in a deposit money bank, which in turn deposits them at the central bank. The resulting increase in bank deposits with the central bank adds to reserve money. No other entity in the economy has this ability.

Given the balance sheet constraint that assets must be equal to liabilities, from Box 5.2 it can be seen that changes in reserve money (RM) reflect changes in the asset side of the balance sheet of the monetary authorities (Box 5.3). For example, an overall surplus (deficit) in the balance of payments adds to (subtracts from) the net international reserves of the monetary authorities which, in the absence of offsetting changes in domestic credit or other net assets, increases (decreases) reserve money. Similarly, if the monetary authorities bring about a net increase (decrease) in their domestic assets by buying (selling) government securities or making (calling in) loans to (from) deposit money banks, the increase (decrease) in these assets, unless offset by a fall in net foreign assets or in other items (net), results in an increase (decrease) in reserve money.[6]

The balance sheet constraint of the monetary authorities is summarized by the identity

$$RM \equiv NFA^* + NCG^* + CDMB^* + CPS^* + OIN^*. \quad (5.1)$$

In terms of flows (changes in stocks), this identity can be rewritten as

$$\Delta RM = \Delta NFA^* + \Delta NCG^* + \Delta CDMB^* + \Delta CPS^* + \Delta OIN^*. \quad (5.2)$$

Dividing both sides of equation 5.2 by the lagged value of reserve money (RM_{t-1}), the growth rate of reserve money $\Delta RM_t/RM_{t-1}$ can be expressed in terms of the contributions of the various asset items, or as

$$\frac{\Delta RM_t}{RM_{t-1}} = \frac{\Delta NFA_t^*}{RM_{t-1}} + \frac{\Delta NCG_t^*}{RM_{t-1}} + \frac{\Delta CDMB_t^*}{RM_{t-1}} + \frac{\Delta CPS_t^*}{RM_{t-1}} + \frac{\Delta OIN_t^*}{RM_{t-1}}. \quad (5.3)$$

or

$$\frac{\Delta RM_t}{RM_{t-1}} = \frac{\Delta NFA^*}{NFA_{t-1}^*} \bullet \frac{NFA_{t-1}^*}{RM_{t-1}} + \frac{\Delta NCG_t^*}{NCG_{t-1}^*} \bullet \frac{NCG_{t-1}^*}{RM_{t-1}} + \frac{\Delta CDMB_t^*}{CDMB_{t-1}} \bullet \frac{CDMB_{t-1}^*}{RM_{t-1}} + \frac{\Delta OIN^*}{OIN_{t-1}^*} \bullet \frac{OIN_{t-1}^*}{RM_{t-1}} \quad (5.4)$$

In other words

$$\textit{Growth rate of reserve money} = \textit{Sum of weighted growth rates of asset items}$$

where the weights are the relative shares of lagged asset items in lagged money stock.

The monetary authorities' control over reserve money tends to be incomplete. For example, changes in net foreign assets, which are a reflection of the balance of payments outcome, cannot generally be considered to be a fully policy-controlled variable. Also, variations in claims on the government are, in many countries, adjusted passively to the government's budgetary position, especially in countries without an independent central bank. Although the central bank could, to some extent, counteract exogenous shocks from the balance of payments and/or resist the monetization of the fiscal deficit, in practice the most controllable factor remains claims on commercial banks.

Interpretation of Balance Sheet Changes

The monetary authorities can influence monetary conditions through their influence on reserve money. There are five main direct instruments available to the monetary authorities to influence reserves money: foreign exchange intervention; open market operations; financing of the budget deficit; rediscount policy; and reserve requirements.[7]

- ***Foreign exchange intervention.*** Monetary authorities intervene in the foreign exchange

[6]This assumes that the government securities bought or sold cannot be used as bank reserves. To the extent that they can, purchases or sales of government securities do not affect reserve money.

[7]It is clear that if the purchase of an asset (e.g., government securities, foreign exchange) is offset by the selling of another asset, the monetary base will not change. In this case we say that the initial action (i.e., the purchase of an asset) has been *sterilized,* in the sense that its impact on the monetary base and hence on overall liquidity conditions in the economy has been offset.

Box 5.3.
Factors Affecting Reserve Money

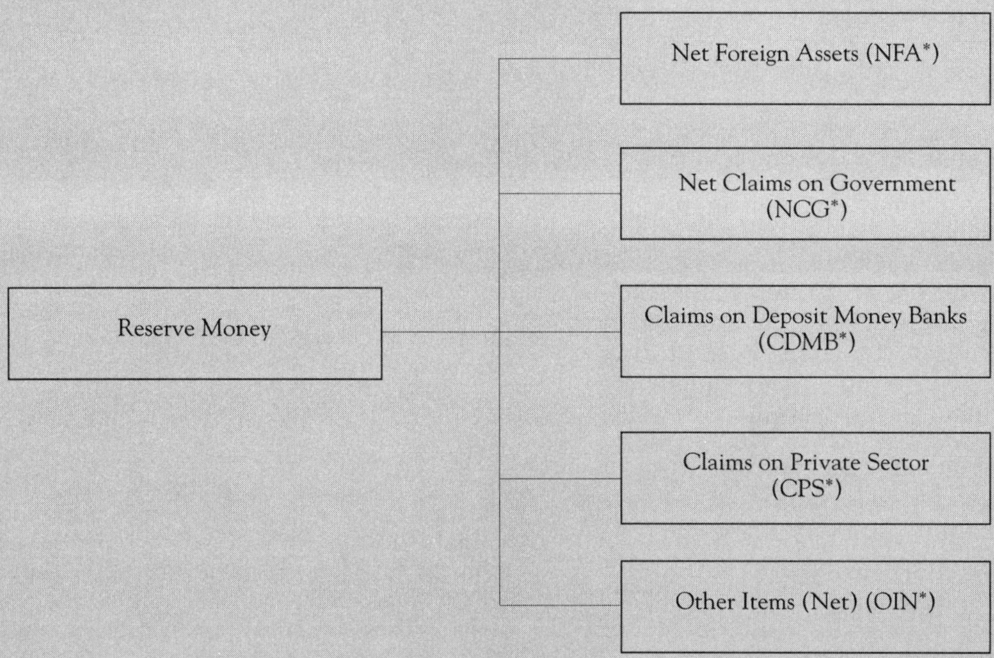

market, inter alia, to defend the exchange rate and achieve a desired amount of international reserves. Their interventions directly affect reserve money and hence have a direct impact on overall liquidity in the economy and the stance of monetary policy. For example, when the central bank purchases foreign exchange from a domestic resident and pays for it by writing a check against itself (or equivalently by printing money), it increases reserve money. Its balance sheet shows an increase in foreign assets and a corresponding rise in reserve money. Conversely, when the central bank sells foreign exchange, foreign assets are reduced, and there is a corresponding reduction in reserve money.

- ***Open market operations***. This is one of the preferred methods of changing the stock of the monetary base. It consists of buying and selling government papers, often securities in the secondary market. For example, when the central bank purchases government securities from the public, the central bank's holding of government securities increases (an increase in its assets), with a counterpart increase in liabilities (i.e., reserve money) in the form of an increase in currency in circulation (if newly printed currency is used to pay for the government security) or an increase in banks' deposits in the central bank (if the central bank writes a check against itself to pay for the purchase). Conversely, a sale of government securities to the public will reduce the central bank's holding of government securities and thus reduces reserve money.
- ***Financing of government deficit***. When the government finances its deficit by borrowing from the central bank (or, equivalently, sells a government security to the central bank), the central bank's holdings of securities increase. When the government borrows from the central bank, central bank claims on the government as well as government deposits with the central bank rise; hence, there is no change in *net* claims on government. But when the government uses the borrowed money to make a payment to the private sector, the stock of reserve money rises, because the government's deposits with the central bank are reduced, thus increasing the central bank's *net credit* to government. A fiscal deficit financed by borrowing from the central bank

thus results in a one-for-one increase in reserve money. For this reason, financing a deficit by borrowing is equivalent to financing a deficit by issuing currency (frequently referred to as deficit financing by printing money, or simply as the *monetization* of the deficit). The central bank's ability to control the reserve money it creates by refusing to lend to the government is therefore one hallmark of an independent central bank.

- ***Discount window***. The discount mechanism is an instrument of monetary control encompassing a variety of arrangements designed to influence the level of central bank credit to the banking system. The most important of the arrangements is the rate of interest charged.[8] The central bank can influence reserve money through the quantity and terms of its lending. The central bank's credit to deposit money banks is in practice the source of reserve money most directly under its control.[9] An increase in the interest rate the central bank charges (i.e., the discount rate) signals its intention to tighten monetary conditions. By making such borrowing more costly, it tends to reduce bank borrowing from the central bank, while at the same time inducing banks to increase their holding of excess reserves. Thus, it tends to reduce central bank assets and hence reserve money. Conversely, a reduction in the discount rate tends to increase banks' borrowing from the central bank and hence reserve money.

- ***Reserve requirements***. The central bank can influence reserve money simply by changing the amount of required reserves banks must hold with it. For example, an increase in the reserve requirement will force the banking system to hold a larger level of reserves for the same level of deposits, thus increasing reserve money. At the same time, however, it will reduce the ability of the banking system to create money.

[8]Others include stipulation of the types of financial assets that the central bank is permitted to acquire in ownership or as a collateral when it makes the credit available, and the maximum amount of credit that the central bank makes available to any one borrower.

[9]In most countries with established financial markets, this type of lending is limited to providing short-term financing to smooth out temporary liquidity needs of banks or to face crises (lender of last resort). This lending often takes the form of collateralized loans against government securities.

Deposit Money Banks

DMBs include all banks and similar financial institutions with appreciable liabilities in the form of deposits (payable on demand) that can be transferred by check or otherwise used to make payments. DMBs have four primary economic roles. First, and most importantly, DMBs provide financial intermediation for savers and investors, a process that transforms the maturities of financial assets. DMBs' important role in this respect consists of using what amounts to short-maturity deposits and producing long-maturity loans. Second, DMBs are the primary creators of deposit money in the economy, a role they fulfill by extending credit. In the context of a fractional reserve system, DMBs contribute to the creation of money in the economy. Third, the behavior of DMBs—in particular their policies on deposit-taking and lending—affects the money supply and liquidity. Finally, acting within the constraints set by the monetary authorities, DMBs help to transmit monetary policy from the monetary authorities to the public. DMBs are able to fulfill this role because, unlike other financial institutions, their deposit liabilities serve as a means of payment—that is, deposits are used to settle deposit holders' obligations.[10]

The definition of DMBs indicates that the line dividing those financial institutions that are regarded as deposit money banks from those that are not is somewhat arbitrary, since it is based on the size and composition of deposits rather than on the nature of the institutions themselves. Analysts need to keep the arbitrariness of this definition in mind in conducting monetary analyses, since it suggests that bank liquidity is not an unambiguous concept.

A typical balance sheet of a deposit money bank is shown in Box 5.5 and a summary analytical presentation is presented in Box 5.6. Most of the items in the box need no additional explanation. Three points, however, are worth noting.

- DMBs typically hold foreign assets, because of their activities in financing foreign trade. Whether these foreign assets are included as part of the net official reserve position of the country is a matter of judgment and depends primarily on the extent to which the monetary authorities control their use.[11]

[10]Money is defined here as a widely accepted means of payment or a medium of exchange. As discussed below, money has other major functions.

[11]For further details, see Chapter 4, Balance of Payments Accounts and Analysis.

> **Box 5.4.**
> **Transactions with the IMF**
>
> Transactions between a member country and the IMF are recorded in the balance sheet of the monetary authorities. SDR holdings are classified as foreign assets; the counterpart of SDR allocations is a liability included in the capital account and in "other items (net)" in the analytical balance sheet of the monetary authorities. A country's reserve position with the IMF is included in the foreign assets of the monetary authorities, while the use of IMF credit is included in foreign liabilities. Examples of transactions with the IMF include paying a quota subscription and purchasing a credit tranche, transactions that leave the net foreign asset position unchanged. In the first case, the increase in the country's reserve position with the IMF is offset by a decline in the country's foreign exchange position. In the second case, there is an increase in foreign exchange from the proceeds of the loan that is equal to the increase in foreign liabilities in the form of use of IMF credit. In contrast, a new allocation of SDRs increases the net foreign assets of the country, because the increase in assets is not matched by an increase in liabilities. See the Appendix to this chapter for more details.

- Unlike their assets, DMBs' liabilities are classified by type of instrument—particularly in terms of liquidity—rather than by sector. This classification system reflects the fact that some liabilities of DMBs are included in the (narrow) money supply on the basis of liquidity, which is determined by their maturity.
- DMBs hold only a fraction of their total assets in the form of reserves with the monetary authorities, as required by law, in an arrangement known as the fractional reserve system. The monetary authorities require DMBs to have a percentage of their deposits available as cash, in part to ensure that the money is readily available should depositors request it and in part to help control the money supply. DMBs sometimes also hold excess reserves as an additional safety margin.

  DMBs must maintain their reserve levels because they accept the obligation to convert deposit liabilities into cash. While demand deposits may be cashed immediately, time and other less liquid deposits can only be cashed after a stated period. It is unlikely that all depositors will seek to withdraw their funds at the same time, and DMBs can borrow from the monetary authorities at the central bank discount rate should reserves run low.

Thus, demand for reserves by the DMBs is an important element in the determination of reserve money and money supply. Changes in reserves can support an expansion or contraction of DMBs' deposit liabilities equal to a multiple of the change in their reserves. Because DMBs borrow at the central bank discount rate, their holdings will depend in part on the interest rate. Another factor that is important in explaining the DMBs' demand for reserves is the efficiency of the payments system. In many transition economies, this is an important determinant of the demand for reserves.

The Monetary Survey

The monetary survey—the consolidated balance sheet for the entire banking system—consolidates the consolidated balance sheet of the DMBs and the balance sheet of the monetary authorities. The assets and liabilities of the monetary survey therefore represent the assets and liabilities of the entire banking system. One important purpose of the monetary survey is to present, in a timely fashion, data on monetary and credit developments for the entire banking system that will allow policymakers to monitor these developments and to adjust monetary policy, if necessary.

Box 5.7 shows an analytical presentation of a typical monetary survey. On the liability side, the monetary survey contains the overall liquidity generated by the banking system, or the stock of money.[12] Narrowly defined, the money stock consists of currency in circulation outside banks (CY) **plus** demand deposits in the banking system. This narrow money is referred to as *M1* in the economic literature.[13]

$$\underset{(M1)}{\textit{Narrow money}} = \underset{(CY)}{\textit{Currency in circulation}} + \underset{(DD)}{\textit{Demand deposits}}$$

A broader definition of money includes, in addition, quasi-money (QM), which consists of time and savings deposits in the banking system. The concept of broad money (M2) covers the liabilities of the banking system. In particular, it includes foreign

[12]Economists rely on a number of criteria to identify a financial instrument as "money." Specifically, a financial instrument is included as part of money if it can serve as means of payment, store of value, unit of account, has a fixed nominal value, is liquid (i.e., immediately available for use), and is the legal tender.

[13]Note that currency in circulation (CY) refers here to the currency in circulation outside banks and not to currency issued.

Box 5.5.
Typical Balance Sheet of Deposit Money Banks

Assets	Liabilities
Reserves	**Demand Deposits**
Cash in vault	Sight deposits
Deposits with monetary authorities	Checking accounts
Foreign Assets	**Time, Savings, and Foreign Currency Deposits**
Claims on nonresident banks	Foreign currency deposits
Claims on nonresident nonbanks	Time deposits
	Savings deposits
Claims on Government	**Money Market Instruments**
Treasury bills	Certificates of deposit
Other government securities	Promissory notes
Loans and advances	Other instruments
Other claims	
	Bonds
Claims on Nonfinancial Public Enterprises	**Restricted Deposits**
	Import prepayments
	Deposits on import letters of credit
	Other restricted deposits
	Foreign Liabilities
	Nonresident banks
	Nonresident nonbanks
Claims on the Private Sector	**Government Deposits**
Discounts	
Loans and advances	**Credit from Monetary Authorities**
Mortgages	
Investments	
Overdrafts	**Liabilities to Nonmonetary Financial Institutions**
Other claims	
Claims on Nonmonetary Financial Institutions	**Capital Accounts**
	Unclassified Liabilities

currency deposits of residents, certificates of deposit, and security repurchase agreements.

$$\underset{(M2)}{\textit{Broad money}} = \underset{(M1)}{\textit{Narrow money}} + \underset{(QM)}{\textit{Quasi-money}}$$

or

$$M2 = CY + DD + TD. \tag{5.5}$$

The identity between assets and liabilities of the banking system implies that the stock of money ($M2$) is identical to the sum of its counterparts, namely net foreign assets (NFA) valued in domestic currency, and net domestic assets (NDA). In other words, for the banking system as a whole

$$M2 = NFA + NDA. \tag{5.6}$$

Since NDA consists of net domestic credit (NDC) and other items net (OIN_b), equation 5.6 can be rewritten as

$$M2 = NFA + NDC + OIN_b \tag{5.7}$$

or, in terms of changes

$$\Delta M2 = \Delta NFA + \Delta NDC + \Delta OIN_b.^{14} \tag{5.8}$$

[14]For purposes of monetary analysis, ΔNFA should exclude the changes in foreign exchange valuation adjustment. This is achieved in practice by valuing the foreign exchange-denominated components in the balance sheet at constant exchange rates and including the valuation adjustments, if any, in "other items, net."

Box 5.6.
Analytical Balance Sheet of Deposit Money Banks

Assets	Liabilities
Net foreign assets	**Deposits**
	Demand (DD)
Reserves	Time and savings (TD)
Required reserves	Foreign currency (FC)
Excess reserves	Liabilities to MA[1]
Domestic credit	**Other less liquid liabilities**
Claims on government (net)	
Claims on other domestic sectors	
Other items (net)	

[1]This item is the counterpart to the gross claims of the monetary authorities on the DMBs.

Algebraic manipulations similar to those involving the accounts of the monetary authorities (equations 5.1–5.4) can also be performed here to derive the contributions of various assets items to the growth of M2.[15]

The above two notions of money (*M1* and M2) are among the most widely used. However, with financial liberalization, even broader definitions (M3, M4, *L*) of the money stock have been found useful in many countries. Although the precise definition differs from country to country, M3 is generally defined to include M2, plus a wider range of instruments and issuing institutions. It includes travelers checks, commercial papers (money market mutual funds, cash vouchers). M4 includes, in addition to M3, liquid government securities, negotiable bonds, and liabilities of other financial intermediaries. Sometimes an even broader concept of liquidity (*L*) is used. This concept (*L*) is often defined to include, in addition to M4, other less liquid financial assets such as treasury bills, government bonds, mortgage bonds, and even some corporate bonds.

Financial innovations, which have tended to blur the distinction between money and near-money assets, have led to a continuing debate on where to draw the line between financial assets that form part of money and those that do not. In the spectrum of financial assets, currency (which carries no interest) is at one end and assets with higher yields but less liquidity at the other. The choice of one or more of these measures of money for purposes of making monetary policy and monitoring monetary developments is also influenced by the stability and predictability of the relationship between the monetary aggregate and nominal aggregate demand in the economy, as well as the degree to which the monetary authorities control the monetary aggregate. This notion implies, however, that no one set of assets will always be included in the money supply and that present definitions of money are likely to change in the future. Reflecting this essentially *empirical test* of which assets constitute money, several monetary aggregates should be analyzed.

Monetary Analysis

The monetary survey, which is the balance sheet of the banking system, highlights two essential relations: the link between a country's external position and the net foreign assets of the banking system, and the direct link between the government accounts and government financing provided by the banking system. The banking system is also clearly linked to the real sector (and the national accounts) through the demand for money and through credit provided to the private sector.

Link to the balance of payments. As discussed in Chapter 4 on the balance of payments, when the transactions of the entire banking system are entered below the line, the overall balance in the balance of payments is financed by the change in the banking system's net international reserves. In principle, the change in net foreign assets is the same whether it is derived from the monetary survey or from the balance of payments accounting identity. Therefore, in the monetary survey

$$\Delta NFA = \Delta M2 - \Delta NDA$$

and in the balance of payments,

$$CAB + \Delta FI + \Delta RES = 0.$$

Since $\Delta NFA = -\Delta RES$, then

$$\Delta NFA = CAB + \Delta FI,$$

[15] $\Delta M2 = \Delta NFA + \Delta NDCG + \Delta CPS + \Delta OIN_b$

$$\frac{\Delta M2}{M2} = \frac{\Delta NFA}{M2} + \frac{\Delta NDCG}{M2} + \frac{\Delta CPS}{M2} + \frac{\Delta OIN_b}{M2}$$

and finally

$$\frac{\Delta M2}{M2} = \frac{\Delta NFA}{NFA} \bullet \frac{NFA}{M2} + \frac{\Delta NDCG}{NDCG} \bullet \frac{NDCG}{M2} + \frac{\Delta CPS}{CPS} \bullet \frac{CPS}{M2} + \frac{\Delta OIN_b}{OIN_b} \bullet \frac{OIN_b}{M2}.$$

Box 5.7.
Analytical Balance Sheet of the Banking System: Monetary Survey

Assets	Liabilities
Net foreign assets (NFA)	**Broad money (M2)** Narrow money (M1) Currency in circulation (CY) Demand deposits (DD)
Net domestic assets (NDA) **Net domestic credit (NDC)** Net claims on government (NCG) Claims on the private sector (CPS) **Other items (net) (OIN)**[1]	Quasi-money (QM) Time and savings deposits (TD) Foreign currency deposits (FC)

[1]In some transition economies, a bank float is significant. For more on this issue, see Tomás Baliño, Juhi Dhawan, and Vasudevan Sundararajan, "The Payments Systems Reforms and Monetary Policy in Emerging Market Economies in Central and Eastern Europe," IMF Working Paper 94/13 (Washington: International Monetary Fund, 1994).

where ΔFI = nonmonetary financing flows.[16] These expressions can be rewritten as

$$\Delta NFA = \Delta M2 - \Delta NDA = CAB + FE = -\Delta RES. \quad (5.9)$$

The monetary survey identity indicates that any excess of domestic credit expansion over the increase in money stock (which, in equilibrium, is equal to the demand for money) is reflected in a decline in the net foreign assets of the banking system (that is, ΔNFA is negative). This relation constitutes the basis of the monetary approach to the balance of payments and provides the theoretical justification for setting ceilings on net domestic assets in IMF-supported programs.

Indeed, the distinction between money of domestic origin (domestic credit) and money of external origin (net foreign assets) and the linkages between the two are at the core of the IMF's financial programming framework. Starting with the monetary survey identity, which expresses the money stock as the sum of changes in its foreign and domestic components, and incorporating a demand function for money that links changes in real money balances to changes in real income and inflation, the framework posits a relationship among the net foreign assets of the banking system, the money stock, and domestic assets. The change in net foreign assets is positive (and the balance of payments in surplus) if the change in the money stock exceeds the change in domestic credit. An increase in net domestic assets that exceeds the desired increase in money is offset by decreases in net foreign assets on a one-for-one basis.[17] In the actual formulation of adjustment programs, targets are set for output, inflation, and other variables in a comprehensive policy package, and the implications of any changes for output, inflation, the balance of payments, and other policy objectives are carefully analyzed. The link between the monetary accounts and the balance of payments is often complicated by exchange rate changes and valuation adjustments (see Box 5.8).

Link to the government accounts. The banking system's net claims on the government appear on the asset side of the monetary survey. The changes in these claims represent the banking system's net lending to the government to finance any deficits. This direct link to the government sector shows how the monetization of a fiscal deficit (that is, the financing of the fiscal deficit through credit from the banking system) has a direct impact on the monetary stock.

Links to the real sector. On the asset side, the credit that the banking system provides to the private sector has a clear impact on developments and growth in that sector. On the liability side, the private sector's desire to hold the cash balances the banking system generates constitutes the private sector's "reaction function," which is an important determinant of the rate of inflation in the economy.

[16]As detailed in Chapter 4 on the balance of payments accounts and analysis, an increase in reserves has a negative sign (–) and a decrease in reserves has a positive (+) sign. In contrast, in the case of net foreign reserves in the monetary survey, an increase in the *NFA* will be positive (+) and a decrease negative (–). Therefore, $\Delta RES = -\Delta NFA$. Also, sometimes only the change in net official international reserves held by the monetary authorities is equated with ΔRES. In this case, ΔRES will be equal only to the *NFA* of the monetary authorities and not to ΔNFA of the banking system at large. However, in countries where the net foreign position of the commercial banks is under the *effective* control of the authorities, it can be argued that the net foreign position of banks should be included with the position of the monetary authorities for the purpose of arriving at ΔRES. In this case, ΔRES has the same coverage as ΔNFA of the banking system. To the extent that *NFA* in the monetary survey is expressed in local currency, valuation adjustment (due to exchange rate variations) would need to be taken into account before comparing ΔNFA from the monetary survey and ΔRES from the balance of payments (see Box 5.8).

[17]For a fuller discussion, see *Theoretical Aspects of the Design of Fund-Supported Adjustment Programs*, IMF Occasional Paper No. 55 (Washington: International Monetary Fund, September 1987); and Chorng-Huey Wong and Oystein Pettersen, "Financial Programming in the Framework of Optimal Control," *Weltwirtschaftliche's Archiv*, Vol. 1, 1979.

Box 5.8.
Valuation Adjustments

In analyzing the balance sheet of the banking system, changes in stocks are often equated with transaction flows. This is not always accurate. In particular, changes between two periods in stocks reflect not only transactions flows, but also revaluation and other factors. Revaluations result from changes in the prices of financial assets and liabilities due to fluctuations in market prices or exchange rates, and other changes, including allocation or cancellation of SDRs and writing off of debts by creditors. Equating changes in stocks over time to transaction flows is particularly misleading when exchange rate changes are significant over the period of analysis. Hence, in these situations, it is important to adjust for the effects of exchange rate changes so as to isolate the transaction flows.

Specifically, changes in stocks over time of those items that are affected by exchange rate fluctuations should be decomposed into changes due to transactions and changes due to valuation.[1] Formally:

Let A_t^R = balance sheet stock item denominated in local currency

$A_t^\$$ = balance sheet stock item in dollars

E_t = exchange rate (local currency units per dollar), end of period

E_t^* = exchange rate (period average)

where:

$$A_t^R = E_t \bullet A_t^\$$$

then

total change in stocks $= (A_t^R - A_{t-1}^R)$

transaction flows[2] $= E_t^*(A_t^\$ - A_{t-1}^\$)$

total change in stocks = transaction flows + valuation

hence

$$\text{valuation change} = (A_t^R - A_{t-1}^R) - E_t^*(A_t^\$ - A_{t-1}^\$).$$

It can be shown that the valuation adjustment (VAd) can also be expressed as

$$VAd = A_{t-1}^\$(E_t - E_{t-1}) + \Delta A_t^\$(E_t - E_t^*).$$

If foreign currency-denominated assets and liabilities in the monetary survey are adjusted for the effects of exchange rate changes, valuation adjustments should be, in this case, reflected in "other items (net)" to ensure that the balance sheet remains in balance.

[1]Changes due to other factors and market price fluctuations are assumed to be negligible in the above illustration.

[2]Transaction flows expressed in terms of local currency. Please note that the average period exchange rate is used to convert dollar-denominated transactions into local currency. This reflects the fact that these transactions are presumed to have taken place throughout the period.

Money Market Equilibrium

Functions of Money

In a market economy, money serves several functions. It can be any of the following:

- A *medium of exchange.* This function corresponds to the transactions motive for holding money.
- A *store of value.* Money is an asset that can be used to transfer purchasing power from the present to the future. This function corresponds to the portfolio (speculative) motive for holding money; demand for money in this role is therefore concerned with the rate of return to money, compared with yields on alternative assets (Box 5.9).
- A *unit of account.* Prices of goods, services, and assets are typically expressed in terms of money (for instance, dollars, rubles, or zlotys).

Monetary policy focuses initially on the quantity of financial assets that serve as transaction balances—usually currency in circulation plus demand deposits (*M1*). However, as the liquidity characteristics of financial assets other than money begin to resemble those of money, broader monetary aggregates become relevant to formulation of monetary policy.

The Quantity Theory and the Demand for Money

The earliest monetary theory—and one of the most influential—is based on the link between the stock of money (*M*) and the market value of output that it finances (*PY*). The so-called quantity equation equates the stock of money in real terms with real output, with a proportionality factor, *k*. Thus,

$$\frac{M}{P} = kY. \tag{5.10}$$

If k is assumed to be constant, this expression provides the *quantity theory of money*. This theory postulates a direct link between the stock of money and the price level (P) whenever the economy is assumed to be at full employment (i.e., Y is fixed). Thus, so long as k remains constant, there is a proportional relation between M and P.

Equation 5.10 can also be rewritten as

$$M \bullet V = P \bullet Y, \tag{5.11}$$

where $V = 1/k$ (the proportionality factor) is the income velocity of money,[18] which is the ratio of the money income (i.e., nominal GDP) to the money stock. Put differently, it is the number of times the *stock* of money turns over in a given period in financing the *flow* of nominal income. Velocity is one of the most studied variables in monetary economics. It is a very useful concept for a policymaker. Indeed, if V can be predicted with confidence, then one can aim at a level of the money supply that is consistent with the attainment of the desired real growth and inflation rate. A closer examination of V reveals that it is not a mechanical link between nominal income and the stock of money. Rather it is a concept very much linked to the demand for money and, in fact, velocity and money demand are inversely related. They are essentially equivalent ways of describing the same phenomenon. Converting equation 5.11 into growth form and using a dot over a variable to denote its rate of change over time, we obtain

$$\frac{\dot{M}}{M} \approx \frac{\dot{P}}{P} + \frac{\dot{Y}}{Y} - \frac{\dot{V}}{V}. \tag{5.12}$$

Assuming a constant velocity, $\dot{V}/V=0$. Equation 5.12 is a simple restatement of the quantity theory equation 5.11. It states that the percentage growth in money supply is equal to the sum of the percentage growth in prices (i.e., inflation), real GDP growth, and the growth in velocity.[19] Assuming constant velocity, the rate of change in money supply necessary to keep prices constant would need to be equal to the rate of growth of real GDP (a proxy for real income). Another way of looking at the implications of equation 5.12 is to note that for a constant velocity, growth in money supply beyond the growth in real incomes will lead to inflation. The higher the growth in money supply, the higher the inflation rate.

In many transition economies, inflation has been a monetary phenomenon, particularly in the early stages of the transition. Several studies have shown that inflation has been strongly correlated with the rate of monetary expansion in virtually all transition economies.[20]

In the above discussion, velocity has been assumed to be constant, but clearly velocity is not constant. In many countries, it has been shown to increase with increases in inflation and interest rates, and to be less sensitive to changes in income.[21]

Demand for Money

It is essential to clarify at the outset the distinction between *real* and *nominal* money balances. The nominal demand for money is the demand for a given number of specific currency units, such as rubles or zlotys. The *real* demand for money, or the demand for real money balances, is the demand for money expressed in terms of the number of units of goods that the money can buy. Therefore, the demand for real money balances is the quantity of money (M) expressed in real terms (M/P), that is, deflated by the index for the general level of prices. The demand for money is fundamentally a demand for real money balances, because people hold money for what it can buy.

There is considerable support in the economic literature for the view that the demand for real cash balances, like the demand function of any other asset, is a function of its price, the price of related assets, income, wealth, taste, and expectations. In a simplified form, the demand for real cash balances is positively related to income and negatively related to the opportunity cost of holding money.

- *Real income*. As real income grows, the demand for real cash balances grows, reflecting the increased level of transactions. As noted earlier, the impact of real growth on the velocity will depend on the income elasticity of demand for real cash balances.
- *Opportunity cost of holding money*. The cost of holding cash balances as opposed to other

[18]Income *velocity* is similar to a related concept called the *transactions velocity* of money, which is defined as the ratio of total transactions to money stock. Transactions velocity is generally higher than income velocity, because a dollar of GDP typically generates transactions worth many more dollars. Transactions velocity, unlike income velocity, is difficult to calculate.

[19]This equation is only approximate since it omits the cross product of changes in the variables. These cross products are very small for small changes in variables.

[20]See Jonathan Anderson and Daniel Citrin, "The Behavior of Inflation and Velocity," in Daniel A. Citrin and Ashok K. Lahiri, eds., *Policy Experiences and Issues in the Baltics, Russia, and Other Countries of the Former Soviet Union*, IMF Occasional Paper No. 133 (Washington: International Monetary Fund, 1995).

[21]If the income elasticity of the demand for money is one, changes in real income do not affect velocity. Velocity will increase (decrease) if the elasticity is less than one (greater than one).

Figure 5.2. Money Multiplier

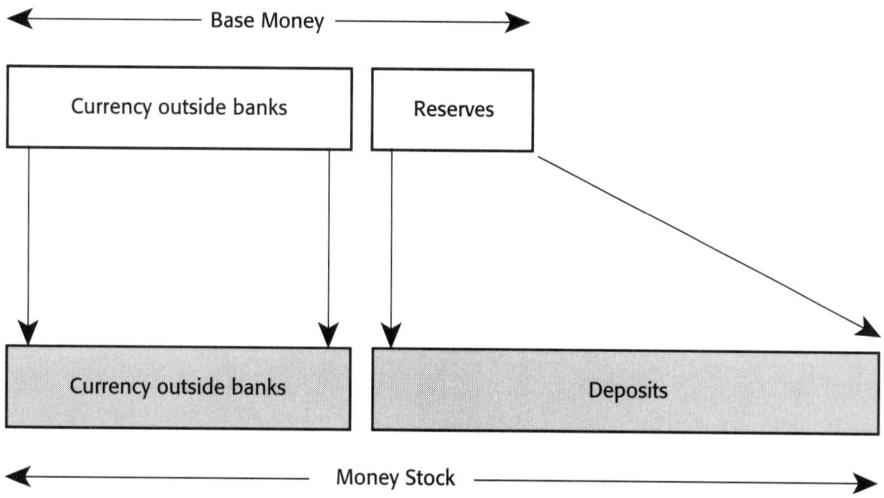

forms of wealth depends on the alternative forms of holding wealth. Thus economists in financially developed countries use the nominal interest rate as the opportunity cost of holding money relative to other assets. Expected inflation is also used as a proxy of the opportunity cost of holding real cash balances. In cases of hyperinflation, the opportunity cost of holding money becomes too high and the demand for money is drastically reduced. See Box 5.10.

The Concept of the Money Multiplier

As seen in the discussion of the balance sheets of the monetary authorities, the initial increase in reserve money serves as a base for financing subsequent monetary expansion by the banking system.[22] (See Figure 5.2.) Under the fractional reserve system, banks use their deposits to make loans, keeping only a fraction of their deposits as reserves.

A simple model for the money supply process starts with the supply of reserve money (*RM*) generated by the monetary authorities. The demand for reserve money comes from the public, which wants to use it as currency (*CY*), and the banks, which need it as reserves. Starting with definitions of reserve money ($RM = CY + R$) and money ($M = CY + DD$), then the multiplier *mm* is simply the ratio of the money stock over base money, where CY = currency, DD = deposits, and R = DMBs' deposits with the monetary authorities, or

$$mm = \frac{M}{RM} = \frac{(CY + DD)}{(CY + R)}. \quad (5.13)$$

Then, dividing the numerator and denominator on the right side by *DD*, and defining *c* as the currency-deposit ratio, and r as the reserve-deposit ratio, we obtain

$$M = \frac{c + 1}{c + r} \bullet RM \quad (5.14)$$

The identity shows how the money supply depends on two parameters, *c* and *r*, and the exogenously given *RM*. The factor of proportionality $(c+1)/(c+r)$ is the *money multiplier* and shows how much money is created by one unit of reserve money. Thus, the *money supply function* can be rewritten as

$$M = mmRM. \quad (5.15)$$

In terms of changes

$$\Delta M_t \approx \Delta mm_t RM_{t-1} + mm_{t-1}\Delta RM_t \quad (5.16)$$

[22]The initial expansion of reserve money by the monetary authorities leads to subsequent expansion by the deposit money banks through the multiplication of resources deposited with them. This is made possible because, of each amount deposited, only a fraction (determined by the reserve requirement) need be kept by the DMBs in reserve; the rest is typically lent and hence will eventually give rise to a deposit that, in turn, will serve as a basis for new loans. At the end of the process the amount of deposit created will be a "multiple" of the original increase in reserve money.

The above equation shows that money supply can increase either because of an increase in the multiplier (*mm*) or an increase in reserve money. In particular, an increase in the money multiplier for the same reserve money target would loosen monetary conditions.

It can be seen from equation 5.14 that the money multiplier (*mm*) is larger (i) the smaller the reserve requirement ratio and (ii) the smaller the currency ratio.

A more general formulation of the money multiplier (with the reserve ratio decomposed into the required reserve ratio on demand deposits (r_d), the required reserve ratio against time and savings deposits (r_t), and excess reserves as a ratio of demand deposits (r_e)) can be obtained by redefining M and RM as follows:

$M2 = CY + DD + TD$

$RM = CY + r_dDD + r_tTD + r_eDD$

CY = currency outside banks

DD = demand deposits

TD = time and savings deposits

r_d = required reserve ratio against demand deposits

r_t = required reserve ratio against time and savings deposits

r_e = excess reserves as a ratio to demand deposits.

The multiplier can be defined as

$$mm = \frac{M2}{RM} = \frac{CY + DD + TD}{CY + r_dDD + r_tTD + r_eDD}. \qquad (5.17)$$

Dividing the numerator and denominator by *DD* and defining *c* and *b* as the ratios to demand deposits of currency outside banks and time and savings deposits, respectively, the value of the multiplier can be expressed as

$$mm = \frac{c + 1 + b}{c + r_d + b\,r_t + r_e}. \qquad (5.18)$$

Equation 5.17 indicates that the value of the multiplier may not be constant over time, weakening the predictability of the relationship between reserve money and the money supply. Moreover, the equation highlights that changes in the multiplier reflect the behavior of three different types of economic agents: (i) the monetary authorities that set the reserve requirements; (ii) the commercial banks that decide how much to hold in excess reserves; and (iii) the nonbank public, which determines the composition of the money stock (the amount of currency held relative to deposits and the relative share of demand deposits in total deposits) in light of the structure of interest rates, inflation, and other variables. Figure 5.3 summarizes the factors that affect the composition of money.[23] Thus the money supply function given in equation 5.15 takes into account the behavior of the public, the banking system, and the monetary authorities. In other words, the monetary authorities do not fully control the money stock, in large part because the public's preference for cash versus deposit and DMBs' desire to hold excess reserves[24] also contribute to the determination of the money stock. However, if the multiplier is constant or at least predictable, then a possible strategy for a central bank to achieve the targeted level of money supply would be first to obtain an estimate of the multiplier, and then to set reserve money so that the targeted money supply is attained using equation 5.15.

Special Issues in Monetary Analysis

There are several issues that need to be kept in mind when analyzing monetary developments in a country. Some of the more important are (i) financial innovation and deregulation; (ii) currency substitution; (iii) the role of the exchange rate; (iv) the complications introduced by capital flows; and (v) seigniorage. These five issues are analyzed in detail below with special reference to the experience of countries in transition.

- ***Financial innovation and deregulation***. As noted earlier, the distinction between monetary and nonmonetary financial assets has increasingly become blurred in many countries, largely because of the innovations brought about by improved information technology and the development of new financial instruments and financial market techniques. In many countries, demand deposits earn interest comparable to the yields of other financial assets as stores of value. The ease with which money can be withdrawn from mutual funds that invest in stocks and bonds has made holding bonds and stocks much more liquid than before. These near-money assets make the demand for money less predictable and more unstable, thereby complicating monetary policy.

[23]It is important to note that when banks lend money and the borrowers gain purchasing power, borrowers incur a debt obligation to the bank. For this reason, loans do not increase the net worth of the borrower, which is calculated as assets minus liabilities. In other words, the money created by the fractional reserve system increases the economy's liquidity, but not its wealth.

[24]In the absence of credit ceilings, excess reserves reflect DMBs' preference for liquidity and are influenced by the exact nature of the reserve requirement (e.g., end-of-period level or weekly average), the penalty imposed by the central bank for violation of the requirement and the opportunity cost of holding excess reserves.

Figure 5.3. Factors Affecting the Money Supply

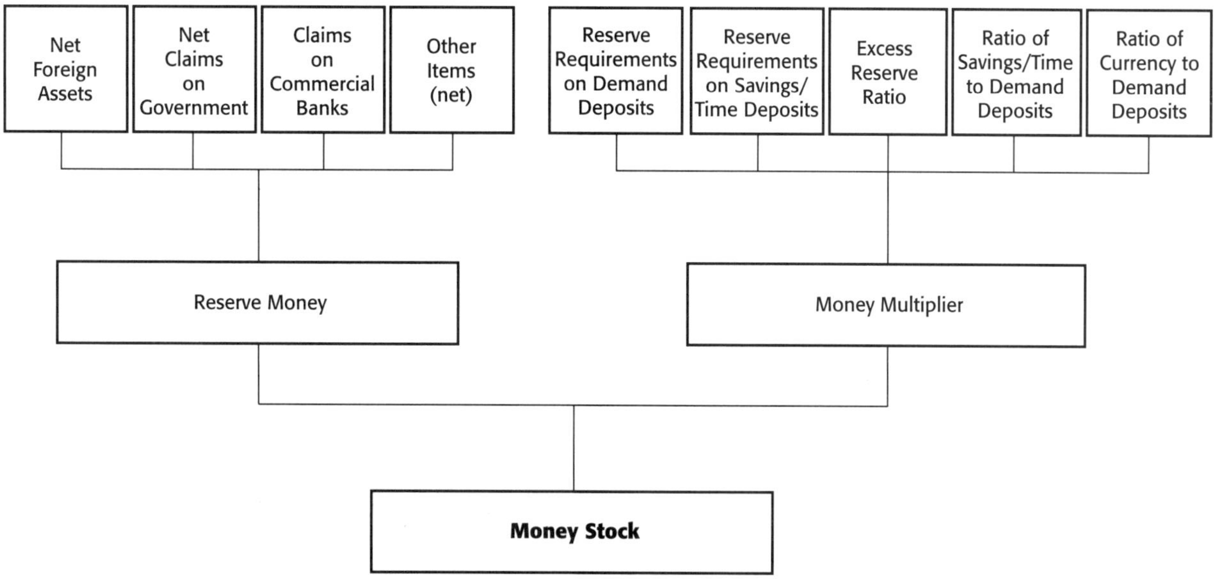

Rapid changes in households' holdings of money and near-money assets can make the velocity of money (either *M1* or *M2*) unstable. Thus, the quantity of money can be an unreliable guide to changes in aggregate demand. Some countries have responded to this problem by shifting to a broader definition of money that includes some near-money assets. However, this approach is an inherently ad hoc exercise, especially since the pace of financial innovation can cause the dividing line between broader monetary aggregates and other assets to shift continuously. More importantly, the broader the monetary aggregate, the less ability the monetary authorities have to control it, since many forms of near money have no reserve requirement and are issued by institutions outside the banking system. The authorities therefore face a dilemma as they try to preserve the link between the intermediate and ultimate targets of policy. They may adopt a broader, "more relevant" monetary aggregate for targeting but will have less control over it. *Relevance* (the link with aggregate demand) and *controllability* therefore need to be finely balanced when intermediate targets of monetary policy are being chosen.

As different measures of money begin to move in different directions because of financial innovation and deregulation, monetary policy is confronted with the problem of choosing appropriate indicators of monetary conditions. Policymakers may, of course, be tempted to use the aggregate that gives the most favorable data for a particular time. However, this approach can backfire and end up misleading policymakers and the public. Besides the monetary aggregates, other indicators of monetary policy have thus been found useful and should be taken into account: nominal and real interest rates, the structure of interest rates of different maturities (as captured by the *yield curve*), and the behavior of the exchange rate.[25] A transition economy undergoing rapid structural and behavioral changes needs to adopt an eclectic approach toward the choice of intermediate monetary targets and monetary indicators.

- ***Currency substitution***.[26] High and variable inflation seriously impairs a currency's ability to function efficiently as a store of value, unit of account, and means of exchange. As a re-

[25]The yield curve depicts a relationship between the maturities of financial assets with similar characteristics and the rates of return on these assets. Depending on expectations concerning future interest rates, the yield curve can be upward sloping (with longer maturities fetching higher interest rates) or downward sloping.

[26]Adapted from *World Economic Outlook* (Washington: International Monetary Fund, October 1994).

sult, the domestic currency in high-inflation countries tends to be abandoned over time in favor of a stable currency (often, but not always, the U.S. dollar), a phenomenon referred to as currency substitution or "dollarization."[27] In many high-inflation countries, the domestic currency's function as a store of value has virtually disappeared, because residents find it less risky and often more profitable to keep assets in foreign currency.

The phenomenon of currency substitution typically occurs in countries with high and variable inflation and has been pervasive in several Latin American economies.[28] These economies have remained highly dollarized even when inflation falls substantially. Although dollarization has the positive result of providing citizens with a reliable store of value, it has also posed formidable challenges to policymakers, by hindering the monetary authorities' control over money. Chronic inflation, fueled by accommodative monetary and exchange rate policies and sustained by formal and informal indexation, has led to increasing dollarization in many transition economies. Depending on institutional constraints and macroeconomic conditions, the dollarization ratio—the ratio of foreign currency deposits to broad money—has generally varied from zero to 10 percent at the start of reform programs to a peak of between 30 percent and 60 percent (Figure 5.4).

To the extent that currency substitution reflects a shift away from domestic money, it will exacerbate the inflationary consequences of a fiscal deficit, making fiscal discipline all the more important in highly dollarized economies. Moreover, currency substitution substantially undermines the authorities' ability to conduct monetary policy, as the foreign currency component of the total money supply cannot be directly controlled. Despite these potential problems, the Latin American experience suggests that combating dollarization with artificial measures, such as issuing indexed domestic financial instruments or forcing the conversion of foreign assets, merely magnifies the eventual inflation "explosion." Normally, sound financial and fiscal policies will increase holdings of assets denominated in domestic currency without government mandates. Finally, foreign currency holdings by residents is a close substitute for local currency and should hence be included in a measure of money.

- ***Exchange rate regimes and monetary analysis***. The discussion so far has not referred explicitly to the exchange rate regime. The nature of the exchange rate regime is, however, closely linked to the operation of monetary policy. Under a fixed exchange rate system, the monetary authorities stand ready to buy or sell the domestic currency for foreign currencies at a predetermined fixed price. Whenever the market exchange rate threatens to depart from this fixed rate, the monetary authorities buy or sell foreign exchange for the local currency to ensure that the rate remains at the fixed level. In terms of the monetary authorities' balance sheet, net foreign assets adjust in line with the foreign exchange intervention, and the monetary base and money supply adjust in line with net foreign assets. Adopting a fixed exchange rate regime therefore dedicates monetary policy to the goal of ensuring that the officially fixed level of the exchange rate is also the equilibrium level. The central bank is then committed to adjusting the money supply to the level needed to ensure that the exchange market clears at the predetermined fixed exchange rate. The monetary authorities are therefore unable to control the money supply; in this sense, by agreeing to fix the exchange rate, they relinquish control over the money supply.

  Under a fixed exchange rate regime, the effects of the central bank's efforts to expand domestic credit go beyond domestic prices and output. An increase in aggregate spending leads to a rise in the current account deficit and puts downward pressure on the exchange rate. The central bank must counter this pressure by selling foreign exchange, resulting in a drop in net foreign assets. The central bank's attempt to increase the money supply is thereby frustrated. Typically, a sound financial program has the opposite effect, improving the net foreign asset position. Using domestic credit ceilings to improve the balance of payments within the financial programming

[27]See Ratna Sahay and Carlos A. Végh, "Dollarization in Economies in Transition: Evidence and Policy Issues," IMF Working Paper 95/96 (Washington: International Monetary Fund, 1995), and Guillermo A. Calvo and Carlos A. Végh, "Currency Substitution in Developing Countries: An Introduction," *Revista de Análisis Economico*, Vol. 7 (June 1992), pp. 3–27. See also Guillermo A. Calvo, *Money, Exchange Rates, and Output*, chapters 8 and 9 (Cambridge, Massachusetts: MIT Press, 1996).

[28]In the absence of data on foreign cash held by the public and on foreign exchange deposited in banks abroad, estimates of the extent of dollarization are based on domestic foreign currency deposits only. For this reason, dollarization ratios frequently underestimate the phenomenon of currency substitution.

Box 5.9.
Interest Rates and Rates of Return

1. Financial Assets and Rates of Return

In general, people hold four types of assets: money; other interest-bearing financial assets (credit market instruments or bonds); equities or stocks; and real (or tangible) assets. The theory of asset demand or portfolio choice suggests that demand for an asset is governed by three characteristics: (i) the expected rate of return, or yield (compared with other assets); (ii) the riskiness of the expected return; and (iii) the liquidity of the asset. The rate of return on a financial asset has two components: the interest or dividend paid on the asset on a regular basis, plus *capital gain* or loss (the increase or decline per period of time in the market price of the asset). As a holding, currency pays no interest. Demand or checking deposits usually pay a zero or low rate of interest compared with less liquid forms of wealth. By holding money, people sacrifice the higher rate of return they could earn from more illiquid assets such as bonds or time deposits. Since the interest paid on money balances is relatively constant, the difference in the rates of return on money balances and alternative, less liquid assets is reflected in the market rate of interest: the higher the rate of interest, the higher the sacrifice for holding money. In an inflationary environment, if alternative financial assets carrying attractive positive real rates of return are not available, people tend to shift their wealth from money to real assets such as property, gold, commodities, or foreign currencies, all of which tend to be more stable in real terms.

2. Nominal and Real Interest Rates

In an environment of low and stable rates of inflation, the behavior of nominal financial variables (such as the monetary and credit aggregates or the spectrum of interest rates) can serve as useful indicators of monetary developments and the stance of monetary policy. However, in general, and particularly in the presence of high inflation, the focus should be on the movements of real (adjusted for the expected rate of inflation) rather than the nominal magnitudes in order to properly assess monetary developments and policies. If prices are rising, borrowers pay back loans in terms of a currency that has lost value. If prices are rising by 10 percent, and one can borrow at 6 percent, the nominal cost of borrowing is 6 percent, while the real cost of borrowing is negative. This real interest rate (R_r) can be expressed as

$$R_r \simeq R_n - P_e$$

where

R_n = nominal interest rate, in percent

R_r = real rate of interest, in percent

P_e = expected inflation rate.

When the inflation rate is low, $(R_n - P_e)$ gives a good approximation of the actual real interest rate. For high inflation, the discrete form below should be used:

$$R_r = \frac{(1 + R_n/100)}{(1 + P_e/100)} - 1.$$

In many transition economies, although the nominal interest rates appear high, the real rates of interest are often negative. Since saving and investment respond to movements in the real rates of return, a negative real return on financial assets suggests a disincentive to save and an incentive to spend, aggravating inflationary pressures and hurting long-term prospects for economic growth.

framework is a simple corollary of this analysis. Under a fixed exchange rate regime, the money supply is rendered *endogenous*—that is, it is determined by the system—rather than being an instrument of policy.

The only way automatic adjustments of the money supply can be offset under a fixed exchange rate regime is through *sterilization* operations by the central bank. Sterilization attempts to offset the impact of a foreign exchange intervention by the central bank with an open market operation in government securities. Thus, a sale of foreign exchange that reduces the monetary authorities' net foreign assets is offset by an open market purchase of securities that raises the monetary authorities' net domestic assets, diluting the impact on reserve money and the money supply. With sterilization, the direct link between an external imbalance and the equilibrating change in the money supply is broken. But sterilization can work only for a short period. Its basic weakness is its dependence on the kind of broad and well-functioning securities market that is not available in many transition economies. More fundamentally, sterilization is limited by the cost of interest payments on the government securities purchased, a cost that can escalate rapidly if the central bank sells too many securities to offset a large foreign exchange inflow. The basic analytics of the monetary im-

Figure 5.4. Selected Transition Economies: Dollarization and Inflation[1]

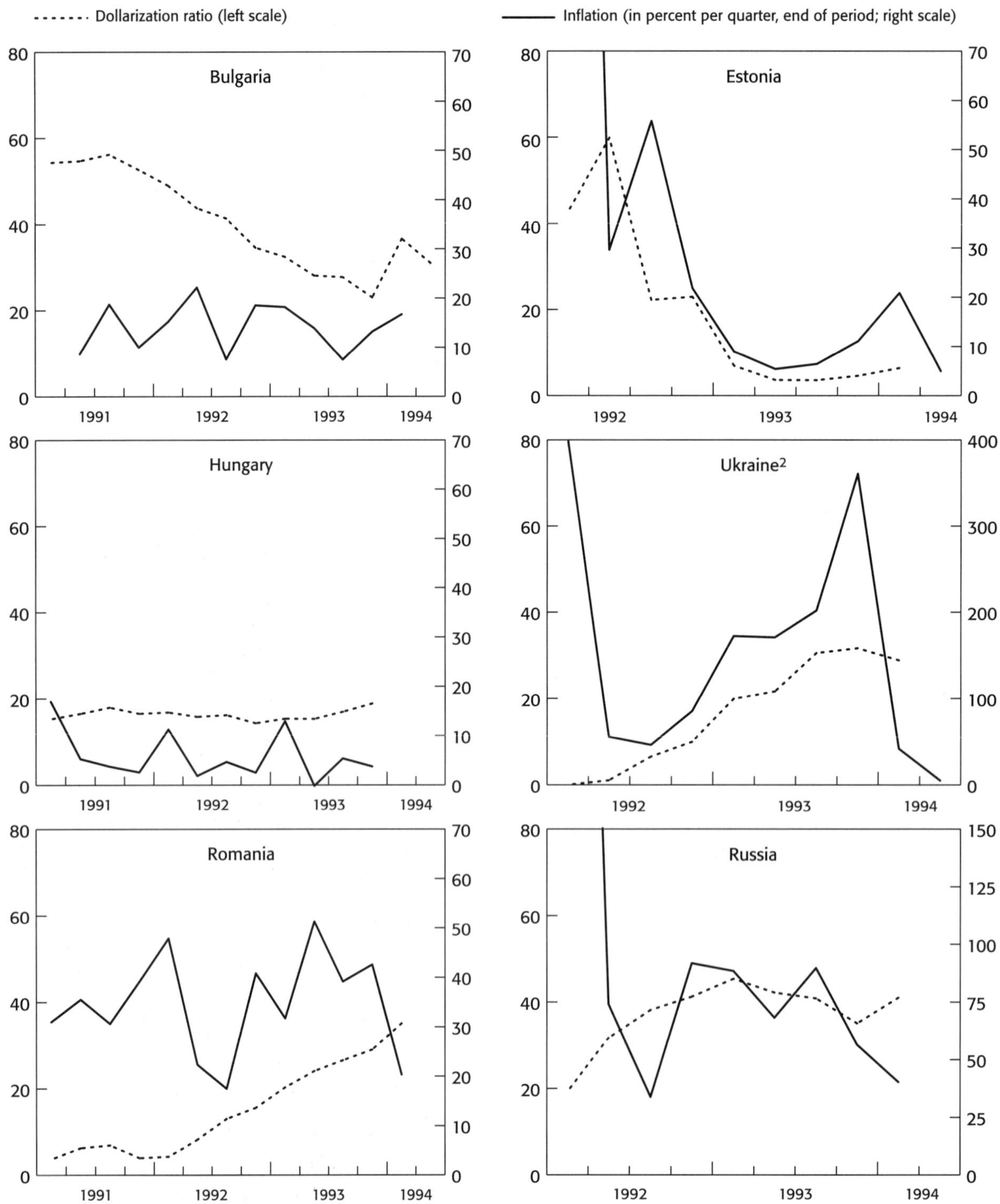

Source: IMF, *World Economic Outlook*, October 1994.

[1]Dollarization is measured by the ratio of foreign currency deposits to broad money (including foreign currency deposits). Note that the inflation scales differ for Ukraine and Russia.

[2]Foreign currency deposits are evaluated at the auction exchange rate.

Figure 5.4 *(concluded)*

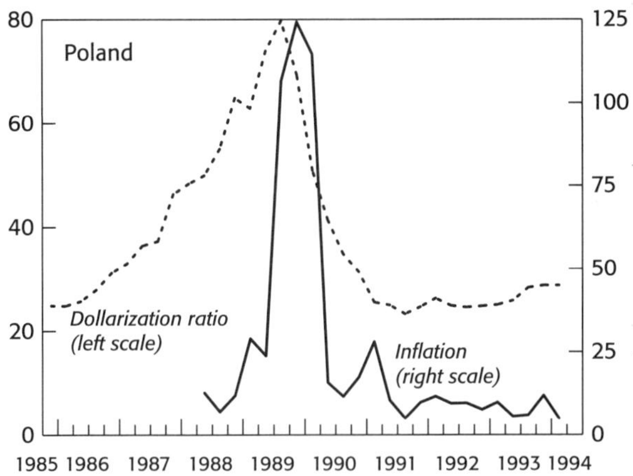

pact of capital inflows under alternative exchange rate regimes are depicted in Figure 5.5.

Despite being required to surrender their independence to control the money supply, countries sometimes choose to tie their exchange rate to the currency of a low-inflation country. In doing so, they seek to impose an automatic discipline on domestic policy and thus to benefit from the credibility of the low-inflation country's central bank. The costs of such an arrangement are the surrender of monetary control to the central bank of the country whose currency is used as the peg and the relinquishing of the exchange rate as an instrument to adjust the balance of payments. *Currency boards* in transition economies (such as those adopted by Estonia and, more recently, Lithuania) essentially create a fixed exchange rate system with no option for sterilization, because reserve money can be created only if it is fully backed by holdings of foreign exchange. Since sterilization is ruled out, adjustments are automatic but not painless. Adjustment will eventually raise nominal and real interest rates and put downward pressure on prices: if prices, and especially wages, are not flexible, output and employment fall.

The primary argument for a floating exchange rate is that a float allows for autonomy in monetary policy and therefore can be used for purposes such as stabilizing demand or prices. Under a pure float, the monetary authorities do not intervene in the foreign exchange market. In practice, however, a "pure" float is largely hypothetical, because most countries that adopt a floating rate regime do intervene when the exchange rate threatens to move too far from its underlying equilibrium level, thereby making the float "dirty." With a floating exchange rate regime, the monetary authorities have full control over the domestic money supply and therefore can determine the domestic inflation rate. Excessive credit creation manifests itself through an additional channel (the depreciation of the exchange rate). In most small, open economies dependent on critical imports, the exchange rate therefore provides an additional channel between the money stock and inflation.

- ***Role of capital flows***. Capital flowing across national frontiers provides intermediation among countries similar to the financial intermediation services banks provide for savers and investors within a country. Capital flows strengthen the link between domestic economic policies and the balance of payments. As

Figure 5.5. Basic Analytics of Capital Inflows[1]

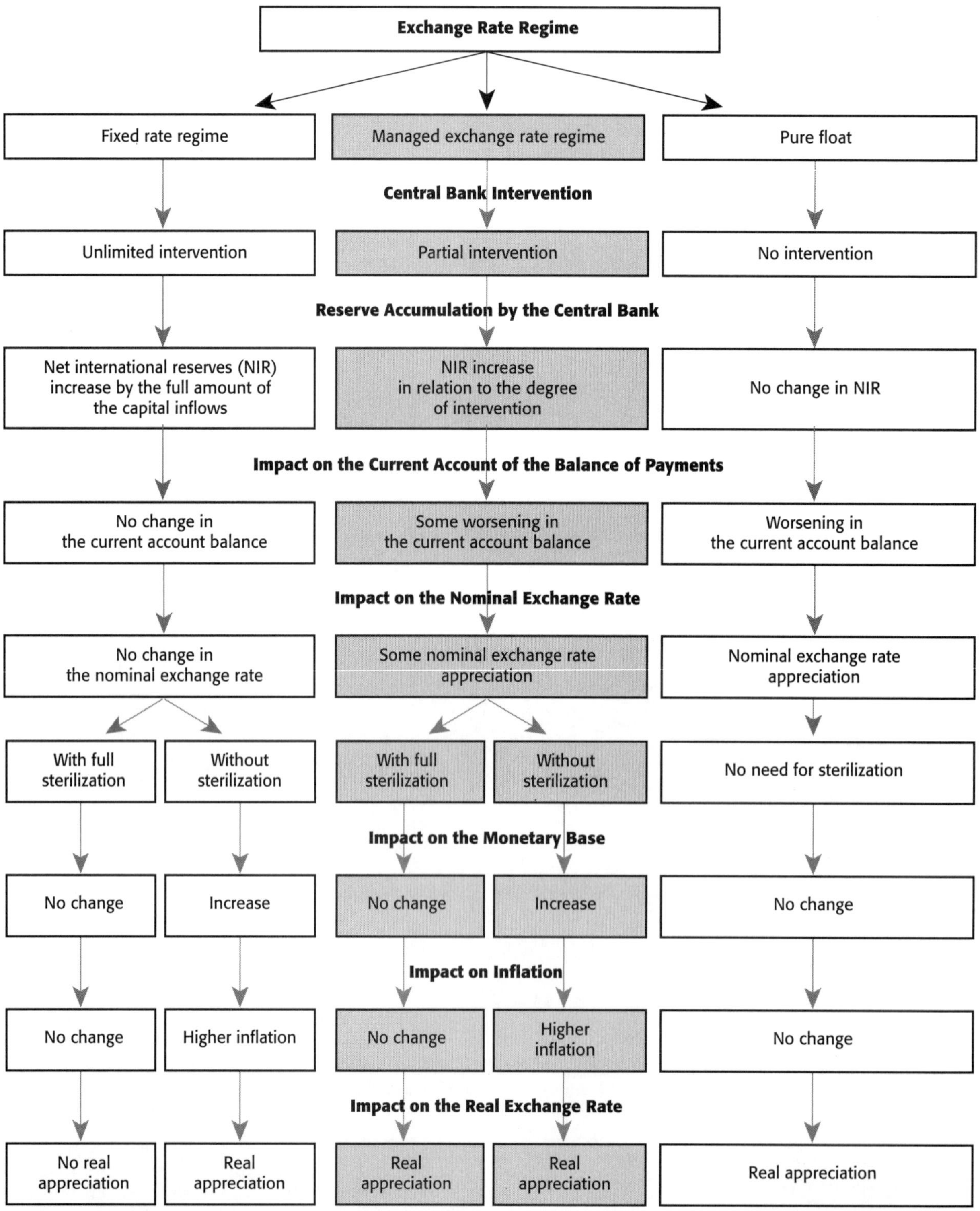

[1]Appropriate use of fiscal policy can help mitigate the effects of capital flows on the real exchange rate.

the world's capital markets have become increasingly integrated in the past two decades, so too have domestic monetary policies and monetary developments in foreign countries. Under perfect capital mobility, the slightest difference between interest rates prevailing in domestic and foreign capital markets provokes very large capital flows. When a fixed exchange rate is added, a central bank cannot hope to influence the level of domestic interest rates. Any attempt by the central bank to tighten monetary policy will induce a huge capital inflow into the country, forcing the central bank to intervene in the exchange market in order to keep the domestic currency from appreciating. The increase in net foreign assets offsets the initial money contraction, forcing domestic interests rates down to the world level.

Under a floating exchange rate regime, the absence of intervention by the monetary authorities implies no change in net foreign assets, and the current account deficit is equal to private and official capital inflows. The link between the money supply and the balance of payments is broken, and the central bank regains control over the money supply. Many real-world cases lie somewhere between the fixed and floating exchange rate regimes and full and zero capital mobility. Thus, even with strict controls over capital flows, traders influence the current account through capital inflows and outflows (for example, by failing to repatriate export receipts or by incorrectly invoicing transactions) and create partial substitution between domestic and foreign assets. The degree of substitution rises as the capital account is opened, and maintaining an independent monetary policy becomes increasingly difficult without some flexibility in the exchange rate. In practice, most countries have responded by undertaking a combination of actions involving (i) a partial intervention to buy some of the capital inflow, thereby allowing some nominal exchange rate appreciation; (ii) partial sterilization to offset part of the impact of the increased net foreign assets on the monetary base; and (iii) some increase in the monetary base and inflation and consequently real exchange rate appreciation.

- ***Seigniorage and the inflation tax.*** An important factor driving money creation in high-inflation situations is the government's attempts to collect seigniorage from money creation. This issue has been dealt with in detail in Chapter 3 on fiscal accounting and analysis.[29]

[29]See, in particular, Box 3.1.

Monetary Analysis in Transition Economies: Some Special Issues[30]

Monetary analysts working with transition economies face special difficulties stemming from the structural and institutional characteristics of these economies. Some of these difficulties are discussed below.

Rapid changes in velocity. Many transition economies have experienced high and variable rates of inflation and accompanying increases in the velocity of money. The increases, however, have generally occurred in large, discrete jumps rather than in smooth trends. In extreme cases (such as Armenia and Georgia in late 1993), velocity has risen as much as threefold in one quarter. The initial large increases in velocity have generally taken a long time to reverse, with real money balances remaining at low levels for prolonged periods. In countries with very high inflation, real money balances have tended to reach the minimum level necessary for transactions purposes and have gradually stabilized at that level. Earlier hyperinflations suggest that real balances do not return to their pre-inflation levels for some time, so that even with actual sharp reductions in inflation, the demand for real balances remains subdued (see Box 5.10). Countries that have maintained an aggressive interest rate policy to ensure a positive real rate of return on domestic monetary assets have succeeded in restoring confidence in the domestic currency relatively quickly.

Lack of competition among banks. The shift to indirect methods of monetary controls is hampered by a lack of competition among banks. Demand for bank reserves is not sensitive to interest rates, because many banks have not yet started behaving like profit-maximizing commercial entities. Many transition economies have therefore found it necessary to rely on nonprice rationing of central bank credit, often through auctions, with banks reallocating reserves among themselves in a market for cash balances. Competition in the banking system is limited for a number of reasons. Like many enterprises, many banks are state owned, and there are few branch networks. Banks continue to depend on central bank funds, large shares of preferential credits, and credit ceilings. Many banks rely heavily on central bank refinancing, reflecting the surplus of credits over deposits transferred from the "monobank" of the centrally planned era, the lack of well-developed interbank markets to recycle

[30]For a comprehensive analysis of monetary policy issues in a transition economy, see David K. Begg, "Monetary Policy in Central and Eastern Europe: Lessons After Half a Decade of Transition," IMF Working Paper 96/108 (Washington: International Monetary Fund, 1996).

funds, and a large share of subsidized loans. (A monobank not only served as the central bank, but had a monopoly on commercial banking functions.)

Interenterprise arrears.[31] When countries tighten credit policies without getting enterprises to harden their individual budget constraints, the result is often a sharp increase in disintermediation, or the movement of funds from the banking system to financial institutions outside the system. In transition economies, enterprises use payments arrears to each other as a substitute for bank credit. Use of these "interenterprise credits" has risen rapidly in many transition economies since 1990 (for instance, in Romania and states of the former Soviet Union, such as Russia). Romania's experience demonstrates that providing bank credit to clear the arrears is not a lasting solution to the problem unless enterprises are convinced that a decisive hardening of the budget constraint will take place thereafter. Preventing new arrears requires positive real interest rates, improved payments systems, more managerial accountability, and effective bankruptcy legislation, and possibly enterprise restructuring and privatization.

Absence of money and financial markets. The lack of such markets in the initial stages of the transition to a free market economy precludes the use of open market operations as an instrument of monetary control. Exacerbating the problems are the absence both of an interbank clearing system and of confidence in the creditworthiness of interbank transactions.

Interest rate problems. The large stock of loans with long maturities at low and fixed interest rates (such as loans for housing) has complicated the process of liberalizing interest rates. Moreover, weak financial discipline tends to undermine the role of interest rates. For instance, there may be a systematic tendency for higher interest rates to feed into higher monetary growth (and hence into higher inflation) if enterprises are allowed to borrow from banks to pay interest obligations.

A large spread between deposit and lending rates. The spread has tended to remain large, as banks pass on a variety of costs to their clients. These costs are associated with (i) the large number of nonperforming loans; (ii) the large share of credits that continue to be extended at preferential rates; (iii) the central bank's heavy reliance on noninterest paying reserve requirements in the initial stages of reform, which lower the banks' rate of return on assets; and (iv) high administrative costs resulting from inefficiencies in the system. In the absence of competition, there is little pressure for banks to abandon the old "cost-plus" system of pricing.

High financing needs of the government sector. Where the formulation of monetary policy is not divorced from the political process, the monetary authorities must frequently subordinate their objectives to accommodate the government's financing need. In countries that face high budget deficits and have limited sources of nonbank domestic financing, this situation has typically been associated with a high inflation outcome.

[31]See Daniel A. Citrin and Ashok K. Lahiri, eds., *Policy Experiences and Issues in the Baltic Countries, Russia, and the Other Countries of the Former Soviet Union*, IMF Occasional Paper No. 133 (Washington: International Monetary Fund, December 1995).

Box 5.10.
Money and Hyperinflation[1]

The term "hyperinflation" is generally used to refer to a sustained increase in the general price level at an extremely high rate. A widely accepted definition is that proposed by Philip Cagan in a seminal study of hyperinflation, namely a monthly rate of price increase of 50 percent or more, sustained for several months. The historical episodes of hyperinflation—such as those in Germany after the first and second world wars, in Austria during the interwar period, in Hungary and in Latin American countries such as Bolivia—provide laboratory experiments for studying the consequences of high and variable rates of monetary growth and inflation.

Studies of these hyperinflations have found several common features in them. First, the real demand for money falls drastically. By the end of the hyperinflation in Germany in the 1920s, real money demand was only one-thirtieth of its level two years earlier. Second, relative prices become very unstable. In Germany, real wages changed (up or down) on average by a third each month. This large variation in relative prices and real wages and the inequities and distortions caused by them took a heavy toll on economic and social stability. Third, at high rates of inflation, inflation tends to be highly variable. In the case of German hyperinflation during 1921–1923, monthly rates of inflation ranged from zero to 500 percent. In such an environment, the nominal interest rate no longer is a useful measure of the alternative cost of holding money, because lending at prescribed nominal interest rates virtually disappears. The best indicator of the cost of holding money in hyperinflation is the expected rate of inflation.

[1]Adapted from Robert Barro, *Macroeconomics* (New York: John Wiley & Sons, Inc., 1993), pp. 201–3.

Background for Monetary Analysis

Institutional setup. With the enactment of the Banking Act in 1989, the National Bank of Poland (NBP) ceased to be the monobank, and its commercial functions were devolved to nine commercial banks. The NBP was granted considerable autonomy, although it was required to submit a draft of the guidelines for monetary policy to parliament each year. Since October 1991, monetary policy has been conducted in the framework of a crawling peg exchange rate arrangement. Although the commercial banks were initially fully owned by the government, considerable progress is being made in privatizing them, and by mid-1996, two had already been sold to the private sector. There are also four large specialized banks dealing with foreign trade, agroindustry, housing construction, and foreign currency deposits that remain in the public sector. In the last five years, a number of private banks have been set up, several with foreign participation.

Inflation performance. Inflation declined sharply from the very high rates of 1989–90 to about 40 percent annually in 1992–93, suggesting that the policy of using the exchange rate as a nominal anchor in the early stages of the stabilization program had some success. The progress in reducing inflation slowed somewhat in 1994 (see Figure 5.6).

Credit expansion. The reduction in inflation has been brought about despite the extension of large credits to the government to finance budget deficits. Most of the credit to the government has been granted by the NBP, making such credit the primary source of expansion in the monetary base. Credit to the nongovernment sector, including the state enterprises, has been relatively sluggish, indicating some crowding out (Figure 5.7).

Velocity of money. The reduction in inflation has been achieved despite significant deficit financing, because the demand for broad money has risen sharply. The fall in inflation has restored the role of money as a store of value to a significant extent, and the private sector has, therefore, channeled its savings into bank deposits. In fact, the velocity of money fell throughout 1991–93 (Figure 5.8).

Interest rates. The deregulation of interest rates has been an important factor in the shift of savings into bank deposits. Lending rates by banks have been influenced mainly by the central bank's refinance rate. Real interest rates on deposits have generally remained negative for short-term deposits, but lending rates have been significantly positive (Figure 5.9). As noted, the spread between the lending and deposit rates of banks has remained wide.

Currency substitution. The earlier period of high inflation and negative real interest rates had re-

Figure 5.6. Poland: Money and Inflation[1]
(Year-on-year percent change)

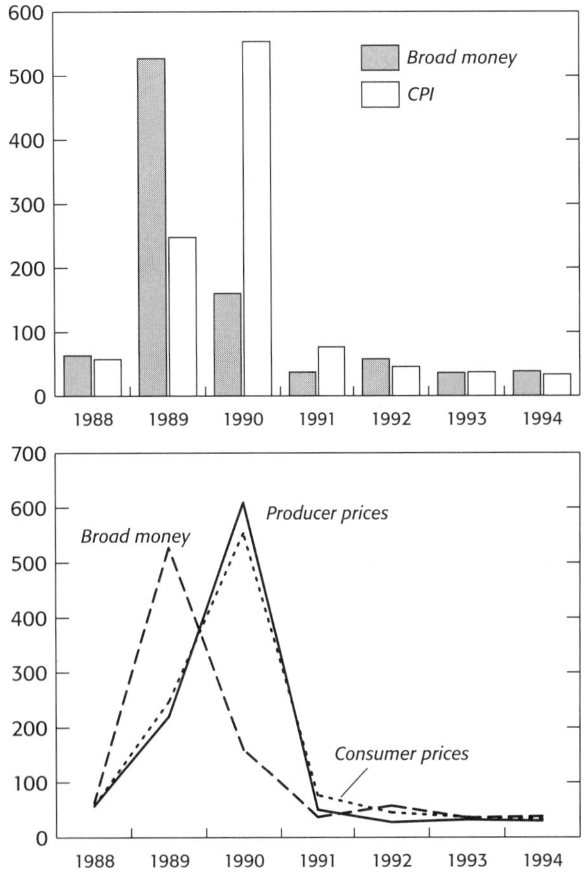

Sources: IMF, *International Financial Statistics* and Tables 2.5 and 5.1.

[1]Broad money is defined as zloty broad money plus foreign currency deposits. Inflation is measured by the CPI.

Figure 5.7. Poland: Credit to Government and Nongovernment

(In constant January 1992 prices)

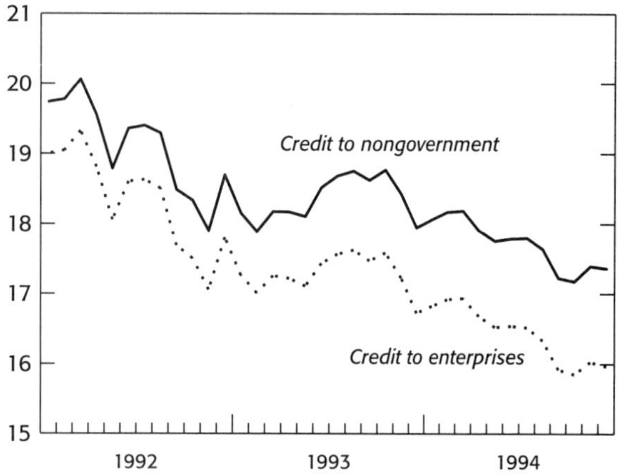

Sources: IMF Institute database and Table 5.1.

Figure 5.8. Poland: Velocity of Money[1]

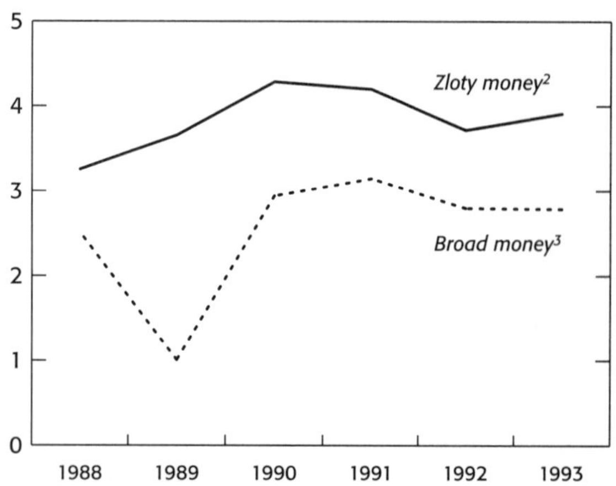

Sources: IMF Institute database and Table 5.1.

[1]Velocity is measured as nominal GDP divided by average of broad money or zloty money.

[2]Zloty money comprises of currency and all zloty deposits.

[3]Broad money comprises of currency, zloty deposits (demand, savings, and time), and foreign currency deposits.

sulted in a rapid increase in dollarization, with the ratio of foreign currency deposits to broad money rising to 80 percent in 1989. Since then, the ratio has fallen sharply, although it did rise somewhat in 1993 (Figure 5.10).

Exercises and Issues for Discussion

Exercises

1. The purpose of this exercise is to familiarize you with the consolidation of monetary statistics. Tables 5.4 and 5.5 of the appendix to this chapter present illustrative data for Transitia on the consolidated balance sheet of the deposit money banks (Table 5.4) and on the balance sheet of the monetary authorities (Table 5.5).

   (a) On the basis of this information, construct the balance sheet of the banking system (i.e., the Monetary Survey). Use the format provided in Table 5.6 to guide you in presenting the monetary survey in its analytical format (Table 5.7).

   (b) Explain why the sum of the other items (net) (OIN) of the monetary authorities' balance sheet and those of the consolidated balance sheet of the DMBs do not yield the "OIN" for the banking system.

   (c) Assume that the reserve requirement ratio is the same for all deposits (demand deposits, time and savings deposits, and money market instruments). What is the implied reserve requirement in Tables 5.4 and 5.5?

   (d) Suppose now that the reserve requirement on all foreign currency deposits is 10 percent. What is the implied reserve requirement ratio for the deposits in national currency?

   (e) Calculate the currency-to-deposit ratio (using the same definition of deposit as in question 1.c above). Using this ratio and the reserve requirement ratio computed in 1.c, calculate the money multiplier, assuming that it can be approximated by the formula given in equation 5.14. Compute the actual multiplier and show that equation 5.14, in this case, overstates the multiplier.

   (f) Suppose the central bank sells, through an open market operation, 40 million T$ worth of treasury bills to the public against a check drawn on one of the commercial banks. Show what happens to the balance sheet of the central bank. What if the sale was against outright cash? Explain why reserve money is also reduced in this case.

2. On the basis of the balance sheet of the National Bank of Poland, calculate for 1993 the contributions to the growth of reserve money from net foreign assets, net claims on the general government, domestic credit to other sectors, and other items (net). On this basis, discuss the factors that affected reserve money in 1993.
3. Verify that broad money growth decelerated in 1993. What factors contributed to this deceleration?
4. Compare the growth rates of reserve money, money, and broad money in 1992–93. What factors might account for any differences between the growth rates of these aggregates in any given year? Would such differences be important in analyzing monetary developments?
5. (a) How much did the general government borrow in 1993 from the monetary authorities? From the banking system?
   (b) It has been argued that this monetization of the deficit represents an inflation tax. Do you agree?
   (c) Estimate the inflation tax in Poland in each of 1991, 1992, 1993, and 1994, and comment on the observed trend.
   (d) How much seigniorage did the NBP receive during the period?
6. It has been said that one consequence of the introduction of the treasury bill market in Poland in May 1991 has been that commercial banks have become reluctant to lend to the nongovernment sector.
   (a) Is this corroborated by the figures in the balance sheets of commercial banks?
   (b) Calculate the increase in bank credit to the nongovernment sector in real terms in 1991–94.
7. Using the information for Poland in Tables 5.1 and 5.2, calculate the broad money multiplier and the velocity during the period 1990–94 including and excluding foreign currency deposits in each case, and comment on these developments.
8. On the basis of the information provided in Tables 5.1 and 5.2, can you detect any systematic link between the growth in broad money and that of prices?
9. How would you interpret the changes in the velocity of money depicted in Figure 5.8? How are they related to the interest rate developments shown in Figure 5.9 and the inflation developments shown in Figure 5.6?

Figure 5.9. Poland: Nominal Interest Rates
(In percent)

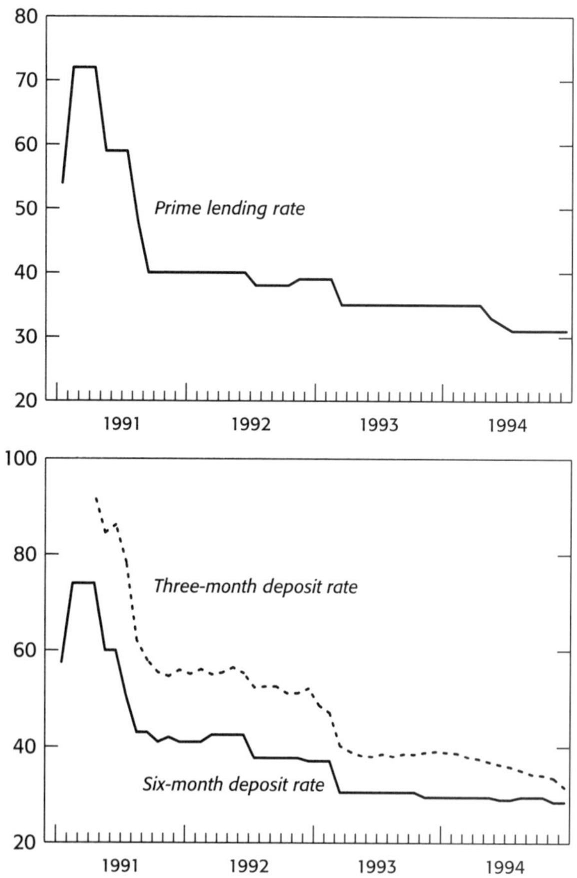

Sources: IMF Institute database and Table 5.3.

Figure 5.10. Poland: Foreign Currency Deposits
(In billions of U.S. dollars)

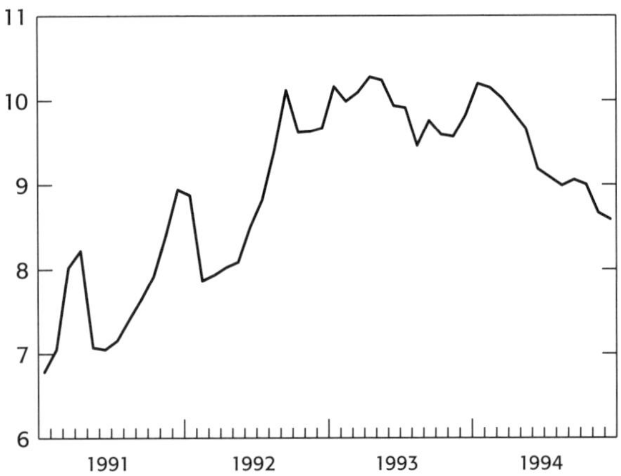

Sources: IMF Institute database and Table 5.1.

10. Assuming that money velocity in 1995 is constant at its level in 1994 and that real growth is expected to be 6 percent in 1995, calculate the stock of money consistent with this rate of growth and an inflation rate of 30 percent. Assuming that other items net and net foreign assets of the banking system remain constant in 1995, what would be the overall credit level consistent with the above growth and inflation rates? Suppose now that credit to the nongovernment sector grows in real terms in line with overall economic growth, what is the level of bank financing that can be made to the budget in 1995? What would happen if, as a result of large capital flows, the banking system increased significantly its holding of foreign exchange. Discuss all available policy responses to this capital flow problem. Explain how this complicates the conduct of monetary policy, how it affects the fiscal adjustment, focusing attention on the impact on inflation and the nominal and real exchange rates.

Issues for Discussion

1. Using Figure 5.8, discuss the implications of the changing role of foreign currency substitution in Poland for monetary developments and the conduct of monetary policy. How is the inflationary impact of a given fiscal deficit affected by changes in dollarization? Explain.

2. Explain the importance of the concept of monetary base in monetary analysis and discuss how various actions by the central bank affect the growth of the monetary base. Would you agree or disagree with the statement that the control over its monetary base is the most effective means of conducting monetary policy by a central bank?

3. What are the principal obstacles to the conduct of an effective market-oriented monetary policy in a transition economy? What can be done to remove these obstacles? Discuss this question on the basis of your own country's experience.

4. Discuss how volatile capital flows complicate the conduct of monetary policy in an open economy. Can monetary policy still retain its ability to influence the rate of inflation in the face of volatile capital inflows? Explain highlighting the role of the exchange rate.

5. Explain why under a fixed exchange rate regime policymakers target the net domestic assets rather than broad money directly. Would this also be true in the case of a crawling peg or an exchange rate band?

Table 5.1.
Monetary Survey[1]
(In trillions of zlotys; end of period)

	1990	1991	1992	1993	1994
Net foreign assets	**74.3**	**71.3**	**128.0**	**186.9**	**275.1**
(In millions of U.S. dollars)	(7,822)	(6,507)	(8,118)	(8,757)	(11,287)
Net domestic assets	**116.2**	**189.6**	**283.1**	**372.4**	**497.9**
Claims on general government (net)[2, 3]	−10.4	86.6	183.1	282.3	395.5
Total state government	—	97.9	201.6	308.4	428.4
Rest of general government	—	−15.7	−18.5	−26.1	−32.9
Claims on nongovernment sector	118.2	187.6	248.9	332.0	415.6
Other items (net)	8.4	−84.5	−148.9	−241.9	−313.2
Money and quasi-money (broad money)	**190.5**	**260.9**	**411.1**	**559.2**	**773.0**
Zloty broad money	130.7	196.6	309.2	398.3	552.4
Zloty narrow money	94.2	107.9	149.7	196.4	274.5
Currency in circulation	39.3	56.2	78.0	99.8	122.7
Demand deposits (zlotys)	54.9	51.7	71.7	96.6	151.8
Quasi-money	96.3	153.0	261.4	362.8	498.5
Savings and time deposits	36.5	88.7	159.5	201.9	277.9
Foreign currency deposits	59.8	64.3	101.9	160.9	220.6
Demand deposits	—	21.4	28.8	47.0	75.3
Time and savings	—	42.9	73.1	113.9	145.3
Memorandum items:					
Gross domestic product	**560.3**	**808.8**	**1,149.4**	**1,557.8**	**2,104.1**
Inflation (percentage change)					
End-period	249.3	60.3	44.3	37.6	29.5
Period average	585.8	70.3	43.0	35.3	32.2
Exchange rate (zlotys/U.S. dollars)					
End-period	9,500	10,957	15,767	21,344	24,372
Period average	9,500	10,576	13,626	18,115	22,723

Sources: Juha Kahkonen and others, *Poland–Statistical Tables*, IMF Staff Country Report No. 96/20 (Washington: International Monetary Fund, 1996); and Liam P. Ebrill and others, *Poland: The Path to a Market Economy*, Occasional Paper No. 113 (Washington: International Monetary Fund, 1994).

[1]The figures for reserves and net credit to general government in 1994 include the impact of the net financing cost of the debt reduction operation with external commercial creditors.

[2]Beginning in 1994, the accounting of treasury bills newly purchased by the National Bank of Poland to finance the budget deficit was changed from face value basis to a cash value basis. Accordingly, to compare net credit to government across years, the net credit to general government has been adjusted in all years to show the cash value of securities.

[3]The change in the stock of net credit to general government can be reconciled with the flow change in financing in the fiscal table after adjustments are made for valuation effects on the dollar-denominated debt of the government and capitalized interest on the bonds issued to recapitalize the state-owned banks.

Table 5.2.
Accounts of the National Bank of Poland
(In trillions of zlotys; end of period)

	1990	1991	1992	1993	1994
Net foreign assets					
Zlotys	33.2	32.4	54.3	77.2	114.5
Millions of U.S. dollars	–	–	3,443.0	3,616.0	4,697.0
Net domestic assets	82.5	68.3	81.2	82.4	81.7
Net domestic credit	67.3	65.2	132.3	164.3	227.2
Claims of general government (net)[1]	–8.8	30.9	101.9	116.6	158.4
Claims on commercial banks	76.1	33.3	34.3	40.3	44.0
Claims on nonfinancial sector (net)	. . .	–7.4	–11.5	0.1	0.2
NBP securities	. . .	8.4	7.6	7.3	24.6
Other items (net)	15.2	3.1	–51.1	–81.9	–145.5
Reserve money	**85.3**	**100.7**	**135.5**	**159.6**	**196.1**
Currency issues[2]	47.8	68.3	95.2	121.8	147.8
Currency in circulation	(39.3)	(56.2)	(77.9)	(99.8)	(122.7)
Currency in banks' vaults		12.1	17.3	22.0	25.1
Deposits of commercial banks	37.5	32.4	40.3	37.8	48.3
Memorandum items:					
Money multiplier			3.0	3.5	3.9
Gross official reserves (millions of U.S. dollars)			4,287.0	4,281.0	6,029.0

Sources: Juha Kahkonen and others, *Poland–Statistical Tables*, IMF Staff Country Report No. 96/20 (Washington: International Monetary Fund, 1996); and Liam P. Ebrill and others, *Poland: The Path to a Market Economy*, Occasional Paper No. 113 (Washington: International Monetary Fund, 1994).

[1]To simplify the analysis, all credits to the government are assumed to be denominated in zlotys.

[2]Including cash in vault.

Table 5.3.
Interest Rates[1]
(In percent)

	NBP Rates			Market Rates				
					Treasury Bills		WIBOR[3,4]	
	Refinance	Six-month Intervention[2]	Prime Deposits[3]	Lending	13-week	26-week	52-week	3-month
1991								
March	72.0	...	74.0	72.0	...	...	...	...
June	59.0	...	60.0	59.0	...	...	...	67.3
September	40.0	...	43.0	40.0	...	...	...	48.4
December	40.0	...	41.0	40.0	...	...	...	47.0
1992								
March	40.0	...	42.5	40.0	46.5	49.0	54.4	46.3
June	40.0	...	42.5	40.0	45.7	48.6	52.0	46.6
September	38.0	...	37.7	38.0	42.4	44.3	47.1	44.6
December	38.0	...	37.0	39.0	41.4	42.9	45.9	44.2
1993								
March	35.0	...	30.5	35.0	28.6	27.4	36.5	35.3
June	35.0	...	30.5	35.0	33.0	34.6	38.1	33.5
September	35.0	...	30.5	35.0	33.4	34.7	38.2	34.0
December	35.0	...	29.5	35.0	33.7	35.1	38.3	34.4
1994								
March	35.0	27.0	29.5	35.0	29.8	33.0	38.0	33.4
June	33.0	26.5	29.0	32.0	28.9	29.5	31.1	32.2
September	33.0	26.5	29.5	31.0	26.8	27.6	29.3	30.6
December	33.0	26.0	28.5	31.0	27.0	27.4	26.3	28.4
1995								
January	33.0	26.0	28.0	28.0	27.0	27.2	26.3	28.9
February	35.0	26.0	29.0	28.0	26.9	26.8	26.3	29.1
March	35.0	28.0	29.0	28.0	28.1	27.5	27.4	30.3
April	35.0	27.8	27.5	28.0	27.3	27.6	27.6	29.7
May	33.0	27.1	26.5	28.0	25.3	26.4	26.2	28.2
June	31.0	26.6	25.0	26.0	25.0	25.9	25.9	27.6
July	31.0	26.5	24.0	26.0	25.2	26.0	26.1	27.6
August	31.0	26.5	23.8	26.0	25.1	26.0	26.1	26.7
September	29.0	26.1	23.0	24.0	24.6	25.5	25.3	26.2

Sources: Juha Kahkonen and others, *Poland–Statistical Tables*, IMF Staff Country Report No. 96/20 (Washington: International Monetary Fund, 1996); and Liam P. Ebrill and others, *Poland: The Path to a Market Economy*, Occasional Paper No. 113 (Washington: International Monetary Fund, 1994).

[1]The NBP refinance rate and the deposit and lending rates are end-period values, while all the other rates are monthly averages.

[2]One-day reverse repo rate.

[3]Midpoint of the range of rates offered by principal commercial banks.

[4]Warsaw interbank offered rate.

Table 5.4.
Consolidated Balance Sheet of the DMBs
(In millions of Transitia dollars)

	1994		1994
Assets	12,000	Liabilities	12,000
Foreign assets	2,400	Demand deposits	5,000
Claims on nonresident banks	2,000	Sight deposits	3,000
Claims on nonresident nonbanks	400	Checking accounts	1,400
		Foreign currency demand deposits	600
Reserves	850		
Cash in vault	200	Time and savings deposits	3,700
Required deposits	550	Time deposits	1,000
Other deposits with MA	100	Savings deposits	1,500
		Foreign currency time deposits	1,200
Claims on government	600		
Treasury bills	300	Money market instruments	900
Other government securities	200	Promissory notes	400
Other claims	100	Certificates of deposits	500
Claims on private sector	7,650	Foreign liabilities	1,280
Discounts	4,000	Nonresident banks	520
Loans and advances	2,000	Nonresident nonbanks	760
Mortgages	1,280		
Overdrafts	200	Government deposits	100
Other	170	Credit from monetary authorities	200
Claims on nonmonetary financial institutions	300	Capital accounts	600
Unclassified assets	200	Unclassified liabilities	220

Table 5.5.
Balance Sheet of Monetary Authorities
(In millions of Transitia dollars)

	1994		1994
Assets	4,000	Liabilities	4,000
Foreign assets	1,200	Reserve money	2,850
Gold	20	Currency issued	2,200
Foreign exchange	467	Currency outside banks	2,000
Reserve position in the Fund	340	Currency in DMBs' vault	200
Holdings of SDRs	160	DMBs' deposits in the MA	650
Foreign correspondent banks	213		
		Government deposits	200
Claims on government	1,500		
Loans and advances	400	Foreign liabilities	400
Treasury bills	560	Deposits of foreign central banks	250
Other government securities	450	Swap facilities	50
Other claims	90	Use of Fund credit	75
		Other debts	25
Claims on nonfinancial public enterprises	300		
Loans and advances	200	Capital account	150
Bills and securities	100	Capital	100
Other claims	0	Reserves	50
Claims on the private sector	30	Unclassified liabilities	400
Claims on deposit money banks	200		
Rediscount and secured advances	60		
Loans and overdrafts	100		
Other claims	40		
Claims on nonmonetary financial institutions	100		
Rediscount and secured advances	20		
Loans and overdrafts	60		
Other claims	20		
Unclassified assets	670		

Table 5.6.
Balance Sheet of the Banking System
(In millions of Transitia dollars)

	1994		1994
Assets		Liabilities	
Foreign assets		Currency outside banks	
MA		Demand deposits	
DMBs		Of which: foreign currency	
		Quasi-money	
Claims on government		Time and savings deposits	
MA		Of which: foreign currency	
DMBs		Others	
Claims on the economy		Government deposits	
MA		MA	
DMBs		DMBs	
Claims on the private sector			
MA		Foreign liabilities	
DMBs		MA	
Claims on public enterprises		DMBs	
MA			
DMBs		Other liabilities	
Claims on other financial institutions		MA	
MA		DMBs	
DMBs			
Other assets			
MA			
DMBs			

Source: Based on data provided in Tables 5.4 and 5.5.

Table 5.7.
Balance Sheet of the Banking System (Analytical Presentation of the Monetary Survey)
(In millions of Transitia dollars)

	1994		1994
Assets		Liabilities	
Net foreign assets		M2 total	
MA		M2 national currency	
DMBs		M2 in foreign currency	
Net domestic assets (NDA)		M1 total	
		M1 national currency	
Net domestic credit (NDC)		Currency outside banks	
MA		Demand deposits	
DMBs		Foreign currency DD	
Net claims on government (NCG)		Quasi money	
MA		QM in national currency	
DMBs		Foreign exchange time deposits	
Claims on the rest of the economy (CPS)			
MA			
DMBs			
Other items (net) (OIN)			
MA			
DMBs			

Source: Based on data in Table 5.6.

Appendix

Accounting for Some Transactions with the IMF

Concepts and Definitions

Quota: Upon joining the Fund, a country is assigned a quota.[1] This is paid in national currency (not less than 75 percent) and in a reserve asset such as a convertible currency (up to 25 percent).

The IMF maintains three accounts with the designated depository of the member (often the central bank). They are the IMF No. 1 Account, No. 2 Account, and the IMF Securities Account.[2]

IMF No. 1 Account: This account is used for the Fund's operational transactions, e.g., purchases, repurchases, repayment of borrowing, etc.

IMF No. 2 Account: This account is used for administrative transactions between the country and the Fund, e.g., payment of publications.

IMF Securities Account: Nonnegociable, non-interest-bearing securities can be substituted by members for their currency (e.g., in the payment of the quota subscription). These securities are encashable by the Fund on demand.[3]

- The *reserve tranche* equals the Fund's holdings of a member's currency (excluding holdings which reflect the member's use of Fund credit) that are less than the member's quota. It is a part of the member's external reserves, and a member may purchase its entire reserve tranche at any time. Purchases in the reserve tranche are not regarded as a use of Fund credit, and are not subject to charges, nor are they required to be repurchased.
- *Credit tranches* are available in four tranches, each equal to 25 percent of a member's quota. A first credit tranche purchase is defined as one that raises the Fund's holdings of a member's currency in the credit tranche by 25 percent of quota. The three subsequent tranches, each equal to 25 percent of quota, are known as upper credit tranches. The distinction between first and upper credit tranches also reflects the higher conditionality that accompanies the use of Fund credit in the upper tranches. In addition to purchases under the Fund's credit tranche policies, members may use the Fund's resources under decisions on compensatory and contingency financing, buffer stock financing, and the extended Fund facility.
- The *Fund's holdings of a member's currency* reflect, among other things, the transactions and operation of the Fund in that currency.
- A member's *reserve position in the Fund* (RPF) comprises the reserve position and creditor positions under the various borrowing arrangements. A member's reserve position in the Fund has the characteristics of a reserve asset. A reserve position in the Fund arises from (1) the payment of part of a member's subscription in reserve assets and (2) the Fund's net use of the member's currency.

[1]This section is illustrative in nature and is not meant to be a formal treatment of IMF transactions. For more precise and formal definitions of the concepts introduced in this appendix and discussion of the transactions with the Fund, see *Financial Organization and Operations of the IMF*, IMF Pamphlet Series, No. 45, Fourth Edition (Washington: International Monetary Fund, 1995).

[2]The member country agrees to make such funds available, on demand, to the IMF. To do this, the country opens the so-called IMF No. 1 Account or issues to the IMF a nonnegotiable security cashable on demand.

[3]A member is required, however, to maintain a minimum balance of one-fourth of one percent of quota in the Fund's No. 1 Account.

Illustrative Examples

1. **Payment of quota**. Assuming a quota of 100 SDRs paid in convertible currencies (25 per-

cent) and national currency (75 percent). This is reflected in changes in the balance sheet of the country's monetary authorities as follows:

Monetary Authorities			
Assets		**Liabilities**	
Foreign exchange	–25	IMF No. 1 Account	75
Quota	100		
Foreign currency	(25)		
National currency	(75)		

or simply

Monetary Authorities			
Assets		**Liabilities**	
Foreign exchange	–25		
RPF	+25		

where RPF, as defined above. In this case:

RPF = Quota – (Holdings – Exclusions), or
= 100 – (75 – 0), or
= 25

Note that exclusions refer to holdings that reflect the member's use of Fund credit. In this case, it is also equal to the reserve tranche.

2. **Drawdown of the reserve tranche**

Monetary Authorities			
Assets		**Liabilities**	
Foreign exchange	0	IMF No. 1 Account	100
Before drawing	–25	Before drawing	75
Drawing	25	Drawing	25
Quota	100		

In terms of RPF:

Monetary Authorities			
Assets		**Liabilities**	
Foreign exchange	0		
RPF	0		

3. **Credit tranche purchase of SDR 40**

Monetary Authorities			
Assets		**Liabilities**	
Foreign exchange	40	IMF No. 1 Account	140
Before drawing	0	Before drawing	100
Drawing	40	Purchase	40
Quota	100		

In terms of the reserve position in the Fund:

Monetary Authorities			
Assets		**Liabilities**	
Foreign exchange	40	Use of Fund credit	40
RPF	0		

where RPF = 100 – (140 – 40) = 0.

Note the following accounting relationships:

Let

NPF = Net position with the Fund
UFC = Use of Fund credit
Q = Quota
H = Fund holdings of member's currency.

Then

NPF = RPF – UFC
= Q – H.

Appendix chart. IFS Money and Banking Sections for a Prototype Economy

(IFS line numbers in parentheses; hypothetical values as of a given date to right of time series descriptor)

Monetary Authorities

Assets		Liabilities	
(11) Foreign Assets	400	(14) Reserve Money	850
(12a) Claims on Central Government	515	(14a) Currency Outside Banks	[650]
(12e) Claims on Deposit Money Banks	85	(–) Banks' Reserves (= line 20)	[200]
		(16c) Foreign Liabilities	40
		(16d) Central Government Deposits	70
		(17r) Other Items (Net)	40

Monetary Survey

Assets		Liabilities	
(31n) Foreign Assets (Net)	320	(34) Money	1,130
(32) Domestic Credit	1,620	(35) Quasi-Money	630
(32an) Claims on Central Government (Net)	[510]	(37r) Other Items (Net)	180
(32b) Claims on Official Entities	[75]		
(32d) Claims on Private Sector	[1,015]		
(32f) Claims on Nonmonetary Financial Institutions	[20]		

Deposit Money Banks

Assets		Liabilities	
(20) Reserves	200	(24) Demand Deposits	480
(21) Foreign Assets	380	(25) Time, Savings, and Foreign Currency Deposits	630
(22a) Claims on Central Government	110	(26c) Foreign Liabilities	420
(22b) Claims on Official Entities	75	(26d) Central Government Deposits	45
(22d) Claims on Private Sector	1,015	(26g) Credit from Central Bank	85
(22f) Claims on Nonmonetary Financial Institutions	20	(27r) Other Items (Net)	140

Nonmonetary Financial Institutions

Assets		Liabilities	
(40) Reserves	35	(45) Time, Savings, and Foreign Currency Deposits	300
(42a) Claims on Central Government	55	(46a) Bonds and Money Market Instruments	150
(42b) Claims on Official Entities	95	(46h) Credit from Monetary System	20
(42d) Claims on Private Sector	315	(47r) Other Items (Net)	30

Financial Survey

Assets		Liabilities	
(51n) Foreign Assets (Net)	320	(55*l*) Liquid Liabilities	2,025
(52) Domestic Credit	2,065	(56a) Bonds and Money Market Instruments	150
(52an) Claims on Central Government (Net)	[565]	(57r) Other Items (Net)	210
(52b) Claims on Official Entities	[170]		
(52d) Claims on Private Sector	[1,330]		

CHAPTER

6 The Flow of Funds: Macroeconomic Interrelations

Macroeconomic aggregates are traditionally derived from an interconnected network of macroeconomic accounts: the national income and product accounts, the balance of payments, government finance statistics (GFS), and the monetary accounts. The basic features of these four accounts and the links between the resource balance of each sector and its financing were reviewed in earlier chapters; this chapter focuses primarily on the links between accounts. A financial program consists of a set of quantitative, coordinated macroeconomic policy measures that are designed to achieve certain economic targets over a specified period. The links between the saving and investment of a sector and the associated financial transactions with other sectors are systematically described in a flow of funds account and provide the basis for formulating a financial program.[1] Understanding these links (which encompass both accounting and behavioral relationships) is therefore fundamental to the design of a financial program.

The four main macroeconomic sectors (private, government, foreign, and banking) all engage in income and expenditure transactions. (By convention, the banking sector's real transactions are assumed to be zero.) A sector's income-expenditure transactions (also referred to as real or nonfinancial transactions) generate changes in financial assets or liabilities. These changes are, in turn, recorded as the sector's financial transactions. Thus, for each sector, the real or nonfinancial transactions (such as imports and exports) and the financial transactions (such as borrowing from abroad or drawing down the country's international reserves) embrace the sector's entire economic relations with other sectors.

In the chapters on the real sector, the fiscal sector, the monetary sector, and the external sector, the identity between the resource balance of each sector and the financing of the resource gap (or, alternatively, the disposal of the resource surplus of the sector) was established. The interrelations between the resource gap of one sector with those of other sectors were also examined. For example, for the private or nongovernment sector, equation 2.13 in Chapter 2 illustrates the equality between the resource gap and its financing, and equation 2.8 shows the relationship between the economywide resource gap and the external current account balance.[2] In this chapter, the interrelationships among economic sectors are examined in a more systematic manner. The discussion of these interrelationships sets the stage for the development of the flow of funds accounts, which provide a record of the real (nonfinancial) and financial transactions among the main macroeconomic sectors in a consistent and comprehensive framework.

Basic Interrelationship Between the Saving-Investment Balance and the External Current Account

Equation 9 in Box 2.2 of Chapter 2 sets out the identity between the economywide resource gap and the current account balance. Thus,

$$\begin{matrix}\textit{Economywide} & & \textit{Current account} & & \textit{Use of} \\ \textit{saving investment} & = & \textit{balance (CAB)} & = & \textit{foreign} \\ \textit{gap } (S - I) & & & & \textit{savings}.\end{matrix} \qquad (6.1)$$

The current account balance of the balance of payments can be viewed in a variety of alternative ways, as shown in Chart 6.1. As a balance of items on the external current account, it equals the sum of all items in the balance of payments that finance the current account balance. In the broader macroeconomic sense, it reflects the gap between the econ-

[1]At a fundamental level, the difference between the flow of funds approach and the traditional market equilibrium approach is that the sectoral balances are treated as constraints in the former, while market equilibria (supply equal to demand) are treated as constraints in the latter. This point and the importance of the flow of funds framework to financial programming are clearly brought out in Chorng-Huey Wong and Oystein Pettersen, "Financial Programming in the Framework of Optimal Control," *Weltwirtschaftliche's Archiv*, Vol. 1, 1979.

[2]Please note that in this chapter, the terms nongovernment sector and the private sector are used interchangeably.

Chart 6.1. Basic Macroeconomic Linkages

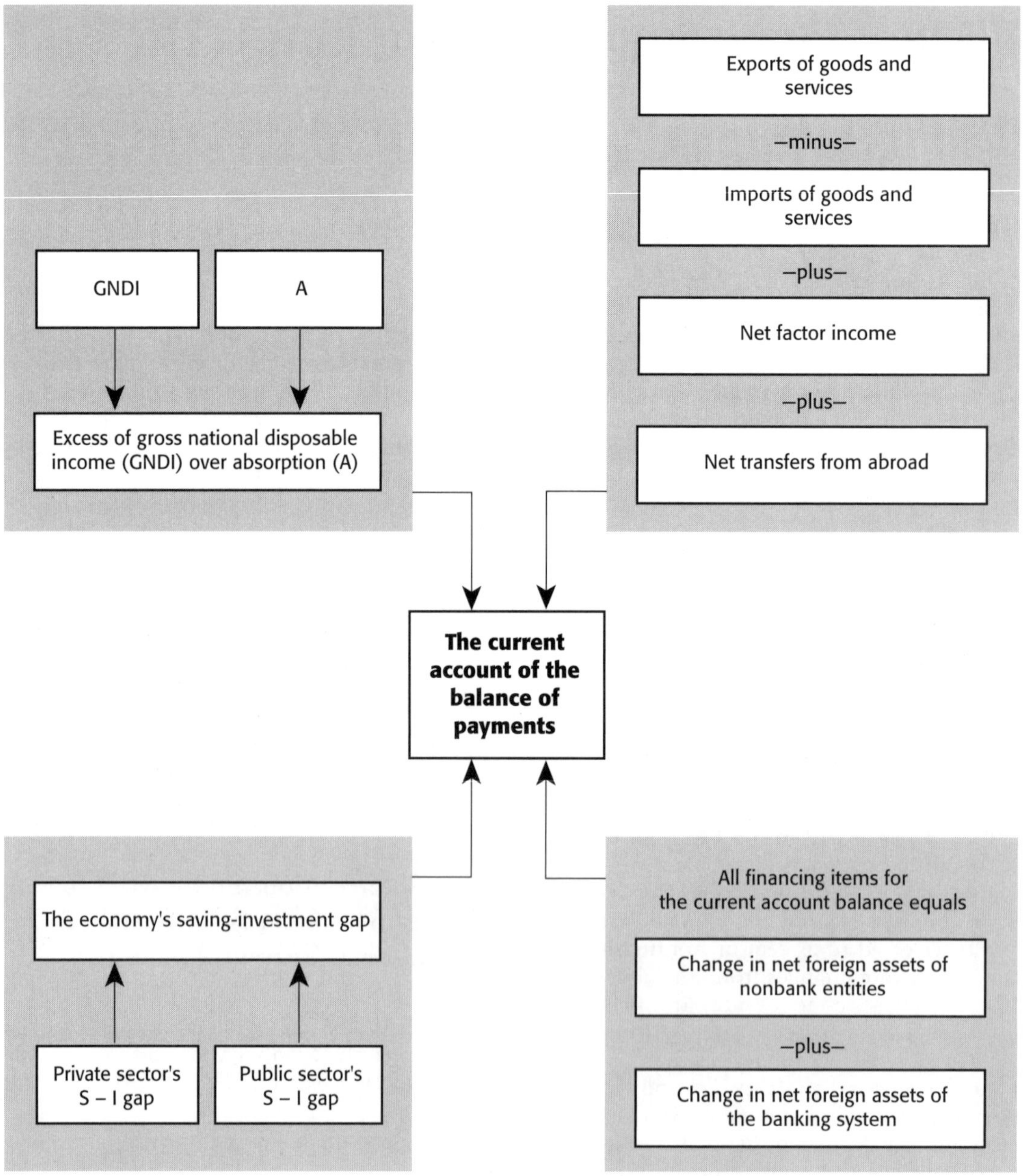

Box 6.1.
Relations Between Sectoral Balances and the Current Account

Sectoral Balances		Current Account Balance
Private	Public	
(1) $(S_p - I_p) > 0$	$(S_g - I_g) < 0$	$CAB < 0$ if $\mid(S_g - I_g)\mid > \mid(S_p - I_p)$[1]
(2) $(S_p - I_p) < 0$	$(S_g - I_g) < 0$	$CAB < 0$
(3) $(S_p - I_p) < 0$	$(S_g - I_g) > 0$	$CAB < 0$ if $\mid(S_p - I_p)\mid > \mid(S_g - I_g)\mid$[1]

[1]Indicates the absolute value of the difference shown in parentheses.

omy's disposable income and absorption and between saving and investment. These latter relationships highlight the importance of the current account balance as a central unifying concept linking the domestic economy with the rest of the world.

Although this identity is central to macroeconomic analysis, it does not make explicit the respective roles of the government and private (or nongovernment) sectors. The link between the fiscal aggregates and the balance of payments can easily be derived from the basic saving-investment gap for the economy as a whole by decomposing saving (S) and investment (I) aggregates into their private and government sector components.

Thus, equation 6.1 can be rewritten as:

$$(S_p + S_g) - (I_p + I_g) = CAB \tag{6.2}$$

where the subscripts p and g refer to the private and government sector, respectively.

This relationship can also be rearranged as

$$(S_p - I_p) + (S_g - I_g) = CAB \tag{6.3}$$

In this form, the equation shows that

Private sector saving-investment gap + *Government sector saving-investment gap* = *Current account balance.*

The significance of this identity cannot be overemphasized. It suggests that there are important relationships among (i) the saving-investment gap of the private sector, (ii) the overall fiscal position of the government sector, and (iii) the current account of the balance of payments. It focuses on the separate roles that the private and public sectors play in a current account imbalance. Complemented by behavioral relationships about the private and government sectors, the identity can be extremely useful in macroeconomic analysis.

Box 6.1 shows three different combinations of private and public sectoral balances and the resulting current account balances. Situation 1 is typical of many countries undertaking adjustment programs: a fiscal deficit is the main source of the current account deficit. This case involves the so-called "twin deficits"; accordingly, reducing the current account deficit will require fiscal adjustment. In many economies, however, a large fiscal deficit is more than offset by an excess of private saving over investment. In Italy, for example, high private saving in recent years has financed a high government deficit, with only a modest current account deficit.

In situation 2, the current account deficit represents both a government deficit and a private sector saving shortfall in relation to private investment.

Situation 3 indicates that a current account deficit coexists with a fiscal surplus and a private saving shortfall. If the current account deficit reflects a private investment boom financed by capital inflow, the policy implications are different from what they would be if the current account deficit reflects a private consumption boom that mirrors a private saving shortfall. The accounting identity provides only a useful conceptual framework for analyzing different behavioral and policy outcomes and deriving appropriate policy implications.

Flow of Funds Accounts

Flow of Funds Framework: The Basics[3]

The interrelations between the various sectors (private, government, monetary, and external) are brought together in this section to set the stage for a

[3]For a more detailed treatment of this topic, see Marcelo Caiola "A Manual for Country Economists," IMF Institute and Research Department (Washington: International Monetary Fund, 1995). See also R.F.G. Alford, *Flow of Funds: A Conceptual Framework and Some Applications* (Crower Publishing, 1986).

full exploration of all such interrelations in the framework of a flow of funds matrix. First, however, it is important to understand the rationale for and uses of a flow of funds matrix. As an analytical tool, the matrix is important for several reasons:

- It summarizes the interrelationships among the different sectors (including the foreign or rest of the world sector) in a systematic and coherent way.
- It helps to bring out inconsistencies in and thereby ensure the consistency of the available data and facilitates macroeconomic analysis.
- It shows which sector of the economy is generating an overall surplus and which is generating a deficit, helps identify the origins and causes of the surpluses and deficits, and sheds light on how the surpluses are utilized and the deficits financed in each sector.
- It is helpful in policy simulations and in analyzing the ramifications of policy options.

At the most aggregative level, an open economy consists of two sectors: the domestic economy and the rest of the world. As discussed for the four sectors covered in this volume, two basic types of transactions can be distinguished for each of these sectors: nonfinancial and financial. The system is "closed" in the sense that the country's exports (X) are the rest of the world's imports (–X), and hence the sum of transactions across sectors must be zero (+ X – X = 0). Similarly, it is possible to derive each sector's resource or saving-investment gap and to trace the gap's financing. Since the financial transactions must cover the gap ex post, the resource gap for each sector will always equal the sum of all financial transactions for the sector. The flow of funds account or table simply combines the nonfinancial transactions, the resource gap, and the financial transactions for each sector in a matrix in which the sectors are in columns and the transactions are in rows. An illustrative flow of funds is shown in Box 6.2 for a small open economy; exports (X) = 100, imports (M) = 300, and borrowing from abroad = 200.

This example illustrates a number of important features embedded in the flow of funds framework.

- As noted, the system is closed, so that the sum across sectors for each transaction (that is, the sum of each row) is identically equal to zero, as is the sum of the resource gaps. The current account of the rest of the world is necessarily the mirror image of the country's current account, since the world as a whole is a closed economy. Specifically, the country can run a current account deficit (–200) if, and only if, the rest of the world is running a surplus of an equal amount (+200).[4]
- For each sector, the sum of real and financial transactions (excluding the resource gap row, which is a subtotal and not a transaction in itself) is also zero. This relationship reflects the fact that ex post, each sector's nonfinancial deficit (surplus) is fully covered (utilized).
- Transactions in the "rest of the world" sector are entered from the point of view of the rest of the world, not from the point of view of the country. Thus, under exports, the rest of the world sector shows –100, reflecting the sector's imports.
- By convention, the signs in the table are as follows: a transaction that increases assets or decreases liabilities of a sector takes a negative sign, and a transaction that decreases assets and increases liabilities takes a positive sign. Thus, the country's foreign borrowing (an increase in foreign financial liabilities) is entered as a +200. Note that for the "rest of the world" sector, net lending (an increase in financial assets) of –200 is recorded (Box 6.3).
- The flow of funds table is, by design, a zero-sum matrix in which each column and each row sums to zero. Thus, the flow of funds system is a quadruple-entry system. Each transaction is recorded with a double entry—that is, as a real transaction, with a counter entry as a financial transaction in each of the two sectors involved.

The above dichotomy, which divides the world into the domestic economy and the rest of the world, can be further refined by disaggregating the domestic economy into three key sectors (the government, the private sector, and the banking sector). However, before analyzing this expanded flow of funds table, it is important to summarize the accounting conventions guiding the construction of a flow of funds table.

The Recording Conventions

The following conventions are used in the flow of funds accounts.

- *Coverage*. The flow of funds accounts record transactions between two sectors. Transactions taking place within a given sector are not shown, since they disappear in the consolidation of the sector. Moreover, some transactions (such as changes in arrears, valuation changes, and other items net) are grouped together for

[4]This equivalence, of course, abstracts from the statistical and measurement problems that are always present in the actual data.

Box 6.2.
Illustrative Flow of Funds of a Simple Open Economy

	Domestic Economy	Rest of the World	Horizontal Check
Nonfinancial transactions			
Exports	100	–100	0
Imports	–300	+300	0
Resource gap	–200	+200	0
Financial transactions			
Foreign borrowing	+200	–200	0
Vertical check	0	0	0

each sector under a balancing item (net errors and omissions).

- *Source.* Whenever data for the same transaction differ (for example, changes in net foreign assets in the balance of payments and in the monetary survey) a single source must be selected. The primary sources used for establishing a flow of funds account are the national income and product accounts and the macroeconomic accounts based on the three linked systems, namely the government finance statistics (GFS), balance of payments statistics (BOPS), and money and banking statistics (MBS).
- *Banking system.* For the purpose of the flow of funds account, this sector is assumed not to have any nonfinancial transactions—that is, its saving-investment gap is identically equal to zero.
- *External sector.* This sector is viewed from the point of view of the rest of the world. Therefore, a current account deficit (+CAB) for the country is a current account surplus (–CAB) for the rest of the world and should be entered as such.

Flow of Funds Framework: Schematic Accounts

To complete the detailed flow of funds, it is important to review, for each sector that constitutes a column in the flow of funds table, the methods used to derive and finance nonfinancial balances. Box 6.4 shows the necessary accounting identities.

The flow of funds account (or table) has as its columns the economic sectors and as its rows the various transactions. It has three major blocks: nonfinancial transactions, saving-investment balances, and financial transactions. The first two blocks are obtained simply by entering the nonfinancial transactions (as summarized in Box 6.3) for each sector and summing them to obtain nonfinancial balances. The third block of the table is obtained by enumerating all the financing transactions for each sector. It should be noted that for all sectors, "other items, net" has been added as a balancing item in order to capture (i) those items in the financing of nonfinancial balances that have not been explicitly entered, and (ii) any errors arising from data that are inconsistent across sectors.

A schematic flow of funds account is shown in Table 6.1. The columns represent the broad economic sectors and the rows transactions among the sectors; the first column is simply the aggregation of all the domestic sectors. The upper part of the table covers transactions in goods, services, income, and transfers, the lower part financial transactions such as borrowing or lending.

Flow of Funds Analysis[5]

The flow of funds account provides a comprehensive framework for describing both the influence of economic activity on the financial system and the role of various financial markets in the generation of income, saving, and expenditure. The identities reflected in a flow of funds account are not, however, sufficient to derive a full picture of a country's financial system. Accounting identities must be complemented by the sectors' behavioral relationships in terms of production, expenditures, portfolio choices, and external trade. But through the interrelationships it presents, a flow of funds account facilitates the analysis of the interactions between the nonfinancial and financial spheres. Such accounts can be

[5]For more details and for an interactive use of the flow of funds, see "Interrelation Among Macroeconomic Accounts," CD-ROM, IMF Institute, International Monetary Fund, 1996.

Box 6.3.
Sign Conventions in the Flow of Funds Account

	Increase	Decline
Assets	–	+
Liabilities	+	–

This assignment of signs for financial transactions can be rationalized as follows: an acquisition of an asset implies the use or disposal of purchasing power, while incurring liability implies acquiring purchasing power.

- A deficit for the external sector, which represents the rest of the world, implies an external surplus for the domestic sector.
- The nonfinancial balance of the banking sector is assumed to be zero; the nonfinancial transactions of this sector are implicitly included in the private sector.

used to trace the impact of fiscal and monetary policy on financial markets, for instance. Flow of funds analysis may be based on past developments or projections; in either case, it is useful to have data covering a period of several years.

The schematic flow of funds table (Table 6.1) follows.

Column 1: Shows the basic national income identity for the overall economy (that is, the aggregation of the domestic economy shown in column 2, and the rest of the world column sector shown in column 6). This basic identity, which defines gross national disposable income (GNDI), has been developed in detail in Chapter 2 and is summarized in equation 1 of Box 6.4. There is no entry for this column in the financial transactions because in a closed system, financial transactions are all identically zero.

Column 2: Shows the aggregate domestic economy or the sum of columns 3, 4, and 5. This column shows, for the domestic economy, the basic identity between the excess of GNDI over absorption and the saving-investment gap for the economy.

Column 3: Shows, for the government sector, the source of the saving-investment gap and (in the lower portion of the column) how this gap is financed.[6] The key equations describing the government position and its financing are shown in Box 6.4, equations 2 and 3, respectively.

Column 4: Shows how, for the nongovernment sector or private sector, the resource gap is derived and financed. This relationship is derived in detail in Chapter 2, equations 2.11 and 2.12 and is shown in Box 6.4, equations 4 and 5.

Column 5: Depicts the resource gap for the banking system, which by convention is identically zero, and its financing, which is the monetary survey identity. This identity is described in equation 5.8 and is depicted in Box 6.4, equation 6.

Column 6: Depicts the foreign sector balance and its financing from the rest of the world's point of view. In particular, this column shows the mirror image of the compiling country's current account balance and its financing. These relations are described in Chapter 5, and are shown in Box 6.4, equations 7 and 8.

Column 7: Provides a horizontal check. It shows that, for each row, the sum of the elements in columns (1), (3), (4), (5), and (6) are zero; column (2) is only a subtotal of columns (3), (4), and (5).

It is also instructive to look at the flow of funds table from the perspective of the rows—that is, in terms of the transactions. As noted, for each column (sector), the sum for all transactions (financial and nonfinancial) is also zero. It is important to keep in mind two features of this table that involve the rows. First, the row summarizing the nonfinancial balances is a subtotal of all the nonfinancial transactions and therefore should not be counted twice during the process of verifying that the sum of a sector's transactions is zero. Second, "net errors and omissions" is included to ensure consistency between and within sectors. These are balancing items, some of which we have previously encountered—for example, "errors and omissions" in the balance of payments and "other items, net" in the monetary survey.

- *Nonfinancial balances*. For the overall economy, the income-expenditure balance $(S - I)$ is also called the "resource gap" because it indicates

[6]The derivation of the government saving-investment gap in terms of the government's disposable income and its consumption is as follows. Recall that $S_g = R_g - C_g$ (Chapter 3, equation 3.1). The government's disposable income is now defined as total government revenues and grants (R_g), net of government transfers (TR_g) and interest payments on government debt (INT_g). Government transfers and interest payments are deducted because they constitute income for the private sector (the nongovernment sector) and as such, are included in the disposable income of the private or the external sector.

Box 6.4.
Main Economic Sectors: Nonfinancial Balances and Their Financing

Sector	Accounting Identity	
Economy		
Saving-investment gap	$S - I = CAB$ or $-S + I + CAB = 0$	
Definition of GNDI	$-GNDI + C + I + X - M + Y_f + TR_f = 0$	(1)
Government		
Saving-investment gap	$S_g - I_g = GNDI_g - C_g - I_g$	(2)
Financing of the gap	$F_g = NFB_g + \Delta NDC_g + NB$ $(S_g - I_g) + F_g = 0$ or $(S_g - I_g) + NFB_g + \Delta NDC_g + NB = 0$	(3)
Private sector		
Saving-investment gap	$= S_p - I_p = GNDI_p - C_p - I_p$	(4)
Financing of the gap	$FDI_p + NFB_p + \Delta NDC_p - \Delta M2 - NB = F_p$ $(S_p - I_p) + FDI_p + NFB_p + \Delta NDC_p - \Delta M2 - NB = 0$	(5)
Banking sector		
Saving-investment gap	$S_b - I_b = 0$ by convention.	
Monetary survey identity	$\Delta M2 = \Delta NFA + \Delta NDC + \Delta OIN_b$ or	
Financing of the gap	$\Delta M2 - \Delta NFA - \Delta NDC - \Delta OIN_b \equiv 0$	(6)
Foreign sector (as viewed from abroad)		
Saving-investment gap	$-CAB = -X + M - Y_f - TR_f$	(7)
Financing of the gap	$-F_f = -FDI - NFB + \Delta NFA$	
Balance of payments identity	$CAB + F_f \equiv 0$ $-CAB - FDI - NFB + \Delta NFA + \Delta OIN_f \equiv 0$	(8)

that if the country does not have sufficient resources to cover its expenditures, a deficit on the external current account is generated. If income exceeds expenditures, a surplus is generated.

- *Sectoral balances*. These allow analysts to identify domestic sectors that are facing financing difficulties. Each sector generates (through nonfinancial transactions) either a negative balance (deficit) or a positive balance (surplus). A negative balance may stem from a decline in saving, an increase in investment, or a combination of the two.
- *Financing of nonfinancial balances*. The flow of funds account also provides an overall description of the intersectoral financial flows that are intermediated through the country's financial system, which plays the crucial role of attracting and allocating saving. For the whole economy, the saving-investment balance is matched by the current account balance, which is financed through capital and financial account transactions, changes in net foreign assets, or exceptional financing (such as the accumulation of external arrears). The saving-investment balance of a given sector is financed by the other domestic sectors and the rest of the world.

As noted above, the usefulness of a flow of funds system lies in the fact that the system describes the financing of various economic sectors and the broad categories of market instruments used in financial transactions. By explicitly describing the main macroeconomic identities, the flow of funds helps analysts to formulate behavioral hypotheses and to design a consistent check of financial programs. The system's interlocking nature provides a basis for analyzing the origins of an imbalance in one economic sector and the potential repercussions for other sectors. Examples illustrating these analytical uses of the flow of funds are given below.

External Imbalance

We have seen that for a given period, the sum of savings/investment balances of the government and the nongovernment sectors is equal to the current account balance. This relation gives us important insights into the possible origins of balance of payments problems. An increase in the external current account deficit can be traced to a rise in the saving-investment deficit (or a reduction in the surplus) of either the private or the government sectors. Policy prescriptions differ according to which sector gives rise to the imbalance and whether the increased deficit (or reduced surplus) has been generated by a fall in saving, or a rise in investment, or both. Analysts must investigate the causes of these changes, using economic analysis and policy judgment to determine whether a particular change needs to be reversed and, if so, how it can best be done. Further, the flow of funds table helps to trace the financing of an increased current account deficit, allowing analysts to measure any change in the financing position of the economic sectors. Such financing can come from a rise in net foreign borrowing by either the government or the private sector, an increase in direct foreign investment, or a change in net foreign assets (possibly a drawdown in official reserves).

Fiscal Imbalance

If government expenditures are increased, they must be financed by a rise in taxes; otherwise, the fiscal deficit increases. If taxes are increased to finance increased spending, the government's nonfinancial balance does not change, but the private sector either reduces its savings, cuts its spending, or both. If the private sector cuts its spending, its financial balances remain unchanged, since the nonfinancial balance is unaffected. But if the private sector reduces its savings, its nonfinancial balance worsens, requiring the sector to either increase borrowing from the banking system, run down its cash balances, or borrow money abroad. Maintaining private spending in the face of reduced disposable income causes a deterioration of the country's external current account balance. If, however, extra government expenditure is financed with increased credit from the central bank, the increased deficit leads to a rise in nominal GDP, which in turn results in (i) higher government revenues that partially offset the increase in spending, and (ii) with a marginal propensity to spend less than unity, improves the private sector's nonfinancial balance. As the counterpart of the increase in domestic credit, the private sector increases its holding of money balances (the form in which it holds extra savings). If the extra government spending induces additional private sector spending on domestic as well as imported goods and services, the external current account balance worsens, affecting other economic sectors (see above). Analysts can examine a variety of such effects, depending on the behavioral assumptions about the economic sectors that are used to supplement the flow of funds accounting.

Exercises

1. Tables 6.2 through 6.6 present the basic macroeconomic accounts for Poland. On the basis of these tables, the nonfinancial transactions balances and the flow of funds for Poland have been derived for 1993 (Table 6.6). Using Table 6.6 as a model, prepare the flow of funds for 1994.
2. On the basis of Table 6.6, what can be said about the significant differences in economic developments in Poland between 1993 and 1994? Compare the 1993 and 1994 nonfinancial domestic balances (you may wish to compute ratios relative to GDP). How do they relate to the external sector nonfinancial balance? What factors may have influenced the level of domestic investment and gross national saving during 1993–1994?
3. Suppose that government capital outlays in 1994 were higher by 1 trillion zlotys. How would Table 6.6 change? In answering this question, explore alternative means of financing the increase in government spending (for example, tax increases, reductions in other expenditures, bank borrowing, nonbank borrowing, and foreign financing). Assume that higher government spending also raises output by 1 trillion zlotys—that is, there are no multiplier effects.
4. Assume that the nongovernment saving-investment balance in 1994 remains unchanged from its 1993 level, but that the general government deficit is higher than in 1993. What can you conclude about the current account of the balance of payments in 1994? Suppose that the current account of the balance of payments improves in 1994. Under the above scenario (an unchanged private sector saving-investment balance), what can you conclude about Poland's fiscal position in 1994 compared with the previous year?

Table 6.1.
Schematic Flow of Funds Account

Transactions/Sectors	Overall Economy (1)	Domestic Economy (2)	Domestic Economy: General government (3)	Domestic Economy: Private sector (4)	Domestic Economy: Banking system (5)	Rest of the World (6)	Horizontal Check (7)
Gross national disposable income (GNDI)	−GNDI	**+GNDI**	$GNDI_g$	$GNDI_p$			**0**
Final consumption	C	**−C**	$-C_g$	$-C_p$			**0**
Gross investment	I	**−I**	$-I_g$	$-I_p$			**0**
Exports of goods and nonfactor services[1]	X					**−X**	**0**
Imports of goods and nonfactor services[1]	−M					**M**	**0**
Net factor income[1]	Y_f					**$-Y_f$**	**0**
Net transfers[1]	TR_f					**$-TR_f$**	**0**
Nonfinancial balances	**0**	**(S − I)**	**$(S_g - I_g)$**	**$(S_p - I_p)$**	**0**	**−CAB**	**0**
Foreign financing							
Nonmonetary							
Direct investment	0	**FDI**		FDI		**−FDI**	**0**
Net foreign borrowing	0	**NFB**	NFB_g	NFB_p		**−NFB**	**0**
Monetary							
Change in net foreign assets	0	**−ΔNFA**			−ΔNFA	**+ΔNFA**	**0**
Domestic financing							
Monetary							
Domestic credit	0	**0**	$+\Delta NDC_g$	$+\Delta NDC_p$	−ΔNDC		**0**
Broad money	0	**0**		−ΔM2	ΔM2		**0**
Nonmonetary							
Nonbank	0	**0**	NB	−NB			**0**
Net errors and omissions[2]	0	**$-\Delta OIN_d$**	ΔOIN_g	ΔOIN_p	$-\Delta OIN_b$	**ΔOIN_f**	**0**
Vertical check	**0**	**0**	**0**	**0**	**0**	**0**	**0**

Source: Based on Box 6.4.

[1]Exports, imports, net factor income, and net transfers can also, in principle, be broken down into the general government and private sectors. However, in practice, this breakdown is hard to obtain and, in any case, little useful purpose is served by such a breakdown here, where the focus is on nonfinancial balances and their financing.

[2]Balancing item calculated as the difference between nonfinancial balances and total identified financing. Note also that $-\Delta OIN_d$ is the sum of the changes in OIN in all sectors in the domestic economy and must be offset by ΔOIN_f in a closed system.

Table 6.2.
Components of Aggregate Demand
(In trillions of zlotys; at current market prices)

	1990	1991	1992	1993	1994
Consumption	376.7	663.3	957.4	1,300.3	1,751.0
Public (CG)	(108.1)	(195.2)	(289.6)	(318.3)	(386.9)
Private (CP)	(268.7)	(468.1)	(667.8)	(982.0)	(1,364.1)
Gross investment (I)	143.5	161.0	174.4	242.3	335.8
Fixed investment	117.6	157.7	193.0	239.8	341.1
Public (IG)	(21.6)	(26.1)	(39.3)	(51.0)	(67.9)
Private (IP)	(96.0)	(131.6)	(153.7)	(188.8)	(273.6)
Changes in stock	25.9	3.3	–18.6	2.5	–5.3
Domestic demand (A)	520.3	824.3	1,131.8	1,542.6	2,086.8
Foreign balance (X–M)	40.0	-15.5	17.6	15.2	17.3
Exports of goods and services (X)	160.5	190.3	272.4	357.3	515.0
Imports of goods and services (M)	120.5	205.8	254.8	342.1	497.7
GDP at market prices	**560.3**	**808.8**	**1,149.4**	**1,557.8**	**2,104.1**
Net income from abroad (Y_f)	–31.9	–30.1	–54.4	–63.4	–33.8
Net current transfers (TR_f)	18.4	12.8	39.9	51.5	26.9
Gross national disposable income (GNDI)	**546.8**	**791.5**	**1,134.9**	**1,545.9**	**2,097.2**

Source: Based on Table 2.3.

Table 6.3.
General Government Operations[1]
(In trillions of zlotys)

	1990	1991	1992	1993	1994
Revenues	**254.3**	**341.9**	**503.0**	**742.2**	**977.5**
Tax revenues	210.5	285.6	418.7	608.5	831.5
Personal income tax	17.7	23.3	81.1	140.4	203.1
Social security contributions	43.8	79.0	111.5	146.0	192.4
Enterprise income tax	82.8	59.4	50.6	66.0	70.6
Excess wage tax (Popiwek)	8.8	27.1	17.0	10.0	3.9
VAT, turnover taxes, and excises[2]	37.3	61.2	103.4	177.5	243.0
Customs duties	3.5	17.1	26.8	43.8	75.0
Other	16.6	18.5	28.3	24.8	43.5
Nontax revenue	43.8	54.6	79.5	121.3	140.0
Capital revenue	...	1.7	4.8	12.4	6.0
Expenditure and net lending	**236.1**	**405.8**	**579.2**	**787.2**	**1,019.6**
Current	218.7	366.3	535.0	729.3	961.6
Wages and salaries	57.3	94.1	135.3	185.4	206.7
Purchases of goods and services	28.7	46.7	70.0	99.9	135.3
Interest payments[3]	2.4	12.6	36.7	53.4	86.9
Subsidies	43.1	41.4	37.1	35.3	42.8
Income transfers	85.8	140.4	229.1	320.7	458.1
Other	1.4	31.1	26.8	34.6	31.8
Capital and net lending	16.7	29.5	39.3	50.9	61.0
Net lending	0.7	10.0	4.9	7.0	−3.0
Overall balance	**18.2**	**−63.9**	**−76.2**	**−45.0**	**−42.1**
Financing	−18.2	63.9	76.2	45.0	42.1
Domestic	−16.2	41.9	81.4	46.6	83.0
Banking system	−16.3	41.2	75.6	35.2	66.8
Nonbank	0.1	0.7	5.8	11.4	16.2
Foreign (net)[4]	−4.1	−0.9	−2.8	−5.9	−43.0
Change in arrears[5]	−2.6	12.9	−6.4	4.3	2.1
Other[6]	4.0	...	4.0	...	...
GDP	**560.3**	**808.8**	**1,149.4**	**1,557.8**	**2,104.1**

Source: Table 3.1.
[1]Comprising the state budget, extrabudgetary funds, and local governments.
[2]1993 data include revenues from the VAT that replaced turnover taxes in July 1993.
[3]Interest obligations on external debt are recorded on a cash basis, interest obligations on domestic debt are recorded on an accrual basis.
[4]Assume net repayment remains unchanged in U.S. dollar terms from previous year.
[5]Excludes external interest payments arrears, which are recorded on a cash basis above the line.
[6]Unallocated financing.

Table 6.4.
Balance of Payments in Convertible Currencies[1]
(In billions of zlotys; unless otherwise indicated)

	1990	1991	1992	1993	1994
Merchandise exports, f.o.b.	142,633	134,950	190,723	246,092	385,155
Merchandise imports, f.o.b.	−103,797	−134,410	−183,747	−287,630	−404,151
Trade balance	38,836	540	6,976	−41,538	−18,996
Services, net	57	236	344	369	1,295
Receipts	16,844	16,678	21,965	33,440	47,718
Payments	−16,787	−14,182	−17,278	−26,756	−46,423
Income net	−32,015	−31,051	−22,523	−23,404	−33,767
Interest payment due	−37,145	−35,990	−30,890	−32,462	. . .
Paid	−4,503	−9,360	−14,948	−14,981	. . .
Debt relief provided	−24,187	−15,367	—	—	. . .
Arrears incurred	−8,455	−11,263	−15,942	−17,481	. . .
Current transfers, net	18,430	4,230	7,195	16,829	26,859
Unrecorded trade	—	2,929	16,105	31,701	72,964
Current account					
(Excluding unrecorded trade)	**25,308**	**−23,785**	**−3,665**	**−41,429**	**−24,609**
(Including unrecorded trade)	25,308	−20,856	12,440	−9,728	48,355
Capital and financial account	**−41,287**	**−85,497**	**4,128**	**26,575**	**60,920**
Medium- and long-term capital, net	−24,976	−64,080	−3,979	−8,532	704
Disbursements	4,066	8,313	7,658	16,702	20,314
Amortization due	−29,042	−72,393	−11,637	25,234	−19,610
Paid	(−3,506)	(−3,670)	(−6,036)	(−16,358)	(−11,430)
Debt relief provided	(−24,558)	(−30,977)	(2,752)	—	(. . .)
Arrears incurred	(−978)	(−37,746)	(−2,849)	(−8,876)	(. . .)
Direct investment	95	1,237	3,870	10,507	12,316
Short-term capital and other, net[2]	−16,406	−22,654	4,237	24,600	47,900
Overall balance	−15,979	−109,282	463	−14,854	36,311
Financing	15,979	109,282	−463	14,856	−36,311
Change in international reserves (−, increase)[3]	−42,199	13,929	−22,006	−11,503	−57,580
Of which: use of Fund resources, net	4,750	3,405	—	−2,627	13,497
Debt relief (interest and principal)	48,745	46,344	2,752	—	179,512
Change in arrears	9,434	49,009	18,790	26,357	−158,243
Memorandum items:					
Exchange rate (zloty/U.S. dollar; period average)	9,500	10,576	13,626	18,115	22,723
Current account (percent of GDP)					
(Excluding unrecorded trade)	4.5	−2.9	−0.3	−2.7	−1.2
(Including unrecorded trade)	4.5	−2.6	1.1	−0.6	2.3
Exports of goods and services (trillions of zlotys)[4]	160.5	190.3	272.4	357.3	515.0
Imports of goods and services (trillions of zlotys)[4]	120.5	205.8	254.8	342.1	497.7

Source: Based on Table 4.3.
[1]Converted from Table 4.3.
[2]Includes credit extended, cost of debt reduction, short-term capital, valuation changes, and errors and omissions.
[3]Includes both official and commercial banks' net international reserves.
[4]On an accrual basis, including unrecorded trade and statistical discrepancy.

Table 6.5.
Monetary Survey
(In trillions of zlotys; end of period)

	1990	1991	1992	1993	1994
Net foreign assets	**74.3**	**71.3**	**128.0**	**186.9**	**275.1**
(In millions of U.S. dollars)	(7,822)	(6,507)	(8,118)	(8,757)	(11,287)
Net domestic assets	**116.2**	**189.6**	**283.1**	**372.4**	**497.9**
Net domestic credit	107.8	274.2	432.0	614.3	811.1
Claims on general government (net)[1]	−10.4	86.6	183.1	282.3	395.5
Claims on nongovernment sector	118.2	187.6	248.9	332.0	415.6
Other items (net)	8.4	−84.5	−148.9	−241.9	−313.2
Money and quasi-money (broad money)	**190.5**	**260.9**	**411.1**	**559.2**	**773.0**
Money	94.2	107.9	149.7	196.4	274.5
Currency in circulation	39.3	56.2	78.0	99.8	122.7
Demand deposits	54.9	51.7	71.7	96.6	151.8
Quasi-money	96.3	153.0	261.4	362.8	498.5
Savings and time deposits	36.5	88.7	159.5	201.9	277.9
Foreign currency deposits	59.8	64.3	101.9	160.9	220.6
Memorandum items:					
Domestic money stock	130.7	196.6	309.2	398.3	552.4
Gross domestic product	560.3	808.8	1,149.4	1,557.8	2,104.1
Inflation (percentage change)					
End-period	249.3	60.3	44.3	37.6	29.5
Period average	585.8	70.3	43.0	35.3	32.2
Exchange rate (zloty/U.S. dollar)					
End-period	9,500	10,957	15,767	21,344	24,372
Period average	9,500	10,576	13,626	18,115	22,723

Source: Based on Table 5.1.

[1]To simplify the analysis, all credits to the government sector are assumed to be denominated in zlotys.

Table 6.6.
Flow of Funds
(In trillions of zlotys)

	Overall Economy (1)	Domestic Economy (2)	Domestic Economy: General government (3)	Domestic Economy: Private sector (4)	Domestic Economy: Banking system (5)	Rest of the World (6)	Horizontal Check (7)
(–) Gross national disposable income (GNDI)[1]							
1993	**–1,546**	**1,546**	**333**	**1,213**	**–**	**–**	**0**
1994							
Final consumption[2]							
1993	**1,300**	**–1,300**	**–320**	**–980**	**–**	**–**	**0**
1994							
Gross investment[3]							
1993	**242**	**–242**	**–51**	**–191**	**–**	**–**	**0**
1994							
Net lending[4]							
1993	**–**	**–**	**–7**	**7**	**–**	**–**	**0**
1994							
Exports of goods and services (X)[5]							
1993	**357**	**–**	**–**	**–**	**–**	**–357**	**0**
1994							
(–) Imports of goods and services (M)[4]							
1993	**–342**	**–**	**–**	**–**	**–**	**342**	**0**
1994							
Net income from abroad (Y_F)[6]							
1993	**–63**	**–**	**–**	**–**	**–**	**63**	**0**
1994							
Net current transfers (TRF)6							
1993	**52**	**–**	**–**	**–**	**–**	**–52**	**0**
1994							
Nonfinancial balances (S–I)							
1993	**0**	**4**	**–45**	**49**	**–**	**–4**	**0**
1994							

Table 6.6 *(concluded)*

	Overall Economy (1)	Domestic Economy (2)	Domestic Economy: General government (3)	Domestic Economy: Private sector (4)	Domestic Economy: Banking system (5)	Rest of the World (6)	Horizontal Check (7)
Nonfinancial balances (S–I)							
1993	**0**	**4**	**–45**	**49**	**–**	**–4**	**0**
1994							
Foreign financing							
Nonmonetary Direct investment[6]							
1993	**–**	**11**	**–**	**11**	**–**	**–11**	**0**
1994							
Net foreign borrowing[7]							
1993	**–**	**–9**	**–6**	**–3**	**–**	**9**	**0**
1994							
Monetary							
Change in net foreign assets[8]							
1993	**–**	**–12**	**–**	**–**	**–12**	**12**	**0**
1994							
Domestic financing							
Monetary							
Change in domestic bank credit[9]							
1993	**–**	**0**	**99**	**83**	**–182**	**–**	**0**
1994							
Change in total money stock[8]							
1993	**–**	**0**	**–**	**–109**	**109**		**0**
1994							
Nonmonetary							
Nonbank[10]							
1993	**–**	**0**	**11.0**	**–11.0**	**–**	**0**	**0**
1994							
Other items (net)[11]							
1993	**–**	**6**	**–59**	**–20**	**85**	**–6**	**0**
1994							
Vertical check							
1993	**0**	**0**	**0**	**0**	**0**	**0**	**0**
1994							

Source: IMF Institute staff calculations based on Tables 6.1–6.6. The figures have been rounded.

[1]Government gross disposable income is derived from Table 6.1 and proxied as follows: GDN = total revenue - (interest payments + subsidies + income transfers).

[2]Government consumption (CG) is derived from Table 6.2 and proxied as follows: CG = (wages and salaries + purchases of goods and services + other current expenditures). Discrepancies with government consumption as shown in Table 6.3 are minimal and may be partially explained by differences in timing (i.e., cash basis in Table 6.3 as against transaction basis in Table 6.2).

[3]As shown in Table 6.2. Excluding net lending.

[4]As shown in Table 6.3. Recorded here as a nonfinancial item (GFS convention) as opposed to a financing item (SNA convention) in order to match the total of government nonfinancial operations with the general government overall balance.

[5]As shown in Table 6.2. Including adjustment on trade data (as shown in Table 6.4) to reflect unrecorded trade and recording of trade on a transaction basis. It should be noted that the detailed BOP (Table 6.4) is on a cash basis and refers only to convertible currencies.

[6]As shown in Table 6.4.

[7]Includes only medium- and long-term net capital as shown in Table 6.4. Government net borrowing as shown in Table 6.3.

[8]As shown in Table 6.4. Excluding valuation adjustment stemming from the impact of changes in the exchange rate.

[9]As shown in Table 6.5.

[10]As shown in Table 6.3.

[11]Calculated residually.